Financial Engineering

Financial Engineering
A Handbook of Derivative Products

S. ECKL, J. N. ROBINSON and D. C. THOMAS

Basil Blackwell

Copyright © S. Eckl, J. N. Robinson and D. C. Thomas 1990

First published 1990
First published in USA 1991

Basil Blackwell Ltd
108 Cowley Road, Oxford, OX4 1JF, UK

Basil Blackwell, Inc.
3 Cambridge Center
Cambridge, Massachusetts 02142, USA

All rights reserved. Except for the quotation of short passages for the purposes of criticism and review, no part of this publication may be reproduced, stored in a retrieval system, or transmitted, in any form or by any means, electronic, mechanical, photocopying, recording or otherwise, without the prior permission of the publisher.

Except in the United States of America, this book is sold subject to the condition that it shall not, by way of trade or otherwise, be lent, re-sold, hired out, or otherwise circulated without the publisher's prior consent in any form of binding or cover other than that in which it is published and without a similar condition including this condition being imposed on the subsequent purchaser.

British Library Cataloguing in Publication Data
A CIP catalogue record for this book is available from the British Library

Library of Congress Cataloging in Publication Data
Eckl, S.
    Financial engineering: a handbook of derivative products / S. Eckl, J. N. Robinson, and D. C. Thomas.
      p.   cm.
    Includes bibliographical references.
    ISBN 0–631–17388–9:
      1. Corporations—Finance. 2. Forward exchange. 3. Futures.
4. Swap (Finance) 5. Options (Finance) I. Robinson, J. N.
II. Thomas, D. C. III. Title.
HG4026.E27   1991
658.15′224—dc20
90–287 CIP

Typeset in 10 on 12 point Times
by Hope Services (Abingdon) Ltd
Printed in Great Britain by
Antony Rowe Ltd, Chippenham, Wiltshire

Contents

Preface

Acknowledgements

1 The Growth of Financial Engineering   1

  1.1 Introduction   1
  1.2 Volatility and the Demand for Financial Engineering   2
  1.3 The Supply of Financial Engineering Instruments   9
  1.4 The Variety of Uses of the Instruments   10

2 The Identification and Measurement of Exposure   11

  2.1 Introduction   11
  2.2 The Measurement of Economic Exposure   12
  2.3 A Brief Digression on Company Valuation   12
  2.4 Economic Exposure Once Again   13
  2.5 The Measurement of Accounting Exposure   14
  2.6 Economic and Accounting Exposure: a Summary   21
  2.7 A Cautionary Tale   22
  2.8 Identifying Exposure: a Case Study   25

3 The Principles of Pricing Financial Instruments   42

  3.1 Introduction   42
  3.2 Some Preliminaries: Markets and Traders   42
  3.3 The Spot Market for Currencies   45
  3.4 The Spot Market for Interest Rates: Loans and Deposits   46

4 Forward Contracts — 54

4.1 The Forward Market for Currencies — 54
4.2 The Forward Market for Interest Rates — 58
4.3 A Comment on Synthetic Forward Contracts — 64
4.4 The Value of a Forward Contract at Expiration — 65
4.5 Contract Settlement — 68

5 Futures Contracts — 71

5.1 Introduction — 71
5.2 Currency Futures — 72
5.3 Interest Rate Futures — 76
5.4 Stock Market Index Futures — 79
5.5 The Value of a Futures Contract at Expiration — 79
5.6 Contract Settlement — 81

6 Swap Contracts — 84

6.1 Currency Swaps — 84
6.2 Interest Rate Swaps — 87
6.3 The Value of a Swap Contract at Expiration — 90
6.4 Contract Settlement — 91
6.5 A Brief Note on Commodity-Indexed Swaps — 91
6.6 Variations on the Swap Theme — 92

7 Share Options — 95

7.1 Introduction — 95
7.2 Expiration Values — 96
7.3 Pricing Call Options — 98
7.4 Sensitivity of European Call Option Values — 114
7.5 Dividends: Option Values and the Decision to Exercise — 122
7.6 Pricing Put Options — 124
7.7 The Payoff to an Option at Expiration — 129
7.8 Contract Settlement — 131

8 Currency, Interest Rate and Other Options — 132

8.1 Introduction — 132
8.2 Currency Options — 134
8.3 Interest Rate Options: Some Preliminaries — 137
8.4 Interest Rate Options: Practical Considerations — 140
8.5 Interest Rate Options: Pricing Caps and Floors — 143
8.6 Compound Options — 147
8.7 Path-Dependent Options — 150

Contents vii

9 Using Derivative Products 155

    9.1 Introduction 155
    9.2 The Building-Block Approach 155
    9.3 Financial Engineering 167
    9.4 The Instruments Viewed as Insurance Policies 178
    9.5 Some Comments on the Use of Derivative Products 181
    9.6 Case Study: Financial Engineering with Currency Options 183

10 The Corporate Hedging Decision 185

    10.1 Introduction 185
    10.2 Some Statistics 186
    10.3 Portfolio Theory 189
    10.4 The Corporate Hedging Decision 202
    10.5 Quantifying Corporate Exposure 207

11 Further Uses of Derivative Products 212

    11.1 Introduction 212
    11.2 Exploiting Opportunities for Arbitrage 212
    11.3 Matching Borrowing Costs to Ability to Pay 214
    11.4 Time and Tax Transformation 217
    11.5 Reducing Posted Borrowing Rates 218
    11.6 Conclusion 221

12 A Brief Look at the Future 223

Notes 225

References and Further Reading 233

Index 237

This book is dedicated to our wives and, of course, Rhianne

Preface

This book results from the authors' experience in explaining derivative products in a variety of contexts, ranging from MBA programmes at the Management College, Henley and at the City of London Polytechnic to in-house training programmes for the Chase Manhattan Bank and to various Euromoney conferences on financial engineering and risk management.

The authors found that newcomers to the field often felt that it would prove difficult to understand. However, this is partly because the market seems to be full of new-fangled instruments, often with specialized and strange sounding names, whereas underneath the gloss things are much simpler. We hope that in this book we have demystified the jargon and, by showing that the instruments are much more similar to each other than first meets the eye, we have given an easy-to-understand guide to the use of derivative products in financial engineering.

Acknowledgements

We owe a debt of gratitude to our many colleagues and students at the Chase Manhattan Bank and the City of London Polytechnic who have encouraged and criticized our attempts to explain derivative products and financial engineering. In particular, we should like to thank Andrew Bevan, Judi Dunn, Michael Hampton, Lynn McFadden, Clifford Smith, Charles Smithson, Nick Warren, Sykes Wilford and Pat Wilson. The authors write in a personal capacity and their views are not necessarily those of their respective employers.

S. Eckl, J. N. Robinson and D. C. Thomas

1
The Growth of Financial Engineering

1.1 Introduction

Financial engineering is not a new phenomenon. For centuries the solving of financial problems and the exploitation of opportunities for making profits or reducing tax liabilities have occupied the minds of entrepreneurs and others. However, recent years have witnessed a growth in the field of financial engineering on a scale which has not been seen before.

As the Bank for International Settlements (1986:1) has pointed out:

> A sharp acceleration in the pace of innovation, deregulation and structural change in recent years has transformed the international financial system in important ways. Major new financial instruments . . . have either been created or have dramatically increased their role in the financial structure; international credit flows have shifted away from loans through large international banks into direct credit markets; the volume of daily transactions has multiplied; financial markets have become far more closely integrated worldwide; capital has become much more mobile.

Cooper (1987: vii) suggests that, although the changes can be summarized as new instruments, securitization and globalization, the new financial instruments are the vehicles by which securitization and globalization are achieved:

> Securitisation results from the substitution of notes, commercial paper, certificates of deposit and traded bonds for direct lending. Globalisation results from the increased use of the Euromarkets and swap transactions which arbitrage international anomalies in interest rates.

1.2 Volatility and the Demand for Financial Engineering

One of the key explanations of the growth of risk management has been the increased volatility of the financial world. Recent years have seen fluctuations in the economic environment on a scale and with a duration which has rarely – in some cases never – been seen before. There has been exceptional volatility in many of the prices that are key to the operation of a successful corporation.

Since the breakdown of the Bretton Woods exchange rate system, exchange rates have fluctuated widely, as indicated by Figure 1.1. The upper part of this figure shows the Deutschmark/pound spot exchange rate over the period 1963–89, the lower part shows the volatility (measured in terms of month-to-month percentage changes) in the same exchange rate.

Interest rates, too, have shown large fluctuations as governments have taken on board the monetarist/Keynesian debate and as the relative importance of the various anti-inflationary policies has changed. These variations are illustrated by the three month Eurodollar interest rate for 1957–89 shown in Figure 1.2.

Commodity price fluctuations have been similarly large, as indicated by the crude oil prices for 1957–89 shown in Figure 1.3.

Stock markets have also been exceptionally volatile. For example, the British market reached what was an all-time high in August 1987 and then, in October of the same year, recorded the greatest single day drop since the crash of 1929 (see data for the period 1957–89 in Figure 1.4).

Financial volatility is adding greatly to the variability of the environment faced by corporations, individuals and even whole nations. As a result these entities face increased environmental risk.

At this point we can distinguish between two kinds of risk. Environmental risk is the risk that a firm's (or an individual's or a nation's) performance will be affected by unanticipated changes outside the firm's control. In contrast, core business risks are risks that most firms must take, resulting as they do from decisions on marketing, production technology, labour force and capital input. These are the risks that most firms believe will determine their profitability and which most firms believe they know how to manage.

However, profitability depends not only on how well a firm manages its core business risks but also on how well it copes with volatility in its wider operating environment. Such volatility can negatively affect even the most technologically competitive firm in an industry, and at worst can put a firm out of business.

Depending upon its core business, the firm may be exposed to several

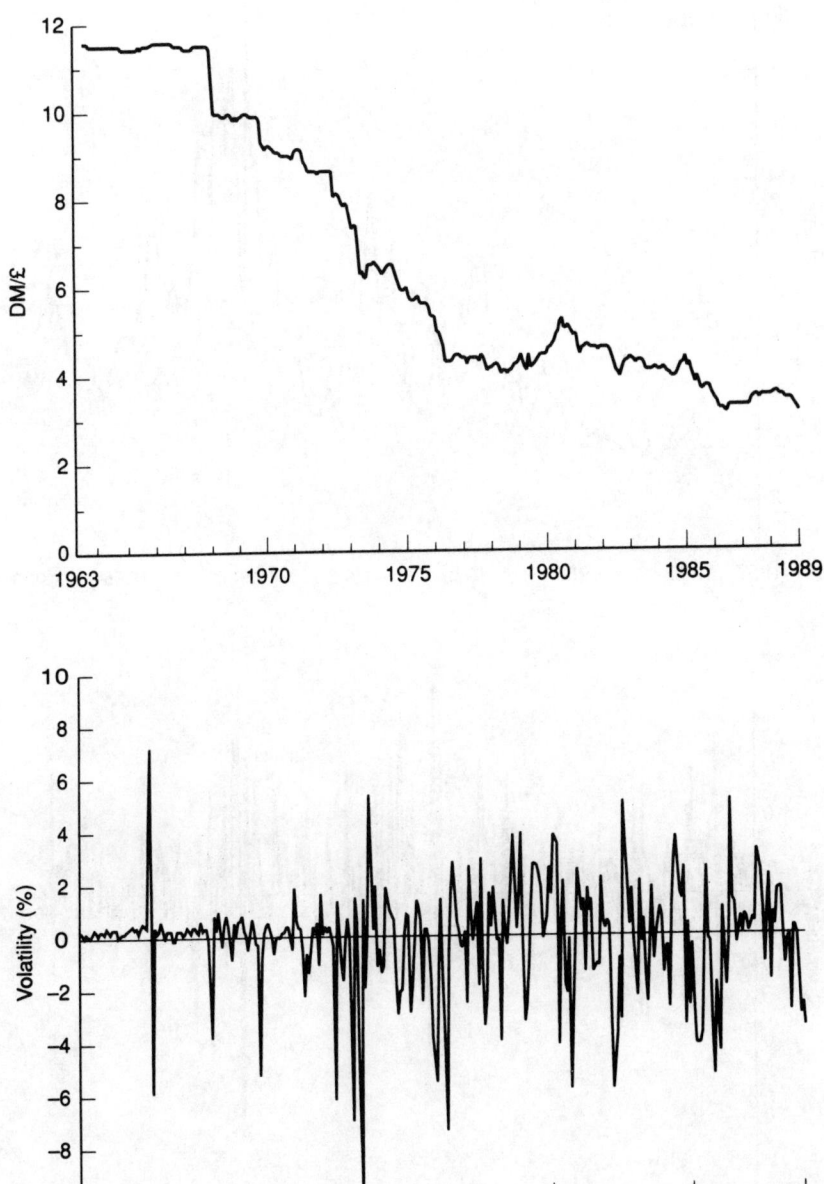

Figure 1.1 Deutschmark/pound spot exchange rate and volatility 1963–1989

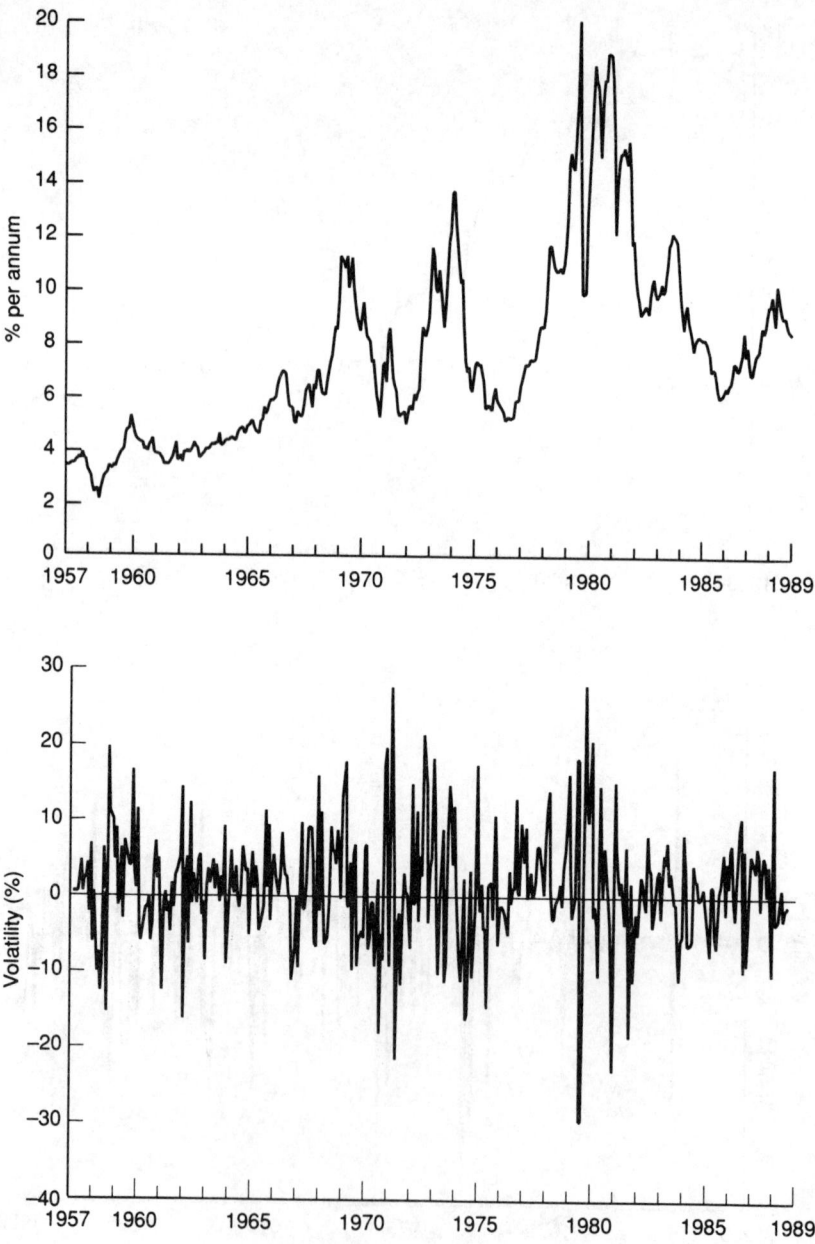

Figure 1.2 Eurodollar three month interest rate and volatility 1957–1989

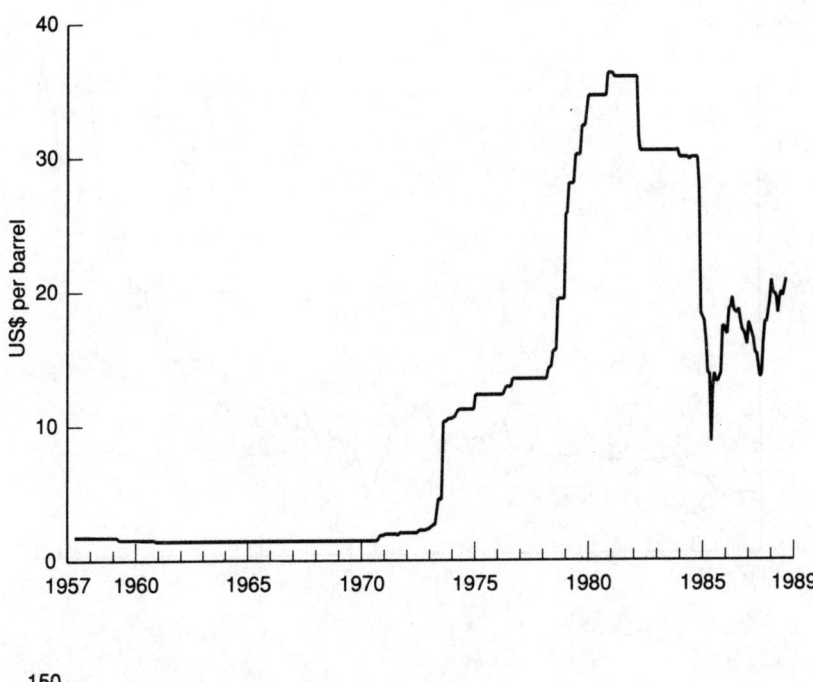
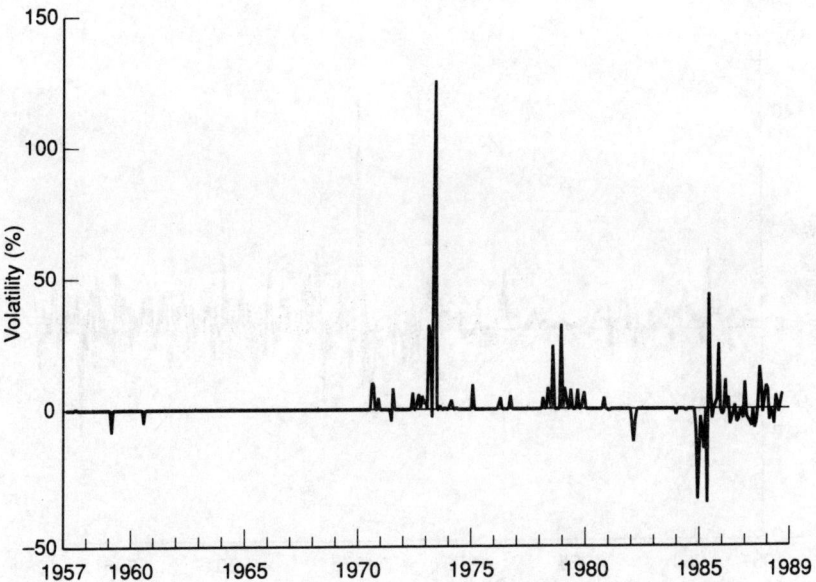

Figure 1.3 Crude oil prices and volatility 1957–1989

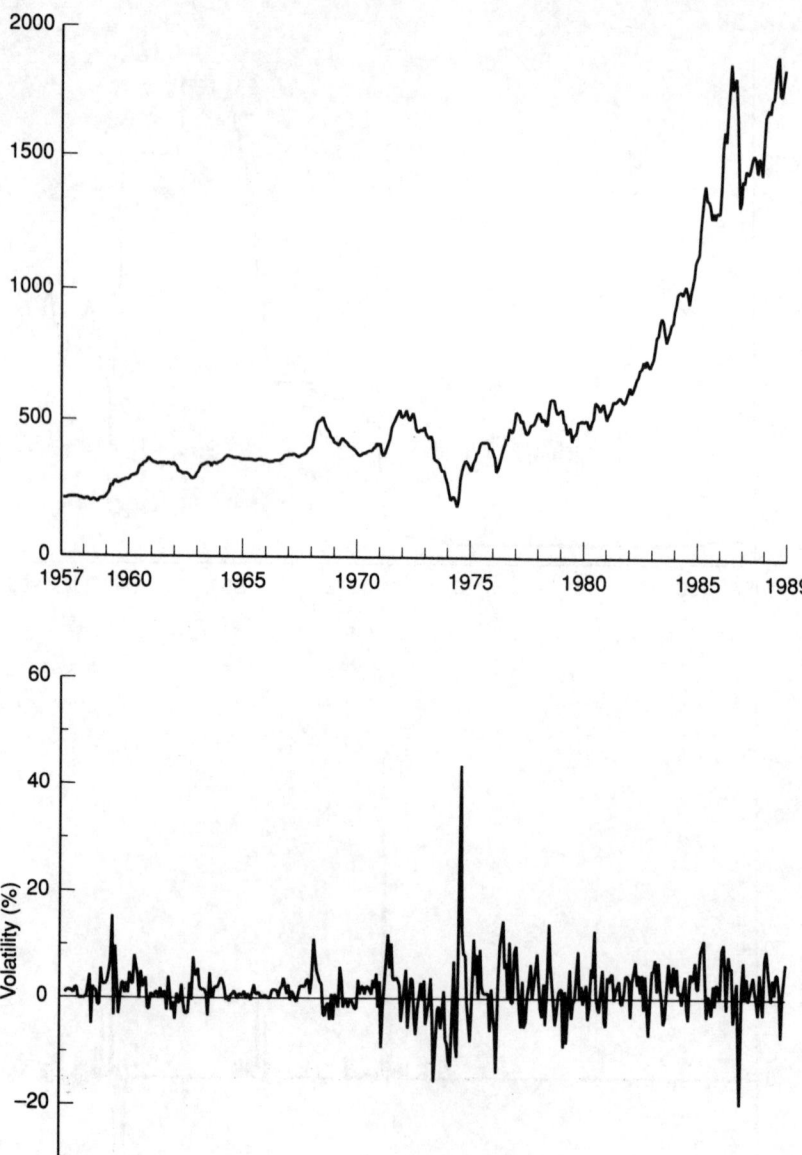

Figure 1.4 UK stock market index and volatility 1957–1989

different variables in the economic environment in which it operates. Price changes may result from a monetary policy shift in Bonn or new government regulations in Tokyo. These changes, which management can neither anticipate nor control, constitute the risks that the firm must face every day and which may, in the last analysis, be the most important determinant of its profitability.

Consider the case of a relatively uncomplicated manufacturing company buying raw materials, processing them into its finished product and selling the product in overseas markets as well as in its home market. This company faces many different exposures springing from exchange rate variability. It is exposed to movements in the international exchange price of its own home currency. An appreciation of its home currency will reduce its competitiveness in overseas markets while at the same time making its home market more attractive to its competitors abroad. The company will also be exposed to movements in many overseas currencies through their impacts on its overseas competitors, both actual and potential. For example, in the days of stable exchange rates, some companies dealing only with the domestic market were not aware that they faced a foreign exchange exposure. However, when their domestic currency appreciated to unprecedentedly high levels they found themselves exposed to competition from imports provided by foreign-based companies; this sharply reduced their profits and, in some well-known cases, forced them out of business.

The company might also be exposed to movements in the prices of its raw materials that result from a change in the international exchange price of the US dollar, the currency in which many of these prices are expressed. In addition it may well be exposed to changes in domestic and overseas interest rates. Owing to the relationship of the interest rate differential between two countries and the exchange rate, the currency risk and the interest rate risk may have to be evaluated jointly.

Each of these influences can be summarized pictorially in the form of a *risk profile* or *exposure profile*. To give an example, Figure 1.5 shows the impact of the US dollar exchange rate on a company. Part (a) of the figure shows that the stronger the exchange rate of the US dollar, the worse will be the performance of the company. Part (b) expresses the same ideas in the form of deviations from one selected exchange rate, and shows that fluctuations taking the dollar above that rate will worsen performance while fluctuations taking it below that rate will improve performance. We have labelled the selected rate the 'forward rate' for reasons which will become apparent later.

The risk profile identifies and measures financial risk. The steepness of the slope of the risk profile indicates the sensitivity of the firm's

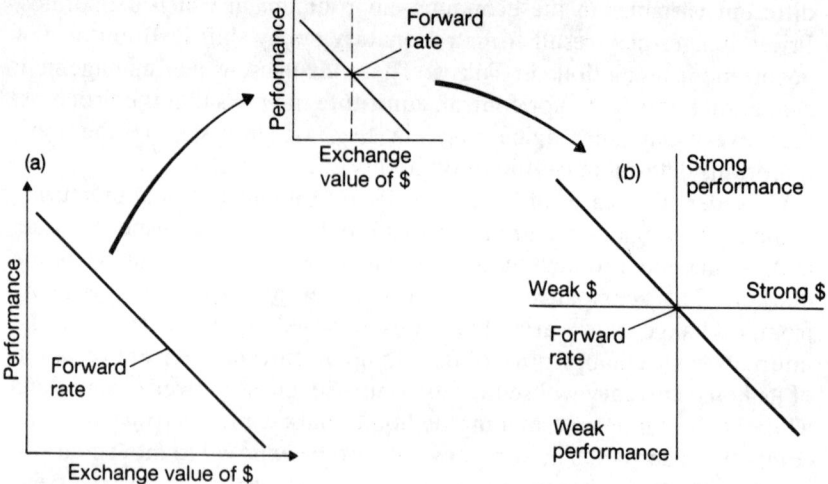

Figure 1.5

performance to a change in a particular exchange rate. We shall have much more to say about exposures in Chapter 2.

A change in the environment (shown by a movement along the horizontal axis) leads to a corresponding change in performance (shown by a movement along the vertical axis). As Figure 1.1 showed, exchange rate fluctuations in the past were confined to a narrow range; now they have a truly huge range.

As might have been expected, firms reacted in two ways to the new economic environment. They devoted more resources to examining their own structure and the characteristics of their competitors in order to identify as many as possible of the factors which influenced their operating environment. They also devoted more resources to forecasting exchange rates so that appropriate action could be taken in advance of those changes. The first part of their effort tended to produce useful results but the second did not. As time went by firms discovered that, although the explicit and implicit forecasts contained in the marketplace proved to be wildly inaccurate, their own forecasts were on average no better than those of the market, and in many cases were significantly worse.

These discouraging results have led to a change in emphasis. Firms still try to identify the key factors influencing their environment but then, instead of forecasting, tend to look for ways of protecting themselves in advance against unexpected adverse changes in these factors.

Thus the emphasis has changed towards the *management* of risk.

Nowadays companies first aim to identify their exposures – or, in terms of Figure 1.5, to draw an exposure profile for each of the factors in the environment which influence their performance. Next, they pay particular attention to those which appear especially threatening to the firm.

Danger might arise in one of two ways. The exposure profile may be especially steep, thus showing that even small changes in a particular currency's value can have a large impact on corporate performance. On the other hand, the range of possible fluctuations in a currency may be so wide that, even if the profile is relatively flat, the environment can still have a large impact on performance. Of course it is quite possible for a company to be very sensitive to changes in its environment *and* for the environment to fluctuate over a wide range; this is the worst possible outcome.

Finally, having identified the dangers, companies then seek ways of manipulating their exposure profiles so that they have a more satisfactory shape. This manipulation can be done in one of two ways. First, the operating characteristics of the firm itself can be changed, for example via an acquisition of another company with another exposure profile or a relocation of production facilities overseas. Secondly, financial instruments can be used, often in the form of off-balance-sheet derivative products; such instruments allow the firm to leave its operations unchanged while protecting itself against the impact of fluctuations in its environment.[1] The ability to separate financial price risks from the underlying physical operations of a company and manage them separately through the use of derivative products may indeed prove to be the greatest financial innovation of the 1980s.

In general, the costs of the first method are higher than those of the second. Thus the greater the expected volatility of the environment, the greater will be the tendency to use the second method rather than the first.

1.3 The Supply of Financial Engineering Instruments

A further factor explaining the growth of financial engineering is the ease with which the financial system has been able to supply the necessary instruments. One of the main reasons for this, which we shall explore in Chapter 9, is that the instruments are much less different than first meets the eye. Many complicated looking instruments, some of which have strange sounding 'trade' names, can be broken down into just a few simpler instruments, while even the simpler instruments can be broken down into small basic components. This is sometimes characterized as the building-block approach to financial engineering. Because banks and other participants in the financial system find it relatively easy to manipulate the basic components, they find it correspondingly easy to offer the apparently more complicated instruments.

1.4 The Variety of Uses of the Instruments

A third factor explaining the growth of financial engineering is the versatility of the instruments. Many of them were invented or developed to do a particular job but, once available, were found to have a wide variety of other uses as well. This is something which we discuss at greater length in Chapter 11.

2
The Identification and Measurement of Exposure

2.1 Introduction

In this chapter we examine the ways in which firms are affected by changes in the price of economic variables and how those effects are measured. Here, as indeed throughout the book, we will be concentrating on seeing the effect on the firm of changes in the price of three particular economic variables: interest rates, foreign exchange rates and commodity prices. We start by identifying the ways in which firms might be affected by volatility in the prices of these economic variables.

Faced with changes in any one of the prices, firms may well wish to review, and possibly revise, their short term operating plans and their longer term strategic decisions. For any such review to be meaningful, it is of course necessary to have identified the ways in which changes in the prices of the economic variables are likely to impact upon the level of the firm's future operations and on the firm's future competitive position. The essential point to note here is that this type of analysis is forward looking. The task is to identify, today, how susceptible the firm will be, in the future, to changes in the price of economic variables. The task is otherwise known as identifying the firm's economic exposure.

The second type of exposure is known as accounting exposure and is based on the firm's historical cost financial statements. Accounting exposure is reflected in the extent to which the profit and loss account and the balance sheet capture the effect of changes in the price of economic variables. The fact that it is based, in the main, on historical cost means that it will naturally be rather more restricted than the measure of economic exposure.

We now move on to discussing the ways of measuring each of these two exposures. We start with economic exposure.

2.2 The Measurement of Economic Exposure

To get a feel for the idea of economic exposure, let us consider the situation of a UK-based firm supplying consumer goods facing a sudden and unexpected one-off increase in interest rates. What are the likely future repercussions for the firm? If the firm has borrowed money from the bank, then the future interest payments will increase, the firm's customers will take longer to pay, and the firm's suppliers will want to be paid more quickly. The result is that the firm will possibly have to borrow still more money if it is to continue trading at the planned levels. Future profits will almost certainly decline. Perhaps even more importantly, there may well be a decline in the future demand for the firm's products – and that will depress projected profits even further.

The task of measuring the future impact of such an interest rate increase on the firm is not a trivial one. Just the first step of trying to project the effect of the increase as it impacts upon future profits, assuming future sales are fixed, is difficult enough. But trying to project future profits when the interest rate increase might impact on the firm's future level of activity is another and higher level of difficulty again.

2.3 A Brief Digression on Company Valuation

Before going any further into the measurement of economic exposure, it might be useful to say a few words about the ideas underlying company valuation.

For simplicity, we set out in Figure 2.1 the flows relating to an all-equity financed company. The market value (market capitalization) of the firm will be the present value of the net cash flows which are expected to be generated by using the firm's assets in the future.[1] We can write this in the following shortened form:

$$V_e = \sum_{j=1}^{\infty} \frac{NCF_j}{(1 + {_0R_j})^j}$$

where V_e denotes the market value of the firm, in this case its equity; NCF_j denotes the expected future net cash flows; ${_0R_j}$ denotes today's discount rate, of which more in Chapters 3 and 10;[2] and j denotes the periods over which the expected future net cash flows are summed.

There are a number of different models suggesting alternative ways of calculating the expected future net cash flow figure. The figure is usually computed thus:

Identification and Measurement of Exposure

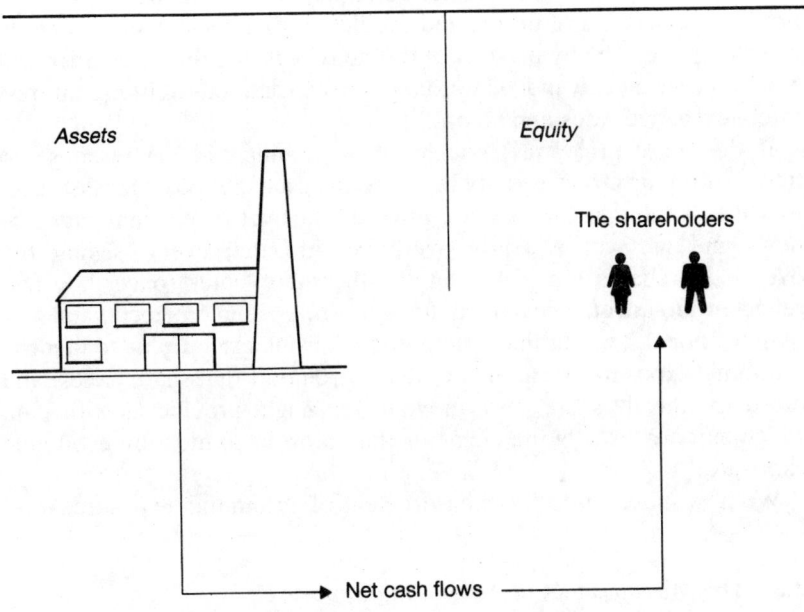

Figure 2.1

	Projected net profit after tax
plus/minus	Non-cash items that have been charged/credited to the profit and loss account
minus	Expenditure necessary to maintain/increase the earning power of the assets.

2.4 Economic Exposure Once Again

The notion that the firm's share price is the present value of the expected future net cash flows is an important one. The share price, at any one point in time, will embody the expectations (at that same point in time) of the firm's expected future net cash flows; it will embody the expectations (at that same point in time) of future interest rates; it will embody the expectations (at that same point in time) of future exchange rates; and so on. There's a lot of information in the price of a share!

Consider now what will happen if expectations of future interest rates change. One response will be that there will be frantic activity among the financial community to calculate the impact of the change on both the firm's expected future profits and the discounting factor, and hence on its share price. The by-product of this activity is that the share price will respond very quickly indeed to changes in expectations of future interest rates, exchange rates and so on.

If the share price was thought to move sluggishly in response to information, arbitrage activity would soon ensue. Suppose, for instance, that it was thought that a share price did not yet reflect some adverse news and was consequently overpriced. In that event, selling the overvalued shares today and buying the shares later (once they had reflected the adverse news) would soon bring about 'correct' values.

In Section 2.2 we outlined the potential problems in trying to identify economic exposure. It should be clear to you now that share prices, and more specifically share price movements, might provide us with data which embody exactly the elements that allow us to measure economic exposure.

We now move on to the measurement of accounting exposure.

2.5 The Measurement of Accounting Exposure

We have already noted that published financial statements are, in the main, drawn up using the historical cost convention. The statements are therefore, by definition, largely backward looking. Thus the profit and loss account for, say, the year ended 31 December 19X1 details the results of trading activities over the previous twelve months. The balance sheet at 31 December 19X1 purports to show the financial position of the company at that date, measured in monetary units which have been generated by verifiable historic transactions adjusted for certain accounting conventions and practices.

2.5.1 Changes in Foreign Exchange Rates

First, we consider the measurement of accounting exposure to changes in the foreign exchange rates. For the UK, the Statement of Standard Accounting Practice number 20 (SSAP 20), issued by the Accounting Standards Committee in April 1983, outlines the methods of accounting for such exchange rate variability.

The firm's financial statements can be affected by foreign exchange rate changes at two levels:

- At an individual company level, when the company enters into transactions denominated in a different currency from its domestic unit of trading. This is known, not unreasonably, as transaction risk.

- At a group level, where a holding company owns a subsidiary (or branch) whose assets and liabilities are denominated in a foreign currency. The restatement of the subsidiary's accounts for consolidation purposes gives rise to what is known as translation risk.

Exposure to transaction risk

Consider, for example, a UK company importing goods from France. Suppose that the company bought, on credit, goods costing 11,000 francs and that the spot rate at the time was FF/£ 11. The UK company would record the goods as an asset of £1000 with a corresponding liability to the French supplier for £1000.

Let us now suppose that, when the UK company came to settle, the spot rate had moved to FF/£ 11.50. The liability in the UK importer's books would now be settled at a cost of £956.52.

Thus the UK importer would have recorded an asset of £1000 initially and would have discharged the £1000 liability with a cash payment of only £956.52. The company is therefore £43.48 better off, and this amount flows through the profit and loss account as a foreign exchange gain. This gain reflects the fact that there is a realized saving of £43.48.

Exposure to translation risk

SSAP 20 outlines two methods of dealing with the accounting for foreign currency denominated subsidiaries: the temporal method and the closing rate (or net investment) method. Each of these methods will now be briefly reviewed.

The temporal method Use of this method is intended to be limited to those subsidiaries which can be viewed as a direct extension of the holding company's activities.

Consider a UK holding company with a subsidiary having foreign currency denominated assets and liabilities. The temporal method involves the translation of the subsidiary's assets and liabilities into sterling using exchange rates dependent upon the nature of those items. SSAP 20 distinguishes between monetary and non-monetary items; the foreign currency denominated monetary assets and monetary liabilities are converted into sterling at the exchange rate ruling at the balance sheet date, and non-monetary items are converted at the historic rate ruling when the transactions were first entered into the subsidiary's books. Whilst the mechanics of converting foreign currency into sterling at determined exchange rates present no problems, there is a more fundamental problem of attempting to distinguish a monetary asset from a non-monetary one! In general, monetary items are those denominated in terms of a specific number of cash flow units. Thus debtors/receivables, creditors/payables, debt and cash all rank as monetary items. As we have already noted, these items get converted at the rate ruling on the balance sheet date.

The amount giving rise to foreign exchange gains or losses under the temporal method will therefore be the balance on the net monetary items. Thus if the subsidiary held a constant balance of, say, $150,000 net monetary assets throughout a year when the spot exchange rate moved from $/£ 1.90 to $/£ 1.75, the monetary assets would be converted in the group accounts to £78,947 at the start of the year but would be converted at the year-end rate of $/£ 1.75 to give a figure of £85,714 in the group balance sheet at year end. The gain of £6767 would flow through the group profit and loss account.

Gains/losses on foreign exchange can also arise under the temporal method through the mismatching of the rates used between the profit and loss account and the balance sheet.

For the purpose of our example, we will now drop the assumption that the subsidiary has an opening balance on net monetary assets.

If the subsidiary sold goods for, say, $500,000 during the year, different rates could be applied in the profit and loss account from those applied in the balance sheet. In accounting terms the subsidiary's journal entry would be as follows:

debit	Monetary assets (debtors/receivables or cash)	$500,000
credit	Sales revenue	$500,000

The monetary assets will, in the sterling group balance sheet, be converted at the closing rate while the sales revenue might, in the group profit and loss account, be converted at the average exchange rate of the period. Assuming (unrealistically!) that there were no expenses, this profit would then flow through to the equity in the balance sheet.

Using the exchange rates above and assuming that the rate moved evenly from $/£ 1.90 to $/£ 1.75 (with an average exchange rate of $/£ 1.825), the subsidiary's accounts converted to sterling would appear as follows:

Subsidiary company balance sheet at year end converted to sterling

Monetary assets	£285,714	Equity	£273,973

This gives a gain of £11,741. It is, of course, unlikely that the firm would wish to keep the assets of $500,000 all in monetary form. However, it

Identification and Measurement of Exposure

should now be clear that foreign exchange gains or losses can also arise where the closing rate varies from the average rate for the period.

The closing rate (net investment) method The closing rate translation is, by far, the most widely used method of consolidating the accounts of a foreign subsidiary. Under the closing rate method, all of the subsidiary's assets and liabilities are converted at the foreign exchange rate ruling at the end of the period. Thus, in contrast to the temporal method, the amount exposed to foreign exchange rate changes is effectively the subsidiary's equity. This treatment reflects the assumption underlying the use of the closing rate method, which is to regard the holding company's interest in the subsidiary as an investment in an organization which operates autonomously. The holding company's investment in the subsidiary is then seen as being an investment in the equity of the entity as a whole rather than in the individual assets and liabilities that comprise the subsidiary.

The following example illustrates the mechanics of the method. Let us assume that a UK holding company acquired 100% of the equity of a German company on 1 January. The cost of the investment was £2 million. At the time of the investment the spot exchange rate was DM/£ 3.

Extracts from the individual company balance sheets on 1 January appear as follows:

UK holding company balance sheet at 1 January

Assets: investment in German subsidiary £2,000,000	

German subsidiary company balance sheet at 1 January

Assets	DM 7,500,000	Equity	DM 6,000,000
		Liabilities	DM 1,500,000

The group balance sheet appears as follows:

UK group balance sheet at 1 January

Assets (from German subsidiary)	£2,500,000	Liabilities (from German subsidiary)	£500,000

Note that the equity (assets less liabilities) of the German company at the date of acquisition exactly equals the sterling cost of the investment in the UK holding company's books.

We shall now assume that the German company does not trade over the subsequent twelve months; in other words, the German company's balance sheet does not change over the period. However, let us assume that the foreign exchange rate ruling on 31 December is DM/£ 3.2. The group balance sheet at 31 December would now appear as follows:

UK group balance sheet at 31 December

Assets (from German subsidiary)	£2,343,750	Liabilities (from German subsidiary)	£468,750

The net assets (assets minus liabilities) are now £1,875,000 compared with £2,000,000 at the start of the year; this represents a translation loss on foreign exchange over the year of £125,000. In other words, the amount exposed was the net assets employed in the German subsidiary, which by definition is equal to the German company's equity. This loss would be shown as a movement in group reserves and would not flow through the profit and loss account.

It might be useful to reflect here upon the nature of these foreign exchange gains and losses. In the case of the transaction gains and losses, these items are represented by cash flow movements. In our example of the UK company importing from France, the £1000 liability was discharged by a cash payment of £956.52, representing a cash flow saving of £43.48.

However, in our translation example using the closing rate (net investment) method, the nature of the translation loss is far more uncertain. If the German company's assets and liabilities were all liquidated (at their book values) on 31 December and the proceeds repatriated to the UK at that date, there is no doubt about the nature of the loss. The loss would be represented by the reduced amount of funds flowing back to the holding company and thus, in this case, the exposure is an economic exposure.

In the more usual case where the German company continues to trade, the relationship between translation gains and losses and economic gains and losses is not so straightforward.

We assume initially that the cost of the investment in the German company (£2,000,000 at DM/£ 3.00) is equal to the present value of the expected future net cash flows of the German company. Therefore at the time of purchase, the economic value and the book value of the investment are identical.

There are some instances in which the accounting translation gain/loss might be related to economic gain/loss. One such instance would be the case where the Deutschmark present value of the German subsidiary's future cash flows was insensitive to changes in the DM/£ exchange rate and where there was no change in either German or UK interest rates.

More often than not, however, it is the case that the translation gain/loss is a poor measure of the change in the company's value in economic terms. Consider for instance the case where the German company is in a position, following a depreciation in the Deutschmark, to increase its expected future cash flows by an amount which maintains its market value in sterling terms. Thus although the depreciation of the currency gives rise to an accounting translation loss, the company does not suffer any gain or loss in economic terms.

Alternatively, consider the case where the German subsidiary exports from Germany and faces foreign competition in its home market. In this case, the depreciation of the Deutschmark might conceivably cause such an increase in the German subsidiary's expected future cash flows that the sterling equivalent present value of the flows also increases. Despite this economic gain, a translation loss would be recorded in the financial statements.

We now move on to examine the measurement of accounting exposure when the two other price variables change. We consider interest rate changes first.

2.5.2 Changes in Interest Rates

Some of the impacts of an interest rate change are easily discernible from the financial statements, others less so. If a company has borrowed variable rate funds (perhaps with the interest rate reset on a monthly basis) then, in the event of rates increasing, the interest expense in the profit and loss account will increase and the reported profit will decline. However, as we discussed above, interest rate changes might also affect the demand for the company's products and this will be reflected in the sales revenue figure. The task of trying to identify the impact of such a change on sales is not easily achieved. Clearly, one would need to refer to the financial statements going back over a number of years; even then the difficulty of isolating the 'interest rate' effect on sales, free from all other confounding influences, would make the exercise highly problematic.

Changes in interest rates might also impact on the accounting values used for certain assets in the year-end balance sheet. Consider a company holding a fixed coupon security at the balance sheet date. If interest rates have increased since the security was purchased, the security's market value would have declined. In this instance, the accounting concept of prudence would suggest that the security now be recorded at market value, rather than at cost, with the write-down from historic cost to market value flowing through the profit and loss account. However, in the event of interest rates having fallen since the purchase of the security, the appreciation in the security's value would not normally be recognized in the accounts. Having said that, though, there have been recent cases of financial institutions valuing their dealing positions of readily marketable securities in the balance sheet at market value when the market value exceeds the original cost. In such cases the need to show a true and fair view has been thought to be more important than the application of the prudence concept.

2.5.3 Changes in Commodity Prices

In the case of a company affected by, say, oil price changes, the historical cost profit and loss account would reflect the increased or decreased cost of the resource produced or consumed in the accounting period. An oil price change might also affect the demand for the company's products, but again it would be very difficult to isolate the specific oil price effect from the published accounts.

For both oil producing and oil consuming companies, the stock of oil at the end of the accounting period would normally be valued in the balance sheet at the lower of cost or net realizable value, again reflecting the application of the prudence concept. Thus, in the event of oil prices falling, the likelihood would be that the stock would be written down to the net realizable value via a charge in the profit and loss account. In all other cases, the stock would normally be held at cost.

The book values of fixed assets could also conceivably be affected by changes in external prices. Consider a company holding fixed assets whose market value might be directly linked to the oil price. In the case of an oil producer, one possible example could be capitalized exploration outlays. Given that fixed assets are normally held at cost or valuation and subsequently depreciated, let us assume that initially the asset is held at cost. If, following a oil price change, the market value of the fixed asset dropped significantly and the drop in value was thought to be permanent, the asset would normally then be written down to its estimated recoverable amount. This write-down would again flow through the profit and loss account. Conversely, if the asset's market value appreciated following an oil price change, the asset could be revalued and held at valuation rather than at a figure based on historic cost. Such write-ups would normally be credited to reserves and would not normally flow through the profit and loss account. However, it should be noted that revaluations can occur for any number of reasons; it is not an automatic accounting practice following a favourable change in interest rates or commodity prices! Indeed, recent accounting surveys suggest that the practice of revaluing fixed assets upwards is declining in all but the largest listed companies.

2.6 Economic and Accounting Exposure: a Summary

It is appropriate here to summarize the main differences between the two measures of exposure. A classification of exposures is given in Table 2.1; accounting exposure is shown divided into translation and transaction exposures.

Table 2.1 Classification of exposures

	Translation exposure	Transaction exposure	Economic exposure
Exposed items	Balance sheet (depending on whether the temporal or closing rate method is used)	Future cash flows	Future cash flows
Identification and quantification	Simple conversions	Simple conversions	Complex interactions
Precision of quantification	Precise	Precise	Imprecise
Duration of exposure	Medium to long term (investment horizon)	Short term (transaction cycle)	Long term (product life cycle)

Economic exposure is forward looking. It includes not only estimates of the direct effect of price changes (such as higher future interest expenses, higher future cost of oil consumed) on the value of the company, but also the possible indirect effects of such price changes on the value of the firm via the revised demand for a company's products, the impact on the company's competitive position, and so on.

Accounting exposure is, in the main, constrained within the framework of historical cost and the other accounting concepts. It is therefore very much more restricted in scope and is principally directed at measuring the historical direct effect of changes in interest rates, exchange rates and commodity prices. The effect of such changes as they appear in the profit and loss account can be regarded as a subset of economic exposure but limited to that one year only. However, with hindsight, the indirect effects of such price changes can be seen in terms of the historical fluctuations in the figures for sales revenue. Indeed, over a number of years it may well be that the accounting exposure captures the economic exposure.

Some elements of accounting practice in the treatment of balance sheet items also have similarities to measures of economic exposure. Specifically, the practice of only writing down certain year-end assets to comply with the prudence concept can be seen as a rather asymmetric treatment but one that is in the same spirit as economic exposure. The more recent accounting development of including marketable securities (held as dealing positions) at their market value is one further step towards closing the gap in the measurement of accounting and economic exposure.

Both accounting exposure and economic exposure can be hedged. In the chapters on financial instruments that follow, we have not directed our discussion to either type of exposure in particular. However, the accounting treatment of hedging instruments (which we do not deal with[3]) may, in practice, be an important consideration in deciding which instrument to use to hedge exposures.

2.7 A Cautionary Tale

In principle, perhaps, it is easy to identify exposure. We know that an oil producing country is bound to have an exposure profile such that a worsening in its environment, which in its case would be a fall in the price of oil, would make it worse off. That's fairly obvious and we don't have to do a great deal of work to find that out. What is very important, though, is that there are many hidden exposures which companies don't know about – and they find out about them the hard way. They suddenly find their sales revenues collapsing, with the looming prospect of financial distress, and by then it is often too late.

The reader can probably think of several examples of companies or countries or individuals who have suffered in that particular way. Here we look at such an example – one which shows how the hidden exposures can be just as important as, or perhaps even more important than, the exposures which can be seen and predicted in advance.

Our example comes from the United States, and it concerns a producer of bicycles in the Midwest. This producer argued that, although he faced many exposures of different kinds, he was at least safe from an exchange rate exposure. He said:

> At least it doesn't matter to me what happens to the dollar. I'm quite safe against all dollar movements. Why? Because wherever I look everything is measured in dollars. My business involves buying steel tubes from an American steel producer. I pay for them in dollars. I then bend them around and make my product. My product is sold entirely in the Midwest.

Identification and Measurement of Exposure

I don't even go as far as the East or West Coasts of the United States. My market is here, close to me, in the Midwest. If I look at my income statement, I see the dollar. All my sales are in dollars. My labour force is paid in dollars. If I look at my balance sheet, I see the same. I have machines which I bought from a US manufacturer, I've paid for them in dollars, I have a dollar loan which enabled me to pay for them. Nothing but dollars. I could draw my situation in the form of an exposure profile, but it really wouldn't look very exciting. I would draw it just as a horizontal line. Whatever happened to the dollar, there would be no difference to my performance. I am protected from any dollar movements. I have no exchange rate exposure.

One might think that this sounds logical. One might even think it sounds correct. It isn't correct. That manufacturer always had a foreign exchange exposure, but he didn't see it. Besides, it wasn't important in the days when the exchange rate was stable. But after 1981 the dollar became very strong and went up to levels that hadn't been seen for years. In particular, it rose very sharply against a potential competitor who was in France, but who had never exported to the United States before. At 8.98 francs to the dollar (seen in 1985) the US market looked much more attractive to the French competitor than when there were only 4.23 francs to the dollar (seen in 1980). The French company began to export into the Midwest of the United States and began to eat into the market of our domestic manufacturer. The strong dollar was a serious matter for our US domestic producer. Imports came flooding in from France and his sales revenue collapsed. He *did* have a foreign exchange exposure, and he didn't find out about it until it was almost too late. It was only the falling sales revenue and the prospect of bankruptcy that revealed his exposure!

Now, to some extent, we may be able to estimate exposure profiles from balance sheet figures. Let's go back to our Midwest bicycle manufacturer. If we look at his accounts we can pick up some exposures immediately. We might find that the manufacturer has borrowed money from his bank, and therefore is going to be sensitive to interest rates. If interest rates go up, the manufacturer's net cash flow will fall, and it is a fairly simple matter to calculate exactly how much the net cash flow will fall. So that part of the exposure profile can be quantified.

But that's only the beginning of the story. Remember that the bicycle manufacturer was subject to exchange rate fluctuations, and his sales were influenced by the exchange rate because, as the dollar appreciated, so the US market became more attractive to an exporter in another country. And his particular competition came from a bicycle manufacturer in France. That would not show in his accounts at all. There is no foreign exchange shown in his accounts. We have to go well beyond these financial statements when we are trying to measure corporate exposures.

We also have to know quite a lot about the structure of the industry. Who are the major bicycle manufacturers of the world? Where are they? What currencies are they based upon? How will they react if exchange rates move? It should be clear that the process of measuring corporate exposure requires a much wider range of knowledge than the ability to read the financial statements of any one particular corporation.

But is that the end of the story? Usually it is not. We'll probably find that the manufacturer also has some sensitivity of sales revenue to interest rates. Because as interest rates change, so people's disposable incomes change; and as their disposable incomes change, so their expenditure changes.

There might be a rather closer link in the case of the bicycle manufacturer because, to some degree, bicycles could be a substitute for cars. If cars get very expensive, people might use bicycles rather more. They would probably go on buying cars, but they might not use them quite as much as they otherwise would.

That would mean that, as interest rates go up, we get a substitution towards bicycles. In this respect a rise in interest rates could be good news for the bicycle manufacturer. The total impact of a change in interest rates on his business is, perhaps, a little less bad than a simple look at the balance sheet might suggest. Interest rates go up and, yes, he would have to pay more on his loan; but, against this, his sales revenue might increase to compensate. So the total exposure that he faces is, perhaps, a little less than first meets the eye, and the slope of his exposure profile is likely to be a little flatter than we might have first thought.

Our manufacturer might well also have an exposure to oil prices. When oil prices increased dramatically some years ago, people used their cars noticeably less. For a while people left their cars in the garage, walked more and cycled more – although eventually the effect wore off. A rise in oil prices would increase the demand for bicycles and raise the sales revenue of our Midwest bicycle manufacturer, which would obviously be good news for him. That's another type of exposure that doesn't show in his accounting figures at all.

Even now we haven't reached the end of the story. Because what we have been doing is thinking of each factor separately. Yes, our manufacturer has an exposure to oil prices, another exposure to exchange rates, yet another exposure to interest rates, and so on. But those factors might not really be separate. Sometimes when one of them moves, the other one also moves. There's very often a link, for example, between exchange rates and oil prices. If oil prices go up in the world then this is bad news for all the oil consuming countries, and we tend to see that the exchange rates of the oil consuming countries fall as the price of oil goes up.

Now just compare the situation of the United States and that of France. They are both oil consuming countries, but they are not really in the same situation. France imports all its oil; so when the price of oil goes up, this has a major impact on the economy. The United States generally imports a smaller proportion of its oil requirements; the rest comes from domestic production. So although a rise in the price of oil does seem to damage the United States, it damages France very much more. What we find is that, as the price of oil goes up, the dollar does depreciate a little, but the French franc depreciates a lot because it is France which is really damaged by the rise in the price of oil. Now if the dollar depreciates a little, and the franc depreciates a lot, what is happening to the dollar/franc exchange rate? The dollar is appreciating against the franc.

Now think back to our domestic manufacturer. Oil prices go up. That's good news to the bicycle manufacturer; he sells more bicycles. But as oil prices go up, the dollar appreciates against the French franc, more imports come in, and that's bad news for the manufacturer. So the total impact of the oil price rise is more complicated than even a second look at the problem might suggest.

At first glance, there's no exposure to oil. There is nothing in the balance sheet, nothing in the profit and loss account. At a second look, yes, there is an exposure because oil prices have an impact on the sales of bicycles. A third look reveals an even more complicated exposure, because oil prices have an impact on exchange rates, and exchange rates also have an impact on the sales of bicycles. At least they do for the domestic manufacturer because, the stronger the dollar, the more he finds imports coming in from abroad. In short, the measurement of the total exposure is a complicated process.

2.8 Identifying Exposure: a Case Study

Sections 2.1 to 2.6 followed a rather formal approach; in contrast, Section 2.7 was largely anecdotal. In this section we draw these approaches together using a 'real-life' case study based on a British tour operator.[4]

The purpose of the case study is to identify World Travel Group's principal exposures on the basis of the information that follows. It is assumed that 'today' is shortly after the publication of the 19X9 accounts.

2.8.1 Background

The British tour operations industry

The British tour operations industry has undergone explosive growth over the past twenty years. The number of package tours sold increased by well over 200% during the period from 19X0 to 19X9. Consumer expenditures for package tours increased over 250% during the same period, even though the cost of a typical tour declined by over 14%. Despite this business boom, competition among major tour operators has reduced after-tax profit margins to as low as 2–3% of gross sales.

Although the industry comprises over 700 tour operators, it is dominated by the five major operators listed in Table 2.2. In addition to selling package tours, each major operator runs an air charter subsidiary.

Table 2.2

Tour operator	Air charter subsidiary of operator
Commonwealth Group	Commonwealth
World Travel Group	World Air
Sky Line Holidays Group	North Star
Intercontinental	Regal
Oxford Airways Group	Oxford Air Tours

Package tour market share survey

A reliable guide to the market share held by the five major operators is the Holiday Booking Index, compiled from bookings taken by a representative sample of tour agents. Based on this index, the Commonwealth Group has been the market leader over the past ten years. The five major operators share approximately half of the overall market. The other half of the overall market is divided among a large number of small speciality operators.

Table 2.3 shows estimates of the market share of the five major operators over the last two years.

Tour industry business practices

A 19X8 industry survey provides the following breakdown of direct costs (as a percentage of selling price) for a typical ten day tour:

    Accommodation   35%

Table 2.3

Tour operator	Market share (%) 19X9	19X8
Commonwealth Group	20.5	19.0
World Travel Group	15.5	13.0
Oxford Airways Group	6.0	7.0
Sky Line Holidays Group	5.0	6.5
Intercontinental	4.0	5.5
Percentage of total market	51.0	51.0

Air fare   35% (30% of which is fuel cost)
Travel agents 10%

After overhead costs are met, even with full utilization, the profit margin will be 10% at best. As previously noted, recent profit margins have been much smaller.

Tour operators normally receive payment for tours four to six weeks in advance, and pay accommodation costs four to eight weeks after the tours. However, the sterling prices to be included in the travel brochures are generally fixed some ten to twelve months prior to the tours.

Most of the large tour operators belong to the Association of British Travel Agents (ABTA), a trade organization. In early 19X0, following a number of travel operator bankruptcies, ABTA set up a performance bond system. Each tour operator member is requested to post a performance guarantee bond in sterling to cover the possibility of that operator failing to meet its obligations. The size of the bond is determined annually by the Civil Aviation Authority, based on the size and reputation of the individual operator. The industry-wide bond for 19X8 was £200 million.

British tour operators

Table 2.4 provides an overview of the tour destinations for the British tour operations industry as a whole.

Charter airlines market share survey

Charter airlines now account for 60% of all intra-European flights, with British-based charters carrying 87% of the traffic. Charter airlines, as opposed to scheduled airlines, dominate the market owing to their ability to achieve maximum utilization from their aircraft. For example,

Identification and Measurement of Exposure

Table 2.4 Number of tours to principal destinations from Great Britain (million)

	19X9	19X7	19X5
Spain	5.02	3.69	2.63
France	4.48	5.00	3.84
Italy	1.18	1.07	1.10
Greece	1.05	1.00	0.86
West Germany	1.30	1.10	1.09
USA	0.72	0.97	1.09
Austria	0.61	0.41	0.33
Yugoslavia	0.48	0.27	0.22
Miscellaneous	0.26	0.74	0.84
Totals	15.10	14.25	12.00

the average Boeing 737 operated by a charter airline is in the air nearly fifteen hours a day – twice the number of hours as its counterpart operating on scheduled commercial routes.

The market leader, Commonwealth Airways, has held the top position for the past eight years. In 19X8, the market shares of the British-based aircraft charter market were as shown in Table 2.5.

Table 2.5

Carrier (affiliated tour operator if appropriate)	Market share (%)
Commonwealth (Commonwealth)	27.6
Sun Ways	22.5
Oxford Air Tours (Oxford)	15.1
Regal (Intercontinental)	10.7
North Star (Sky Line)	7.5
World Air (World Travel)	7.4
Hebridair	3.8
Other British airlines	5.4

2.8.2 World Travel Group PLC

Introduction

World Travel Group (WTG) was originally incorporated fifteen years ago. The shares of World Travel Group are publicly traded. The directors of the company hold 45% of the issued shares.

Market details for World Travel Group at 30 September 19X9 were as follows:

Identification and Measurement of Exposure

Shares outstanding 51.6 million
Price per share £1.13
Market capitalization £58.3 million
Annual dividend £0.05
Price/earnings ratio 6.2 (sector average is 11.7)

Sales and pre-tax profits, excluding intercompany accounts, for World Travel Group are generated by its two major subsidiaries as shown in Table 2.6. For summary group profit and loss accounts and balance sheets, see Tables 2.7 and 2.8.

Table 2.6 World Travel Group sales and pre-tax profits: year to 31 March

	Tour operations: Sunnex Vacations PLC (£ million) 19X9	19X8	Charter airline: World Air (£ million) 19X9	19X8
Sales	198.5	155.8	42.2	35.5
Pre-tax profits	6.3	8.7	5.5	7.8

Table 2.7 World Travel Group summary profit and loss accounts: year to 31 March

	19X9 (£ million)	19X8 (£ million)
Sales revenue	240.7	191.3
Gross profit	56.9	52.6
Operating profit	12.3	15.8
Interest expense (primarily aircraft finance)	(5.1)	(4.2)
Investment income	4.6	4.9
Tax	(4.8)	(4.8)
Extraordinary items	13.0[a]	(7.9)
Dividends	(2.5)	(2.3)

Note: [a] Includes credit of £12.4 million profit on aircraft sales.

Sunnex Vacations PLC

Sunnex Vacations PLC is the tour operations subsidiary of World Travel Group. Sunnex offers a wide range of package tours, including ski holidays, educational tours, budget tours, and tours aimed at the youth market. No information is available regarding the contribution to the earnings of Sunnex Vacations PLC by each of these various services.

According to the most current information available, the destinations of tours sold by Sunnex Vacations PLC can be broken down as follows:

Table 2.8 Summary WTG balance sheets: at 31 March

	19X9 (£ million)		19X8 (£ million)	
Current assets				
Cash	18.7		37.8	
Investments[a]	23.0		10.5	
Accounts receivable	41.0	82.7	24.9	73.2
Fixed assets				
Tangible fixed assets	95.5		76.9	
Aircraft finance costs	6.5	102.0	6.9	83.8
		184.7		157.0
Current liabilities				
Accounts payable[b]	54.8		53.4	
Dividends payable	1.4		1.3	
Taxes payable	1.1	57.3	1.0	55.7
Long term liabilities				
Long term finance	57.8		53.6	
Deferred tax	26.6	84.4	22.3	75.9
Owners' equity				
Share capital	5.8		5.8	
Retained earnings	37.2	43.0	19.6	25.4
		184.7		157.0

Notes: [a] Short term British Government securities to support Association of British Travel Agents bond.
[b] Includes cash received in advance: £23.6 million in 19X9, £31.7 million in 19X8.

Spain	56%	Malta	7%
USA	20%	Italy	5%
Greece	7%	Other	5%

The currency movements which may appear most relevant to WTG's operations are shown in Table 2.9.

World Air

World Air was set up at the same time as World Travel Group, as a wholly owned subsidiary. Management policy dictates that Sunnex Vacations uses no more than 50% of World Air's capacity. The balance is shared by up to 25 other tour operators. No single tour operator, other than Sunnex Vacations, utilizes more than 8% of World Air's total capacity.

Capacity on the airline is sold twelve months ahead for summer tours

Identification and Measurement of Exposure

Table 2.9 Currency movements to 19X2–19X9

		peseta/$	$/£	peseta/£
19X2	June	109.2	1.76	191.8
	December	125.9	1.62	203.9
19X3	June	143.3	1.55	222.2
	December	157.9	1.43	226.6
19X4	June	154.7	1.38	213.2
	December	171.7	1.18	203.8
19X5	June	174.7	1.28	223.7
	December	156.9	1.44	226.5
19X6	June	144.5	1.49	215.3
	December	135.2	1.43	193.3
19X7	June	126.7	1.61	204.0
	December	109.0	1.87	204.0
19X8	June	121.5	1.71	207.7
	December	113.4	1.81	205.2
19X9	June	124.3	1.55	192.7
	December	109.4	1.61	176.4

and nine months ahead for winter tours. The charterer pays by instalments prior to departure. Although prices are fixed, the ability of the air charter firms to pass on increases in direct operating costs (such as fuel) to charterers depends greatly on the competitive environment within the industry.

World Air's current fleet consists exclusively of Boeing aircraft, as shown in Table 2.10. In addition, World Air holds the option to sell back the B757 acquired in March 19X6, at a fixed dollar price, in March of the year following 19X9.

Table 2.10

Acquisition date	Aircraft	Cost ($ million)
March 19X5	One B737-200	12
March 19X6	One B757	34
March 19X7	One B757	35
May 19X8	One B757	36
On order Dec. 19X8	Four B737-300	100 (delivery late 19X9)

All aircraft were financed by sterling denominated, sterling LIBOR priced financial leases. The agreements call for interest payments over periods from seven to twelve years at rates not exceeding 2.5% above sterling LIBOR. The repayment schedules in the 19X9 and 19X8 accounts were as shown in Table 2.11.

Table 2.11

	19X9 (£ million)	*19X8* (£ million)
1–2 years	5.9	6.4
2–5 years	16.4	28.0
Over 5 years	35.5	19.2
Total	57.8	53.6

2.8.3. Suggested World Travel Group Exposure Profiles

Before setting out the individual exposure profiles, it is worth spelling out again the underlying assumptions.

First, the market value of the equity is assumed to be the present value of its expected future net cash flows. As outlined in Section 2.3, this can be written mathematically as

$$V_e = \sum_{j=1}^{\infty} \frac{NCF_j}{(1 + {_0R_j})^j}$$

Secondly, in the following discussions of the exposures, individual profiles have been suggested. When you look through the individual profiles, bear in mind that in some cases the slopes could offset each other. There is, for instance, obviously a relationship between expected inflation in two countries and their relative foreign exchange rates. Similarly, it is difficult to tease out the separate effects (to a UK company) of a change in the $/£ exchange rate and the possible subsequent effect in terms of the dollar denominated fuel oil prices that the UK company might have to pay. Is this an oil price exposure or a foreign exchange exposure?

Commodity price exposure

The main commodity price exposure relates to oil price changes.

Operating costs An increase in oil prices will raise industry operating costs significantly. The information given in Section 2.8.1 suggests that fuel costs account for something around 10% (35% × 30%) of the total price of the holiday.

It is likely, however, that the competition is faced with the same sort of cost structure. World Travel Group might, in fact, be somewhat less adversely affected than its competitors; it has recently invested in a

Identification and Measurement of Exposure

modern fleet of fuel efficient aircraft and its costs might rise by less than the industry's average.

Faced with an oil price increase in 19X9, World Air would have limited alternatives. One is to have the additional cost absorbed by World Travel Group and ultimately the shareholders of the group. Another is to pass the additional cost on to the passengers in the form of a fuel surcharge. Although in this way the short term cash flow of the company may be improved, there is always the possibility that cash flow will deteriorate in the future as customers seek out tour operators offering a no-fuel-surcharge guarantee.

World Travel Group's decision might well rest on its competitors' expected response. If competitors do not raise their prices, then passing all of World Air's additional fuel costs on to the customers to protect this year's profit might yet prove to be a costly exercise in terms of lost customer business in the future.

It seems likely that, given World Travel Group's pre-tax profit margin of only some 5%, even a small increase in oil prices will significantly reduce the value of the firm. Consequently, the profile of changes in corporate value with respect to changes in the oil price is likely to be steep, as illustrated in Figure 2.2. We will not, for the moment, attempt to quantify the slope of the exposure profile. At this point we are more

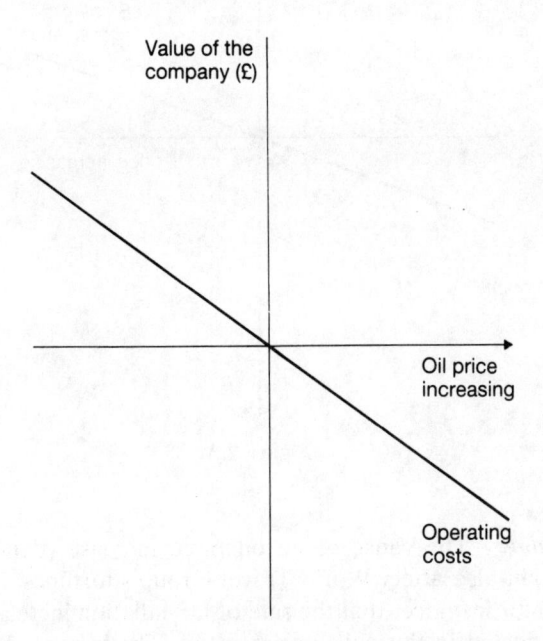

Figure 2.2

interested in the direction of the profile. The matter of attempting to quantify the slopes will be addressed in Chapter 10.

Sterling appreciation Given that the UK oil production in 19X9 was not an insignificant proportion of the world's total output, it is reasonable to assume, given an increase in the price of oil, that sterling would appreciate against other currencies in general and the currencies of non-oil-producing countries in particular.

Thus World Travel Group's peseta denominated cash flow liabilities (for accommodation, hotels and so on) would be reduced in terms of sterling equivalents. It is also likely that British demand for holidays in Spain would increase owing to the increased purchasing power of the British currency abroad.

Figure 2.3 shows the possible exposure profile. As indicated, the slope of the curve would certainly offset that of Figure 2.2, but this secondary appreciation effect would probably be weaker in impact.

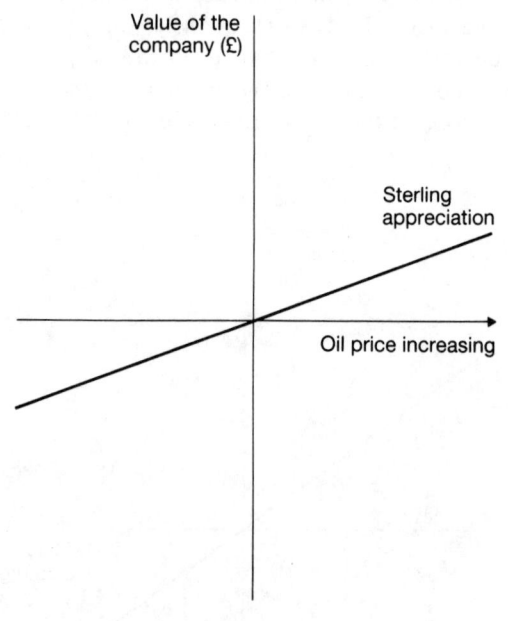

Figure 2.3

Aircraft values The cause of an oil price increase (denominated in dollars) might also affect World Travel Group's fortunes.

Assume, for instance, that the rate of US inflation increased and that this was reflected in the dollar price of oil. The increased cost of fuel

Identification and Measurement of Exposure

might well then depress the market value of aircraft. This might, in turn, increase the value of the option to sell that World Travel Group holds in respect of the Boeing 757 purchased in March 19X6. Alternatively it could be argued that, given the 757 is a very fuel efficient aircraft, its price would increase following an oil price increase because more airlines would switch to 757 fleets. In that instance, the value of the option would fall.

Summing up all these arguments, we suggest that it is likely that World Travel Group's corporate value will be negatively affected in the event of oil prices increasing, as shown in Figure 2.4.

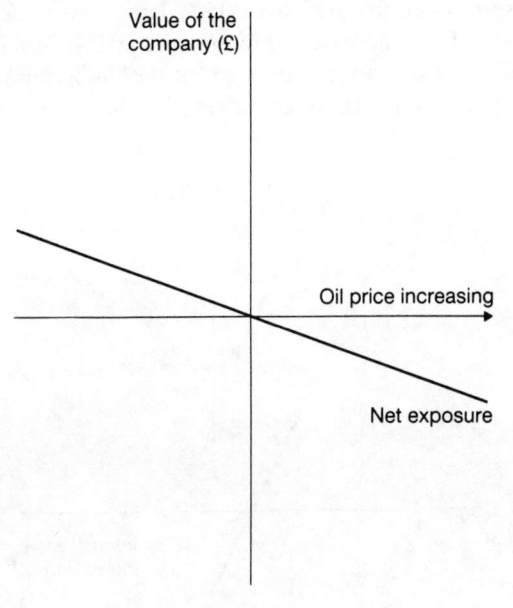

Figure 2.4

Interest rate exposure

If we refer to the equation (repeated at the beginning of Section 2.8.3) used to model the valuation of an all-equity financed firm, it will be noted that interest rates can impact on both the numerator and the denominator. For instance, a change in the interest rate could impact on the numerator in terms of changing the estimate of the firm's future net cash flow. Changes in the interest rate will almost certainly affect the denominator discount rate used to calculate the present values.

36 Identification and Measurement of Exposure

Our approach here will be to see first the possible impact of interest rate changes on the 'absolute' expected future cash flows without taking into account the effect of the changes on the discount rate. By looking at the component cash flows first, we can then sum the elements to get a feel for the direction of WTG's *total* absolute cash flow sensitivity to interest rate changes.

Leasing The company has heavy lease payment obligations linked to sterling LIBOR. In 19X9 the company has a debt/equity ratio of 1.34:1 (£57.8 million:£43.0 million) on the balance sheet, and has lease expenses in the profit and loss account of £5.1 million, some 41% of the operating profit (see Tables 2.7 and 2.8).

These lease obligations are particularly heavy over the longer term and the effect of an increased interest rate will be to increase cash outflows. The exposure profile, in terms of the undiscounted cash flows over future periods, is therefore likely to be steep, as shown in Figure 2.5.[5]

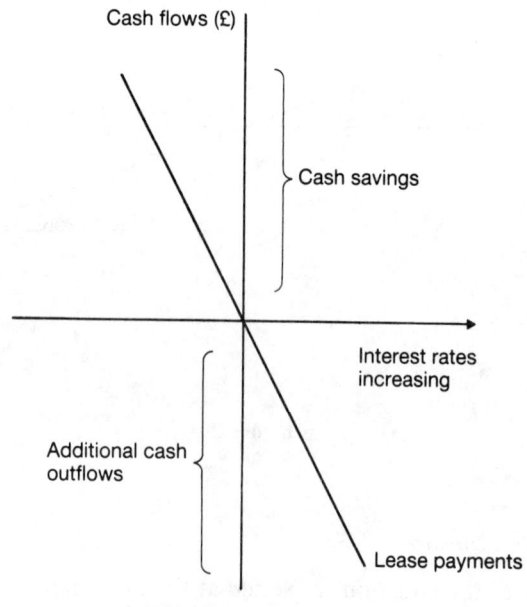

Figure 2.5

Securities You will note that World Travel Group is required to hold, as part of the ABTA bond, substantial short term, British Government securities. The securities represented, in 19X9, some 12% of total assets

Identification and Measurement of Exposure

(see Table 2.8). Given that these securities pay fixed interest, an unexpected change in other interest rates would not affect interest receipts. Thus we would expect that the curve to be flat, as shown in Figure 2.6.[6]

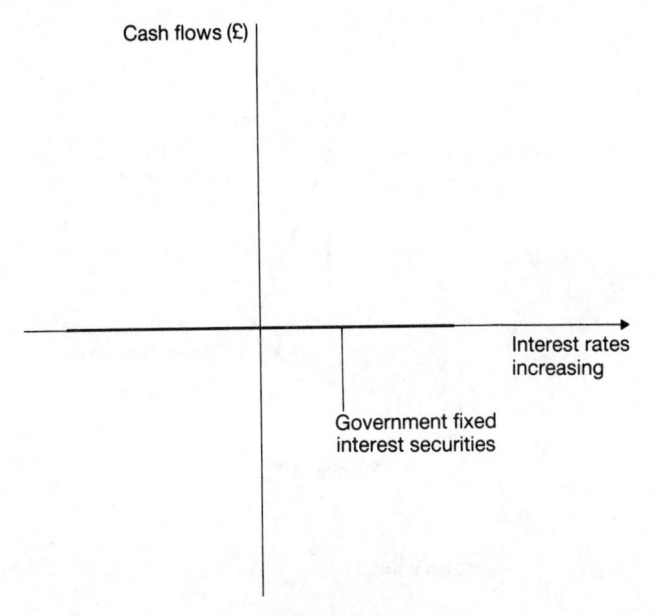

Figure 2.6

Demand for holidays A third potential effect might arise through increased interest rates being used by the government as an instrument to control demand in the economy. This could affect the demand for holidays; it all depends upon how sensitive that demand would be with respect to higher interest rates. Many thousands of holiday packages offered by leading British tour operators were cancelled in 1989 following a significant increase in mortgage rates (from about 8% to about 13%). This is illustrated in Figure 2.7.

Holiday receipts The mitigant to the three points above would be the positive effect of higher interest rates on the short term investment of the group's holiday receipts. World Travel Group receives, on average, the sterling cost of the holiday some five weeks before departure date and settles with its suppliers some six weeks after departure. It is therefore able to invest these essentially free funds over the eleven week period, giving rise to an exposure profile as in Figure 2.8.

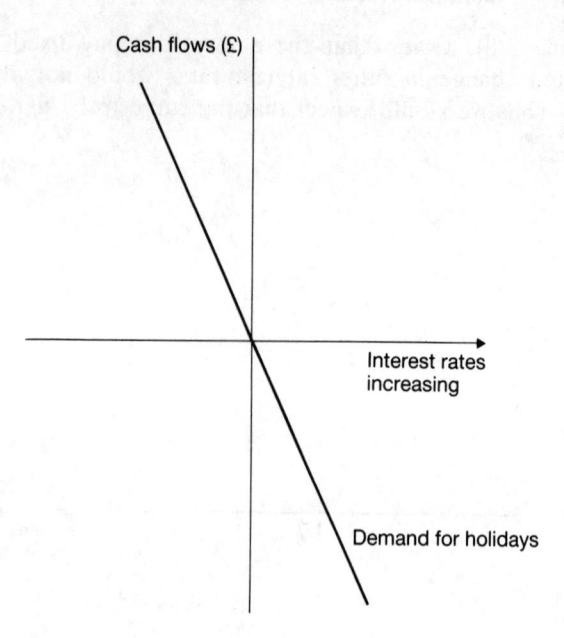

Figure 2.7

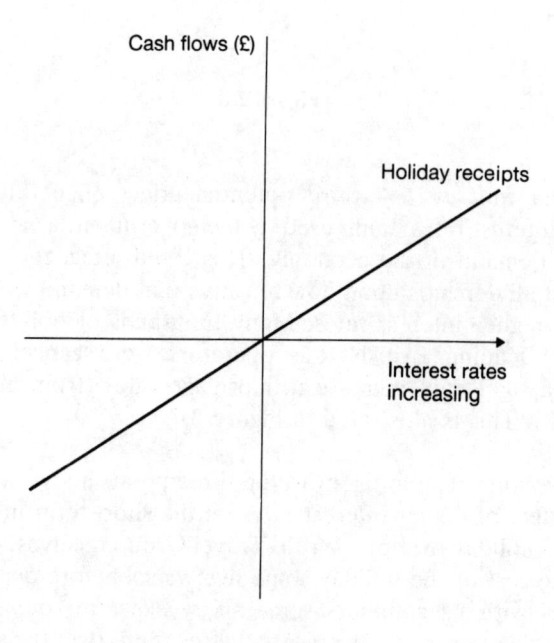

Figure 2.8

Identification and Measurement of Exposure

Having now looked at the individual undiscounted cash flow effects from interest rate changes, it is clear that WTG's net cash flow will be negatively affected when interest rates increase.

Given that interest rate increases will also result in the net cash flows now being discounted by a higher discount factor, it is likely that the value of the shareholders' wealth will fall sharply in the event of interest rates increasing. This is summed up in Figure 2.9.

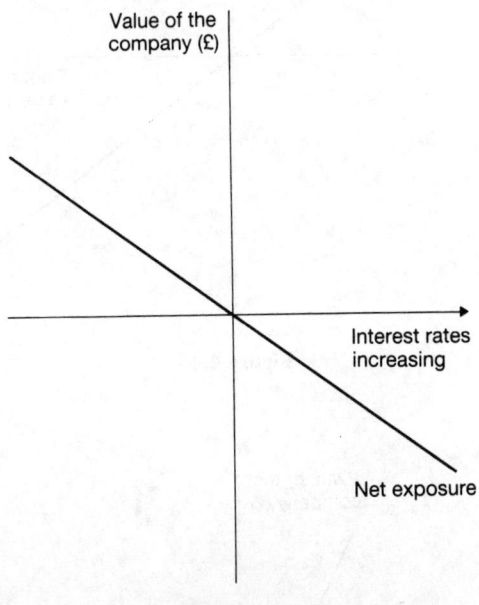

Figure 2.9

Foreign exchange exposure

US dollar versus pound sterling Around 20% of the group's holidays are in the US. An appreciation in the value of the dollar against sterling might have two negative impacts. One is the reduced British demand for holidays in the US owing to the reduced purchasing power of the pound sterling in America. The other is the increased sterling costs of dollar denominated liabilities for oil, purchases of new aircraft, accommodation and so on. The total impact is shown in Figure 2.10.

Spanish peseta versus pound sterling The group has a significantly higher proportion of tourists going to Spain than any other tour operator. Thus the appreciation of the Spanish peseta against sterling might well have the same impact as an appreciation of the dollar against

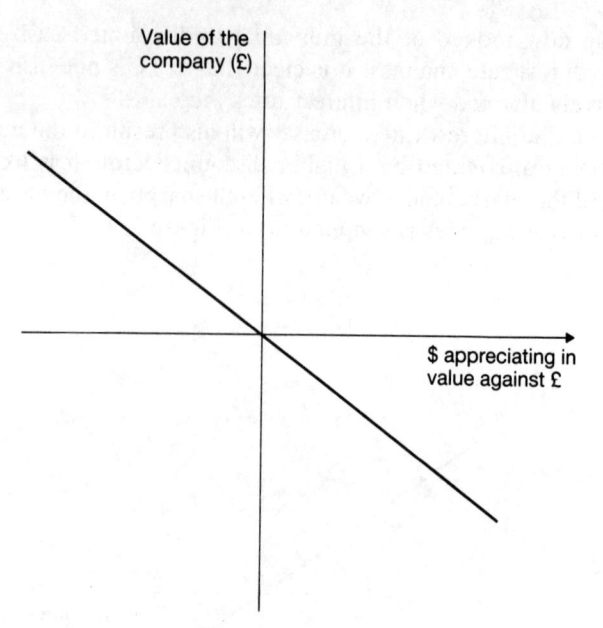

Figure 2.10

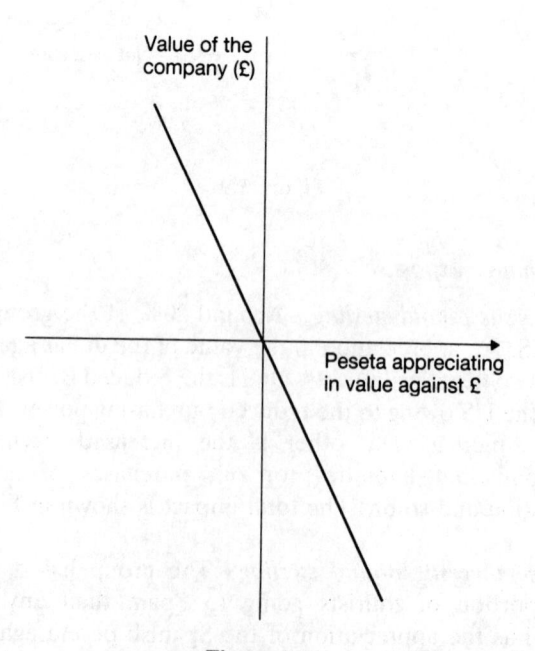

Figure 2.11

Identification and Measurement of Exposure 41

sterling. Given the greater reliance on Spanish holidays than American, however, it is likely that the slope of the Spanish peseta exposure would be steeper that that for the dollar, as shown in Figure 2.11.

Other currency exposure This relates to the same sort of exposure as that faced by the Midwest bicycle manufacturer in Section 2.7. Suppose, for instance, that following an unexpected depreciation of Turkish lira (relative to the movement of the pound against pesetas) it became very cheap for British tourists to go to Turkey. In other words, the purchasing power of British tourists in Turkey improved markedly.

Given that a large percentage of World Travel Group's customers currently go to Spain, such a move could have a significant effect on the group's fortunes as its customers switch to Turkish destinations. The group's exposure depends upon its ability to provide Turkish holidays at short notice. This is illustrated in Figure 2.12.

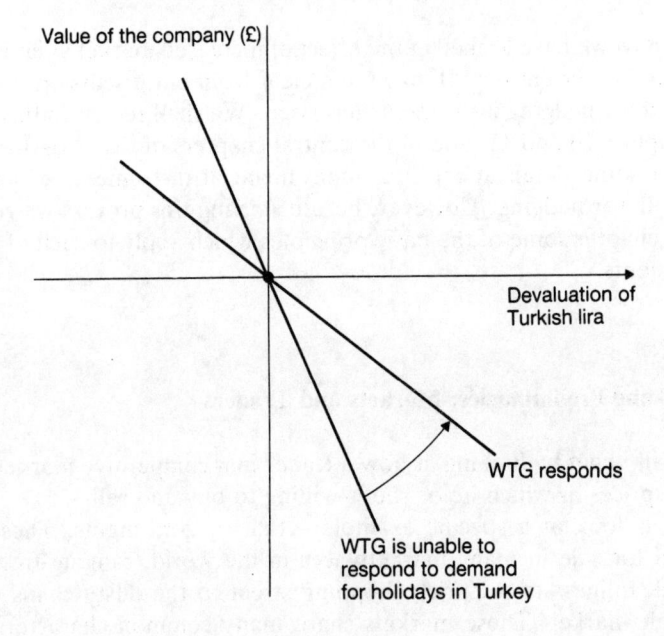

Figure 2.12

Summarizing, we would expect to see WTG's market capitalization being adversely affected in the event of unexpected increases in interest rates, in oil prices and in the event of certain foreign currencies appreciating in value against the pound sterling. As we have already noted above, we have not at this stage attempted to measure the slope of the exposure profile. This task is deferred until Chapter 10.

3
The Principles of Pricing Financial Instruments

3.1 Introduction

Up to now we have looked at the effect of increased market volatility on firms and other entities. It may seem clear from our discussion why the demand for hedging instruments has risen. We shall return to this issue in Chapters 10 and 11, and in the central chapters of the book we shall look in some detail at the individual financial instruments which are available for hedging. However, before starting this process we review in this chapter some of the basic principles which apply to each of these instruments.

3.2 Some Preliminaries: Markets and Traders

We shall begin by looking at how a trader in a competitive market may fix the prices at which he or she is willing to buy and sell.

Let us look at a specific example — that of gold ingots. These are offered for sale in many marketplaces in the world, ranging from the calm cleanliness of a Zurich shopping street to the dusty chaos of an open air market. These markets share many common characteristics. First, the product is readily and unambiguously defined: the ingots are hallmarked to indicate purity and are sold by weight, which may be stamped on the ingot itself or readily verified by a weighing machine. (For the moment we exclude the possibility of false markings and weighing machines!) Secondly, there is a high degree of competition between traders. Often there will be rows of traders in close proximity, each offering similar products so that potential customers can easily shop around before making a trade.

Such a market comes close to the economist's abstraction described as perfect competition. First, no trader has any significant influence over the global price of gold. This is something determined in the global currency and metal markets whose centres may be many thousands of miles away. Secondly, each trader has to match the price of the others. Too high a price will drive too many clients away to other traders; too low a price forces the trader to trade at a loss and go out of business.

So far we have talked of the 'price' of gold, but in practice things are not quite so simple. In most of the markets of the kind we are considering there will be a buying price (often known as the bid price) and a selling price (often known as the asking price, the offer price or the offered price). Thus, if the global price of one ounce of pure gold is $500, traders might be prepared to buy a one ounce ingot for $499 and to sell a one ounce ingot for $501. This difference in price (often known as the bid-offer spread, the bid-ask spread or simply the spread) provides the trader with his profits. Economists tell us that, given freedom of entry and exit to the business of gold trading, the spread will be such that, in the long run, it provides the marginal trader with a normal rate of profit. Thus it will have to provide a gross income in excess of the costs of carrying the stock of gold which this type of business requires.

One last point before we move on. It should be clear that if a trader intends to stay in business, his bid and offer prices should form a band which straddles the global price of gold. If not, the trader will be offering customers huge profit opportunities at his own expense. For example, if he sets prices at $489–$491 when the global price is $500 (that is, when the bid-offer spread is $499–$501 around the central price of $500), customers will flock to him to buy large quantities of gold for $491 which they can then sell on the world market for $499. The trader will deplete his gold stock rapidly; and to service his customers he must buy new stocks at $501 per ounce, only to be selling them immediately at $491, thus making a loss on every ounce! If, on the other hand, his price band is above the global price he still gives profit making opportunities to his customers. If his prices are $509–$511 while the global gold price is $500, customers flock to buy gold on the world market at $501 and to sell it to him at $509!

To put this in slightly more technical terms: by setting his price wrongly, the trader is offering a risk-free arbitrage opportunity to other participants in the market. These other participants will make a profit at the trader's expense by arbitraging between his prices and those of the market. In a competitive world, these opportunities will be seized upon very quickly indeed and the trader will be forced out of business. It is of course possible to argue that, in the second case just discussed, the market price might move up to $540, whereupon the trader could sell his stock (bought for $509) and still make a profit. However, in a modern competitive market the opportunity for the other participants to make a guaranteed $8 per ounce of gold arbitraged would quickly generate many huge transactions, and the trader, building up his stock of gold, would run out of cash and credit long before the world gold price began to move upward. It is the guaranteed, risk-free nature of the arbitrage profit which generates these large and rapid reactions. In market jargon the trader is offering free lunches – and there will be no shortage of customers ready to eat them!

So far we have looked at the impact on a trader if his bid-offer spread fails to straddle the global price. We should now examine the effect of straddling the global price but posting a bid-offer spread which differs from other traders. For example, suppose that each trader posts $499–$501 except for one who posts $498–$502. In such a case, given our assumptions so far, this one trader will have no customers. Those wishing to buy gold and those wishing to sell gold can do so more advantageously by going to another trader. Now suppose our single trader posts $499.50–$501. He will then find that he buys a lot of gold from people taking advantage of the extra 50 cents which he offers, while his sales of gold are unspectacular. He therefore begins to build up a gold stock and, if other traders begin to run short, they will have to raise their bid price to match his. Our trader is acting as a market maker.

Let us now reconsider the determinants of the bid-offer spread. Most real-world markets are somewhat less than perfectly competitive and have some elements of monopoly within them. There may be, for instance, some restrictions such as licensing on the numbers of traders allowed in the market. In such a case, buoyant market conditions may lead to a widening of the bid-offer spread and hence to increased profits for traders. Customers may build up loyalties to particular traders and may be willing to go on trading with trader X even though his bid-offer spread is wider than trader Y's. Traders, too, may distinguish between customers. Old established customers, customers dealing in large volumes, and local customers as opposed to tourists or foreigners, may be charged lower spreads.

So far, we have only briefly considered issues of quality. In some markets, customers will not be readily able to judge quality and may be concerned about the prospect of being sold, for example, 18 carat gold masquerading as 22 carat. Some traders may have a better reputation than others and these will be able to charge higher spreads to reflect their quality status. The less homogeneous the item being traded, the more issues of this kind might emerge. Hence the spreads on gold jewellery, which involve issues such as design, craftsmanship and so on, are likely to be higher than those on gold ingots.

Finally, we should point out that we have not discussed at any length why the world price of gold in our example was $500 per ounce. Ultimately, the world price is determined by a complicated interaction of demand and supply. Fortunately, we do not need to address this issue in the book. This is because we are looking at highly competitive markets from the point of view of a single participant. The collective actions of a large number of market participants will move world market prices but the actions of a single participant will not. The only decision open to a single participant is to set the prices at which that one participant is prepared to buy or sell.

Now, armed with these general comments, we shall consider the pricing of some of the simpler financial instruments. It is worth noting that each of these instruments has a uniform, known quality and is traded on extremely competitive markets.

3.3 The Spot Market for Currencies

The way in which foreign exchange rates are quoted varies from source to source but the principles remain similar. A table with a heading such as 'foreign exchanges' or 'currencies' is presented which reports the trading of a currency, say the pound sterling, against several other currencies. In the table there is a column labelled 'close', showing rates at the close of the previous business day. For example against Deutschmarks one might find the figures 3.1375–3.1425. This indicates that, at the end of the day concerned, banks bid for the pound and offered the Deutschmark at a rate of 3.1375, and offered the pound and bid for the Deutschmark at a rate of 3.1425. In other words, a customer could sell a pound to the bank for DM3.1375 and could buy a pound from the bank for DM3.1425.[1] As can be seen from these figures, the quotations are similar to the gold price quotations discussed in Section 3.2. This is hardly surprising when we consider the nature of the spot currency market, with its clearly defined product, large number of participants, high degree of competition and so on.

It is also worth noting that the bid-offer spread is very narrow. A sum of £100 converted into Deutschmarks and then reconverted into pounds would be returned as £100 × (3.1375/3.1425) or £99.84, indicating a charge of about 0.08% on each of the two transactions. (Note that we are talking here of the charge made to customers able to obtain the banks' best possible rate. Other customers would be quoted less advantageous terms.)

3.4 The Spot Market for Interest Rates: Loans and Deposits

3.4.1 Interpreting the Yield Curve

The pages of the financial press and, more recently, the many screen-based information services usually contain quotations based upon the concept of a yield curve. In this section we examine these quotations in some detail.

A typical set of quotations appears in Table 3.1. Suppose, for example, that the quotations refer to bank deposits and bank loans. The first column shows the time to maturity: the length of time covered by a transaction entered into today. The second column shows the offer or offered rate: the rate which the bank will charge if it makes a loan. The third column shows the bid rate: the rate which the bank will pay on a deposit. The difference between items in the third and second columns is known as the bid-offer spread.[2]

Table 3.1

Time to maturity (months)	Offer rate (%)	Bid rate (%)	Central rate (%)
1	11 3/8	11 5/16	11 11/32
2	11 1/2	11 7/16	11 15/32
3	11 5/8	11 9/16	11 19/32
4	11 11/16	11 5/8	11 21/32
5	11 13/16	11 6/8	11 25/32
6	11 7/8	11 13/16	11 27/32

The table shows that the bank will pay, in arrears, 11 5/16% on a deposit received today and repayable in one month's time, 11 7/16% on a deposit received today and repayable in two months' time, and so on, as shown in the third column. For a one month loan the bank will charge (at least[3]) 11 3/8%, for a two month loan (at least) 11 1/2%, and so on, as shown in the second column.

A set of quotations such as this is known as a yield curve because it is common practice to show bid rates, offer rates or the mean of the two rates (central rates) in the form of a graph with the interest rate on the vertical axis and time to maturity on the horizontal axis. The central rates from Table 3.1 produce the yield curve shown in Figure 3.1.

It is usual practice to quote interest rates on an annual basis. Thus if the one month bid rate is shown at 11 5/16% (or 11.3125%), a depositor of £1000 for one month would not expect to receive back from the bank his initial £1000 plus £113.125 in interest at the end of the month! Rather he would expect to receive his £1000 plus one month's worth of an

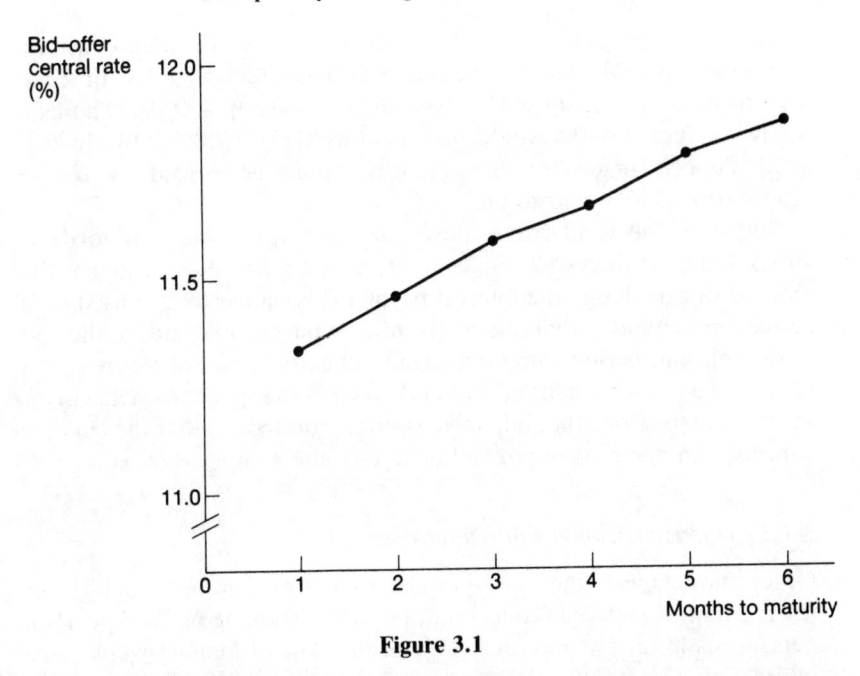

Principles of Pricing Financial Instruments 47

Figure 3.1

annual interest rate of 11.3125%, an amount which would be close to one-twelfth of £113.125.

You will notice that we have just used the rather imprecise words 'close to one-twelfth'. This is because, until we know the market to which the yield curve applies and the exact conventions used to make quotations in that market, we cannot be precise about the calculation of interest. For example, some markets use the convention that each month has 30 days and each year has twelve such months. In such a market a depositor placing his money with the bank for one month would receive *exactly* one-twelfth of £113.125 (that is, £9.4271) in interest because interest would be calculated as £(30/360)(11.3125%) per pound deposited. The total amount to be paid at the end of the month, including the return of deposit, would be £[1 + (30/360)(0.113125)] per pound deposited.

Now let us return to our yield curve and look at the longer maturities, continuing to refer to a market using 30 day months and 360 day years. The yield curve shows the rates paid/charged on deposits/loans arranged today and maintained until the agreed maturity date. Thus the two month deposit rate (11^7/$_{16}$%) is applied to a deposit made today and repaid in two months' time. To calculate the amount of interest to be received, let us assume that all the interest is paid at the end of the two month period. In this case a depositor of £1 for two months would receive £[1 + (60/360)(0.114375)] at the end of two months. It will be easy to see from the yield curve that a £1 deposit made today for three months would be repaid as £[1 + (90/360)(0.115625)], a £1 deposit made today for four months would be repaid as £[1 + (120/360)(0.11625)], a £1 deposit made for five months would be repaid as £[1 + (150/360)(0.1175)], and so on.

Note that the yield curve shows the rates applicable only to deals struck today. It therefore relates to the spot market. Note also that the method of calculating the interest payments is similar to that used on a zero coupon bond in that one single interest payment is made at the end of the relevant period with no intermittent cash flows. For this reason a yield curve in such a market is often known as the spot zero yield curve. In practice, one or other adjective is often omitted, so that the curve is variously known as the spot yield curve or the zero yield curve.

3.4.2 Differing Market Conventions

Other markets use other conventions. Some work on the actual figures for the month and year concerned, so that (assuming no leap year!) a deposit made for one month at 11% at the start of January would earn interest of £(31/365)(0.11) per pound deposited, while a similar deposit made at the start of February would earn interest of £(28/365)(0.11), and so on. One month deposits made on other days of the month would similarly earn interest based upon the actual number of days concerned.

Some markets calculate interest payments on the basis of compounding. On this basis, a deposit made for one month at 12% in a market using the 30 day month convention would lead to an amount to be repaid at the end of the month, including return of deposit of £$(1 + 0.12)^{30/360}$ per pound deposited rather then of £[1 + (30/360)(0.12)]. Hence the interest earned would be £$[(1 + 0.12)^{30/360} - 1]$ per pound deposited.

Different conventions in different markets can lead to a great deal of confusion and can suggest to the unwary that different markets contain very different rates of interest for the same maturity period. This is rarely so. It is important to note that each yield curve expresses the same concept, albeit in a different way. Each curve shows the 'cost' or 'price' of money for different maturity periods. If arbitrage opportunities are to be removed, each maturity period must have a single price of money. However, different yield curves express this price in different ways, in rather the same way as a car speedometer calibrated in miles will show a speed as 50 per hour while a speedometer calibrated in kilometres will show the same velocity as almost 80 per hour.

To illustrate this, consider a comparison between market A, in which interest is calculated in the simple fractional way, and market B, in which interest is calculated using compounding. We might well find the bid rates shown in Table 3.2. The interest rates appear to be different for the same maturities, and it may seem that the two markets offer large arbitrage opportunities. However, the difference reflects only the different calculation method used in each market. The actual amount of interest paid in each market will be the same. In market A, £1000 deposited for one month will earn interest of £1000 × (0.113125/12) or £9.4271. In market B, £1000 deposited for one month will earn interest of £1000 × (1.119178$^{1/12}$ − 1) or £9.4271. Similar calculations for other maturities will confirm the correspondence between the two yield curves.

Table 3.2

Time to maturity (months)	Market A Fraction (%)	Market A Decimal (%)	Market B (%)
1	11 5/16	11.3125	11.9178
2	11 7/16	11.4375	11.9966
3	11 9/16	11.5625	12.0735
4	11 5/8	11.625	12.0812
5	11 6/8	11.75	12.1553
6	11 13/16	11.8125	12.1614

3.4.3 Par Yield Curves

Par yield curves provide another, very important, example of differing market conventions.

So far we have considered interest rates and yield curves in the context of instruments involving a single payment of interest and principal at maturity, sometimes known as zero coupon instruments.

However, many financial instruments, such as long dated bonds, involve regular payments – or coupons – over the life of the instrument. The yields on such instruments can also be shown in the form of a yield curve, known as the par yield curve. At first glance, the par yield curve looks exactly like the spot zero yield curve, but its interpretation is very different. The data in Table 3.3 represent the par yield curve graphed in Figure 3.2.

The rates shown in a par yield curve are those regular interest payments (expressed as an annual rate) which would enable an instrument offering such payments to trade on the market at par, that is at a price equal to its face value. An example may help to clarify this concept.

Principles of Pricing Financial Instruments

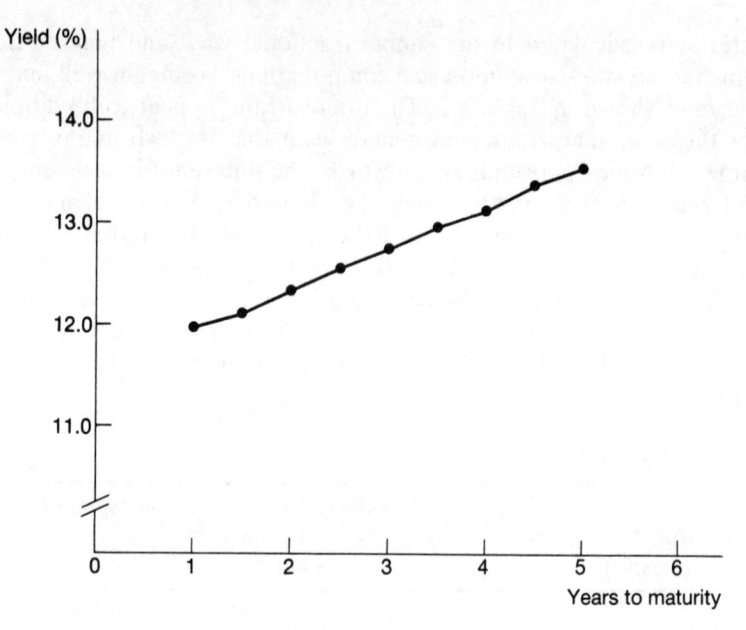

Yield (%)

Years to maturity

Figure 3.2

Consider a newly issued two year bond which pays a coupon at six monthly intervals. Let this coupon (expressed as an annual rate) be denoted as $C\%$. The bond therefore entitles its holder to an amount of $(C/2)\%$ in six months' time, followed by $(C/2)\%$ in twelve months' time, followed by $(C/2)\%$ in eighteen months' time, followed by $(C/2)\%$ plus return of principal at the end of the two year period. This series of cash flows for a bond of face value £100 can be shown as follows:

Months hence	6	12	18	24
Cash payment (£)	C/2	C/2	C/2	(C/2) + 100

The present value of this payment stream is[4]

$$\frac{C/2}{(1 + {}_0R_6)^{0.5}} + \frac{C/2}{(1 + {}_0R_{12})^{1.0}} + \frac{C/2}{(1 + {}_0R_{18})^{1.5}} + \frac{(C/2) + 100}{(1 + {}_0R_{24})^{2.0}}$$

where ${}_0R_j$ denotes today's spot zero rate of interest for a maturity of j months.

All the interest rates shown in the expression are rates applicable today and can be read from today's spot zero yield curve. Suppose that today's spot zero yield curve gives the central rates (those half-way between bid and offer rates) shown in Table 3.4. In this case the present value can be calculated as

Principles of Pricing Financial Instruments

$$\frac{C/2}{(1.1219444)^{0.5}} + \frac{C/2}{(1.1234375)^{1.0}} + \frac{C/2}{(1.125)^{1.5}} + \frac{(C/2) + 100}{(1.1275)^{2.0}}$$

$$= \frac{C/2}{1.059219} + \frac{C/2}{1.1234375} + \frac{C/2}{1.193243} + \frac{(C/2) + 100}{1.2712562}$$

$$= 0.472046C + 0.445063C + 0.419026C + 0.393312C + 78.662349$$

$$= 1.729447C + 78.662349$$

If the bond in question is trading at par (that is at a price of £100) the present value which we have just calculated must be equal to £100. Hence

$$100 = 1.729447C + 78.662349$$
$$C = 12.3378\%$$

As can be seen from Table 3.3, this is the rate shown on the par yield curve for a maturity of two years.

Table 3.3

Time to maturity (years)	Yield (%)
1.0	11.9805
1.5	12.1205
2.0	12.3378
2.5	12.5501
3.0	12.7569
3.5	12.9529
4.0	13.1528
4.5	13.3415
5.0	13.5236

Table 3.4

Time to maturity (years)	Interest rate (%)
0.5	12.19444
1.0	12.34375
1.5	12.5
2.0	12.75
2.5	13.0
3.0	13.25
3.5	13.50
4.0	13.75
4.5	14.0
5.0	14.25

52 Principles of Pricing Financial Instruments

Now let us calculate the rate shown on the par yield curve for maturities of one year. This is the rate which (paid semi-annually) will enable a one year bond to trade at par. Hence we can calculate the rate from

$$100 = \frac{C/2}{(1 + {}_0R_6)^{0.5}} + \frac{(C/2) + 100}{(1 + {}_0R_{12})^{1.0}}$$

$$100 = \frac{C/2}{(1.1219444)^{0.5}} + \frac{(C/2) + 100}{(1.1234375)^{1.0}}$$

$$100 = 0.472046C + 0.445063C + 89.012517$$

$$0.917108C = 10.987483$$

$$C = 11.9805\%$$

Note that the par and the zero yield curves are not independent. Indeed if we are given any one yield curve we can calculate the other. Just to illustrate this point, let us calculate the spot zero rate ${}_0R_{18}$ from the par yield curve:

$$100 = \frac{12.1205/2}{(1.1219444)^{0.5}} + \frac{12.1205/2}{(1.1234375)^{1.0}} + \frac{(12.1205/2) + 100}{(1 + {}_0R_{18})^{1.5}}$$

$$100 = 5.721434 + 5.394381 + \frac{106.06025}{(1 + {}_0R_{18})^{1.5}}$$

$$88.884185 = \frac{106.06025}{(1 + {}_0R_{18})^{1.5}}$$

$$(1 + {}_0R_{18})^{1.5} = 1.193241$$

$$1 + {}_0R_{18} = 1.125$$

$${}_0R_{18} = 0.125 = 12.5\%$$

In this way, using the par yield curve data shown in Table 3.3, the reader can calculate the spot zero rates up to a maturity of five years as in Table 3.4. In each case the two curves will be consistent.

3.4.4 Differing Conventions Once Again

As we have shown in Section 3.4.2, the cash flows associated with loans or deposits will be equal even though the different market conventions lead to different ways of expressing interest rates. In the case of the par yield curve in Section 3.4.3, payments made on loans or deposits according to the par yield curve have the same present value as payments made according to the zero yield curve.

Principles of Pricing Financial Instruments

We shall illustrate this by reference to a two year loan or deposit and we shall use the figures shown in Tables 3.3 and 3.4. The spot zero yield curve shows that the two year rate $_0R_{24}$ is 12.75%. This means that a two year loan/deposit of £100 will incur no interest charges until the end of two years, whereupon it must be repaid as £100 plus the interest charge to make a total of £100 × (1.1275)² or £127.1256. The par yield curve shows that the two year rate, denoted $_0R^P_{24}$, is 12.3378%. This means that a two year loan/deposit of £100 will incur four interest payments, each of 6.1689%, at six monthly intervals and then be repaid as £100. Clearly the present values (and future values) of the two transactions must be the same or there would be a risk-free arbitrage opportunity.

This two year cost of money is the same in each case but, because the interest payment arrangements are different, the figure expressing the rate of interest is different. Let us just show that this is, in fact, the case.

A two year deposit of £100 placed in a zero coupon instrument involves the following cash flows:

Months hence	0	24
Cash flows (£)	−100	+100 (1.1275)²

It is clear that the net present value of these cash flows is zero.

A two year deposit of £100 placed in a six monthly coupon instrument involves the following cash flows:

Months hence	0	6	12	18	24
Cash flows (£)	−100	+6.1689	+6.1689	+6.1689	+106.1689

Using the zero yield curve (Table 3.4), the net present value of these flows can be calculated as

$$-100 + \frac{6.1689}{(1.1219444)^{0.5}} + \frac{6.1689}{(1.1234375)^{1.0}} + \frac{6.1689}{(1.125)^{1.5}} + \frac{106.1689}{(1.1275)^{2.0}}$$

which is equal to zero. Thus the spot zero and the spot par yield curves show different ways of expressing the rate of interest according to the terms under which that interest is to be paid.[5]

With these preliminaries out of the way we are at last able to examine some derivative products. We shall look at forward contracts in Chapter 4, futures in Chapter 5, swaps in Chapter 6 and options in Chapters 7 and 8.

4
Forward Contracts

4.1 The Forward Market for Currencies

4.1.1 Calculating Forward Exchange Rates

Now let us turn to the determination of a price for a one year forward currency contract: a contract involving the exchange of Deutschmarks for pounds sterling in one year's time, at a rate agreed today.

Suppose that the spot DM/£ exchange rate quoted today is 3.1375–3.1425, the one year Eurosterling interest rate is quoted as $12^{3}/_{8}$–$12^{5}/_{16}\%$, and the one year Euro-DM interest rate is $5^{7}/_{16}$–$5^{5}/_{16}\%$. What will be the exchange rate quoted for a one year forward contract?

Let us first ignore bid–offer spreads and work with central rates. Hence we can write the spot DM/£ rate as 3.14, the one year Eurosterling rate as 12.34375% and the one year Euro-DM rate as 5.375%. The principle under which the forward rate is calculated is that, as with other such instruments, the quotation must allow no risk-free arbitrage opportunities. This means that the forward rate must be quoted as DM/£ 2.9452. Suppose a bank quotes a stronger sterling than this, say DM/£ 3.00. Such a bank will be deluged with orders from those wishing to sell sterling one year hence, because by borrowing Deutschmarks today, converting to sterling and depositing in sterling today, it would be possible to make a risk-free profit. For example, DM100 borrowed today must be repaid as DM105.375. Now DM100 can be converted to sterling today to give £100/3.14 = £31.8471, which deposited at 12.34375% will provide £35.7782 at the end of the year. The bank's forward quotation of DM/£ 3.00 allows the conversion of £35.7782 into DM107.3348. This can be used to repay the DM105.375, leaving a guaranteed risk-free profit of almost DM2 per DM100 borrowed. Similarly, a quotation involving a weaker sterling than DM/£

Forward Contracts

2.9452 will also generate a deluge of orders, this time from those wishing to buy sterling one year hence in order to make a risk-free profit from borrowing sterling today, converting into Deutschmarks and depositing the Deutschmarks today.

Referring this argument back to the discussion in Section 3.2, we can see that, without bid–offer spreads, there is just one world price that can be quoted. Any deviation from this price on the part of the trader will offer risk-free arbitrage opportunities.

If we now add some realism and take account of bid–offer spreads, the situation becomes a little more complicated. It is still the case that the price band produced by the bid–offer spread must surround the central rate of DM/£2.9452. If it does not, arbitrage opportunities will still exist. However, given this proviso, a bank can quote quite a wide bid–offer spread. There is however a maximum spread which can be charged, because too wide a spread will induce potential customers to produce their own forward deals.

Consider a potential bank customer in Britain who will receive DM100 next year and who wants to convert this sum into sterling. He can produce a forward for himself by borrowing an amount of Deutschmarks today which will give him a liability of DM100 next year. This will be DM94.8429, that is DM100/1.054375. This liability will be paid off with the DM100 which he will receive next year. He can convert today's borrowed Deutschmarks into sterling (at a rate of DM/£ 3.1425) and deposit the sterling at a rate of 12.3125%. Hence he can arrange today a set of deals which will, in effect, allow him to guarantee a forward rate for his Deutschmarks. The amount of sterling he will receive for his DM100 will be £[(100/1.054375)/3.1425]1.123125 which equals £33.8967, thus giving a forward DM/£ rate of 100/33.8967 or 2.9501.

Similarly, a recipient of £100 in one year's time can arrange a forward rate for buying Deutschmarks by borrowing £100/1.12375 today, converting to DM(100/1.12375)3.1375 today and depositing at 5.3125% to give DM294.0316 in one year's time.

Thus a potential customer can produce forward DM/£ rates of 2.9403–2.9501. These rates show the widest spread which a bank could charge in a competitive market. Wider spreads would induce customers to arrange their own forwards in the way shown above. Competition between banks may lead to the quotation of bands in a narrower range than that shown above, but narrow bands offer no extra opportunities to potential customers. The rates discussed are summarized in Table 4.1.

It is also helpful to show this in a pictorial form as in Figure 4.1. To remove risk-free arbitrage opportunities and to allow banks to stay in business, any movements round this diagram must, after allowing for

Table 4.1

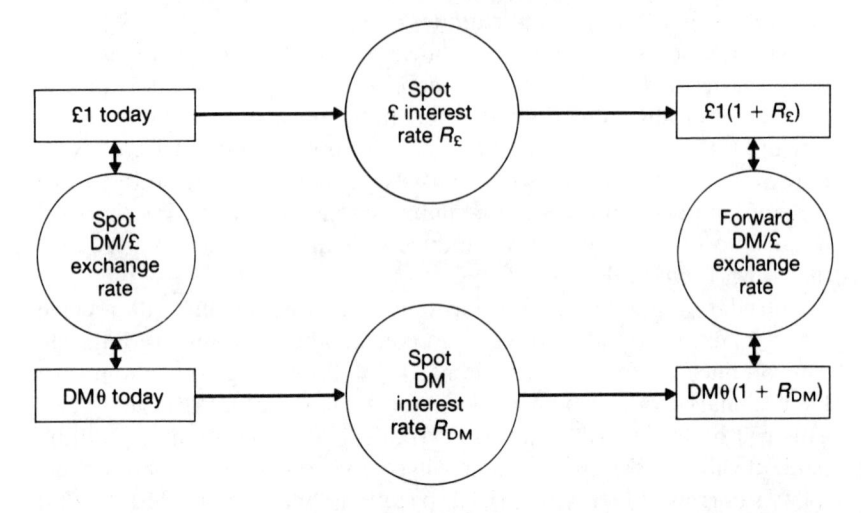

Spot DM/£ exchange rate	3.1375 − 3.1425
Spot twelve month £ interest rate	12.3750%−12.3125%
Spot twelve month DM interest rate	5.4375%− 5.3125%
Limiting range of twelve month forward DM/£ exchange rate	2.9403 − 2.9501

Figure 4.1

the time value of money and after conversion across currencies, produce equivalent amounts. These principles can be applied to many different markets including commodity markets, and to forwards with many different maturity dates.

In terms of a general formula we can see that the forward rates may be calculated from the spot rates in the currency and interest rate markets. If, as in many textbooks, we ignore bid–offer spreads and use central rates, we can write simply that the forward rate showing the number of units of currency x exchanging for £1, $F_{x/£}$, can be expressed as

$$F_{x/£} = S_{x/£} \frac{1 + R_x}{1 + R_£}$$

where $S_{x/£}$ denotes the spot rate and R_x and $R_£$ denote the appropriate interest rates for the two currencies concerned.

If, as in the real world, we take into account bid–offer spreads, the formula becomes more cumbersome:

$$F_{ox/b£} = S_{ox/b£} \frac{1 + R_{bx}}{1 + R_{o£}}$$

Forward Contracts

$$F_{o£/bx} = S_{o£/bx} \frac{1 + R_{ox}}{1 + R_{b£}}$$

where the extra subscripts b and o denote bid and offered rates.

4.1.2 Currency Forward Contracts

In Figure 4.2 we illustrate the documentation involved in a currency forward contract. We should point out that the figure provides *only* an illustration and that the real-life documentation is much more complicated, involving a very careful definition of each of the entities and each of the concepts involved, including the place where the payments are to be made. This exactitude is important should either party enter into a legal dispute. Those actively involved in such deals will often simplify the process by signing one general document setting out all the issues, sometimes known as a master agreement, and then, each time they complete a deal, by exchanging telexes similar to that shown in Figure 4.2 and referring to the master agreement.

Currency forward contract

This document records the agreement between ABC GmbH and the National Bank PLC that, on 14 September 1989, ABC GmbH will pay to the National Bank PLC the sum of 1.8 million Deutschmarks and the National Bank PLC will pay to ABC GmbH the sum of 1 million US dollars.

Figure 4.2

As can be seen from the documentation, the forward contract takes the form of an obligation to pay the agreed sums of money on the agreed date. Contracts can be cancelled by mutual agreement but the party wishing to cancel will usually have to pay a fee to the other. Effective cancellation can also be achieved by entering into another, reverse, contract for the same date. That is, ABC will pay $1 million to the

58   Forward Contracts

National Bank in return for DM1.8 million. In practice, there will be a bid–offer spread in each deal – for example, if the first contract involves a DM/$ rate of 1.80 then the second will involve a rate of 1.7990 – and thus a cancellation cost will be imposed on ABC.[1]

4.2 The Forward Market for Interest Rates

4.2.1 Calculating Forward Interest Rates

As in the case of forward foreign exchange contracts, we shall begin by ignoring bid–offer spreads and using only central rates. Thus our spot zero yield curve can be written as in Table 4.2 (the rate notation will be explained shortly).

Table 4.2

Time to maturity (months)	Yield (%)	Rate notation
1	11.34375	$_0R_1$
2	11.46875	$_0R_2$
3	11.59375	$_0R_3$
4	11.65625	$_0R_4$
5	11.78125	$_0R_5$
6	11.84375	$_0R_6$

As in the currency market, it is possible for a depositor or a borrower to fix a future interest rate today through combinations of borrowing and lending in the same currency. (Note that, without a bid–offer spread, the depositor and the borrower will each face the same interest rate.)

Consider the fixing of the rate for a one month deposit/loan starting in one month's time. This rate will be 11.485179%. How do we know? Because this is the only rate which prevents the market maker in interest rate forwards from making an unlimited loss. If the market maker quotes this rate, two successive one month deals arranged today will be equivalent to a two month deal also arranged today. Suppose a depositor deposits £1 today for one month at 11.34375% and also agrees *today* to deposit the proceeds of £1.009453125 (that is, £1 plus the £0.009453125 interest earned in the month) for a further one month at today's quoted forward rate of 11.485179%. At the end of two months the depositor will have £1.009453125 × (1 + 0.00957098) = £1.019114583. This is exactly equal to the amount he would have if, instead of doing the above deal, he simply deposited £1 for two months at today's two month rate of 11.46875% and so received £1.019114583 at the end of the two month period.

Note that any other forward rate will ruin the market maker. If he quotes a rate above 11.485179%, market operators will borrow for two months today at 11.46875%, deposit for one month today at 11.34375% and arrange today to deposit next month's proceeds at the forward rate which has been quoted. Each pound borrowed and deposited in this way gives a risk-free profit, so that there will be no shortage of operators wishing to enter into the transaction! The market maker is not saved by quoting a rate below 11.485179%. All that would happen now is a reversal of positions: market operators would deposit for two months today at 11.46875%, borrow for one month today at 11.34375% and arrange to borrow next month at the forward rate which the market maker has quoted. Again, a profit!

How did we calculate the correct forward rate R as 11.485179%? By equating the two possible deals to ensure equal returns. That is, the returns from a loan/deposit combination covering one month now, immediately followed by one further month, must equal the returns from a deposit/loan made now for two months. Mathematically,

$$\left(1 + \frac{1}{12} 0.1134375\right)\left(1 + \frac{1}{12} R\right) = 1 + \frac{2}{12} 0.1146875$$

Thus

$$1.009453125 \left(1 + \frac{1}{12} R\right) = 1.019114583$$

$$1 + \frac{1}{12} R = 1.00957098$$

$$\frac{1}{12} R = 0.00957098$$

$$R = 0.11485179 = 11.485179\%$$

Let us now see if we can generalize this result. First, some notation. We shall use the notation $_iR_j$ to denote the rate of interest in period i for maturity in period j. Hence our spot zero yield curve would be denoted as shown in the third column of Table 4.2.

The forward rate which we have just calculated applied to a period starting next month and finishing after a further month. It would therefore be denoted as $_1R_2$. We have calculated the rate by solving for $_1R_2$ in the equation

$$\left(1 + \frac{1}{12}{}_0R_1\right)\left(1 + \frac{1}{12}{}_1R_2\right) = 1 + \frac{2}{12}{}_0R_2$$

We could set out these results in a triangular formation as follows:

Month 0 (%)   Month 1 (%)
${}_0R_1 = 11.34375$ ${}_1R_2 = 11.48518$
${}_0R_2 = 11.46875$

Now ${}_1R_2$ is only one of many possible forward interest rates. The more information we have on today's spot yield curve, the greater the number of forward rates which we can calculate. If we include ${}_0R_3$ in our triangular formation, there are three forward rates which can be calculated:

Month 0 (%)   Month 1 (%)   Month 2 (%)
${}_0R_1 = 11.34375$ ${}_1R_2 = 11.48518$ ${}_2R_3 = 11.62161$
${}_0R_2 = 11.46875$ ${}_1R_3 = 11.60901$
${}_0R_3 = 11.59375$

Here ${}_1R_3$ is the two month interest rate starting in month 1, while ${}_2R_3$ is the one month rate starting in month 2.

We can calculate ${}_1R_3$ by comparing the costs/returns of a one month deal in month 0 followed by a two month deal in month 1 with the costs/returns of a three month deal today; that is,

$$\left(1 + \frac{1}{12}{}_0R_1\right)\left(1 + \frac{2}{12}{}_1R_3\right) = 1 + \frac{3}{12}{}_0R_3$$

This shows that ${}_1R_3 = 11.60901\%$.

We can calculate ${}_2R_3$ in either of two ways. The first is to compare three successive one month deals with a single three month deal; that is,

$$\left(1 + \frac{1}{12}{}_0R_1\right)\left(1 + \frac{1}{12}{}_1R_2\right)\left(1 + \frac{1}{12}{}_2R_3\right) = 1 + \frac{3}{12}{}_0R_3$$

This shows that ${}_2R_3$ is 11.62161%. The second is to compare a one month deal starting in month 1 followed by a one month deal in month 2 with a two month deal starting in month 1; that is,

$$\left(1 + \frac{1}{12}{}_1R_2\right)\left(1 + \frac{1}{12}{}_2R_3\right) = 1 + \frac{2}{12}{}_1R_3$$

As would be expected, this method of calculation also produces a figure of 11.62161% for ${}_2R_3$.

By now some generality should be becoming apparent. In general, a

Forward Contracts   61

forward rate can be calculated from today's interest rates by means of the following formula:[2]

$$\left(1 + \frac{t}{12}\, _0R_t\right)\left(1 + \frac{T-t}{12}\, _tR_T\right) = 1 + \frac{T}{12}\, _0R_T$$

From this we obtain:

$$_tR_T = \frac{12}{T-t}\left[\frac{1 + (T/12)\, _0R_T}{1 + (t/12)\, _0R_t} - 1\right]$$

Application of this formula to the whole of our yield curve gives Table 4.3 (calculations to four decimal places). Each column of this table looks just like another yield curve – and this is exactly what it is! Each column shows a forward yield curve for the month in question.[3]

4.2.2 Forward Rate Agreements

In many markets, forward rates are embodied in the instrument known as a forward rate agreement (FRA). That is, banks guarantee *today* predetermined interest rates which will become applicable in the future.

As with other instruments which are bought or sold, FRAs are quoted with a bid–offer spread. How are these spreads calculated? The issue here is analogous to that of the foreign exchange or currency forward. Too large a spread will induce the customer to avoid the bank and construct his own forward. Consider, for example, a potential customer who will receive £1 million in three months' time and will then deposit it for three months. If he wants to lock in today's forward rate he may ask a bank to quote for an FRA. He can, alternatively, guarantee a forward rate (and so construct his own FRA) by borrowing for three months today and depositing the proceeds for six months today. Let us work through the arithmetic of such a transaction.

Today's spot yield curve has offered–bid rates of

Three months   11⅝–11⁹⁄₁₆   (11.625–11.5625)
Six months   11⅞–11¹³⁄₁₆   (11.875–11.8125)

The potential customer will receive £1 million in three months' time. Hence he can afford to borrow £1/[1 + (1/4) 11.625%] million or £0.971758 million today. This amount deposited for six months will yield £0.971758 × [1 + (1/2) 11.8125%] million or £1.029152 million in six months' time. Hence the FRA rate quoted by the bank must be such that the customer receives at least £1.029152 million after depositing, in three months' time, his £1 million for three months. That is, the minimum rate received must be 4 × 2.9152% or 11.6608%.

Similarly, a customer needing to borrow £1 million for a three month

Table 4.3

Time to maturity (months)	Month 0 (%)	Month 1 (%)	Month 2 (%)	Month 3 (%)	Month 4 (%)	Month 5 (%)
1	$_0R_1 = 11.3438$	$_1R_2 = 11.4852$	$_2R_3 = 11.6216$	$_3R_4 = 11.5101$	$_4R_5 = 11.8219$	$_5R_6 = 11.5874$
2	$_0R_2 = 11.4688$	$_1R_3 = 11.6090$	$_2R_4 = 11.6216$	$_3R_5 = 11.7228$	$_4R_6 = 11.7618$	
3	$_0R_3 = 11.5938$	$_1R_4 = 11.6503$	$_2R_5 = 11.7647$	$_3R_6 = 11.7531$		
4	$_0R_4 = 11.6562$	$_1R_5 = 11.7793$	$_2R_6 = 11.8056$			
5	$_0R_5 = 11.7812$	$_1R_6 = 11.8319$				
6	$_0R_6 = 11.8438$					

period starting in three months' time can guarantee a forward rate by borrowing today for six months and depositing for three. A calculation using the figures above will show that the maximum rate charged must be 11.8451%.

Thus a bank's quotations for a three month FRA starting in three months' time (often called a three against six FRA, following the common notation $_3R_6$) cannot show a wider spread than 11.8451–11.6608.

The general formula used to calculate the bid rate $_tR_{T,b}$ for an FRA will be

$$\left(1 + \frac{t}{12}\,_0R_{t,o}\right)\left(1 + \frac{T-t}{12}\,_tR_{T,b}\right) = 1 + \frac{T}{12}\,_0R_{T,b}$$

That used to calculate the offered rate $_tR_{T,o}$ will be

$$\left(1 + \frac{t}{12}\,_0R_{t,b}\right)\left(1 + \frac{T-t}{12}\,_tR_{T,o}\right) = 1 + \frac{T}{12}\,_0R_{T,o}$$

In Figure 4.3 we illustrate the documentation involved in a forward rate agreement. As in the case of the currency forward contract (Figure 4.2), we have simplified to show only the bare essentials of the agreement.

Forward rate agreement

This document records the purchase by XYZ Company of a £1 million forward rate agreement from the National Bank. Under the agreement, the National Bank will pay to XYZ Company on 14 December 1989 the sum of £25 for each basis point by which the three month interbank offered rate on 14 September 1989 exceeds 8%. Thus, if the rate is 8.1%, the National Bank will pay to XYZ Company £250. Should the three month interbank offered rate lie below 8%, the XYZ Company will pay a similarly calculated amount to the National Bank.

Figure 4.3

4.3 A Comment on Synthetic Forward Contracts

We have shown how the supplier of a product is constrained in his pricing by the existence of substitute products. In the case of a currency forward contract, a supplier's customers can make almost perfect substitutes by borrowing today the currency which they will receive in the future, converting the proceeds today to the currency which they prefer and depositing the proceeds in the preferred currency's domestic money market. Were it not for the fact that this operation would swell the balance sheet, while a forward contract generally does not, the substitute would indeed be perfect in the sense that it would be indistinguishable from the forward contract itself.

Another name for this substitute product is a synthetic forward. It is synthetic in the sense that a forward contract can be replicated without recourse to the forward market.

It is also useful to note that, even if a forward market for a particular product does not exist, that product will still have an implicit forward price. Consider the market for, say, widgets. An individual who will receive widgets in the future may wish to guarantee the price at which he can sell them. If he contacts a widget user, he may be able to agree today a price with that user. However, he may well want to have some idea of the maximum price he could possibly charge before he began any negotiations. That maximum price would be determined by today's widget price, today's interest rate for maturity at the future date in question, and the costs of storing and keeping widgets in perfect condition. This is because the widget user could himself guarantee a future price for widgets by buying them today and storing them until needed. The cost to the widget user would be the storage cost plus the cost of funds employed in buying the widgets. This total cost is often known as the cost of carry.

A simple example may be helpful here. Suppose that today each widget costs £100, that storing a widget for one year costs £2, and that today's one year interest rate is 10%. In this case the maximum price which could be charged today for a widget to be delivered next year is £112.

Finally, it is worth noting that, should a forward market for widgets suddenly come into being today, the rate embodied in the forward contract would be £112. Any other price would offer a risk-free arbitrage opportunity. If the forward rate were £113, market participants would rush to buy widgets today for £100 and to enter into contracts to sell them for £113 next year. This would ensure a risk-free profit of £1. Of course, the process of exploiting the risk-free profit would tend to lower the forward price of widgets relative to the spot price and would therefore remove the opportunity. If, on the other hand, the forward rate were £111, market participants would rush to enter into contracts to buy widgets next year for £111 and would arrange to sell them to the widget users for £112, once again ensuring a risk-free profit of £1 and, once again, so removing the risk-free arbitrage opportunity.

4.4 The Value of a Forward Contract at Expiration

As we shall discuss at greater length in Chapters 9 and 11, many users of forward contracts regard them as providing protection against future fluctuations. By fixing a rate today which will be applicable on a predetermined date in the future, the user gains peace of mind and can turn his attention to other, more pressing, parts of his business. In this general sense the forward contract has a value to its user which might be difficult to express in purely monetary terms. However, we can also consider the monetary value of a forward contract on its expiration date.

4.4.1 Currency Forward Contracts

Consider first a currency forward contract. As we have already discussed, this contract obliges its buyer (and its seller) to exchange a fixed quantity of one currency in return for a fixed quantity of another. For example, the buyer of the contract shown in Figure 4.2 is to pay to the bank DM1.8 million in return for $1 million on 14 September. If the spot exchange rate[4] between the Deutschmark and the dollar on 14 September was DM/$ 1.80, the forward contract would expire with a value of zero. That is, the amounts of money handed over according to the forward contract would be exactly equal to the amounts handed over if an ordinary spot transaction had been made on the same day. However, the stronger the dollar above DM1.80 on 14 September, the greater the value of the forward contract to its owner. If the spot rate is DM2.00, a spot purchase of $1 million costs DM2.0 million, while the owner of the forward contract receives the $1 million for only DM1.8 million. This represents a 'saving' of DM0.2 million. This saving could actually be enjoyed in the form of cash if the owner of the forward contract decided to resell his $1 million on the spot market. By the same token, if the dollar is weaker than DM1.80, the forward contract has a negative value to its owner.

Hence, we can show the Deutschmark value of the contract to its owner at expiration as DM(spot DM/$ rate − 1.80) million. More generally, the value is $DM(S_{DM/\$} - F_{DM/\$})A$, where S denotes the spot exchange rate at expiration, F denotes the forward rate embodied in the contract, and A denotes the amount of dollars involved in the contract.

The value of the contract at expiration, sometimes known as its payoff, is shown graphically in Figure 4.4. As with the exposure profile shown in Figure 1.5, the upper part of the figure shows the value of the contract as a function of the spot lexchange rate. The lower part of the figure centres on the forward rate embodied in the contract, and shows the deviation in value as a function of the deviation in the spot exchange rate from the forward rate.

4.4.2 Forward Rate Agreements

An FRA has a similar payoff although, as indicated in Section 4.2, we have to be careful to distinguish between the various periods involved and to specify the notional amount. Consider a three against six (3v6) FRA. This contract provides a predetermined interest rate; however, if it is to be realized in the form of cash it must be linked to a notional capital sum, the notional principal. Figure 4.3 shows an FRA with a notional principal of £1 million. Suppose that the forward rate for a three month maturity starting in three months' time and expiring in six months' time is 8%. This will be the rate embodied in the 3v6 FRA as shown in Figure 4.3. If in three months' time the actual spot rate for three month money turns out to be 8%, no cash changes hands. However, if the spot rate differs from 8% the owner of the FRA will receive a payment from or make a payment to the seller of the FRA. For example, if the spot rate turns out to be 10%, the owner of the FRA will receive an amount equivalent to 2% of £1 million for the period covered by the FRA. If this amount were payable at the end of the period to which the FRA refers (as we have assumed in Figure 4.3), it would come to exactly £5000. However, because FRAs are usually settled once their value is known, that is at the *start* of the period to which they refer, the amount paid at settlement would be £5000 discounted by the 10% interest rate then prevailing, that is £4878.05.

Hence we can express the terminal value of a t v T FRA as

$$\frac{(T-t)}{12}(S_t - F_t) A$$

The cash payment made at time t can be expressed as the FRA's terminal value divided by $1 + S_t [(T - t)/12]$, that is

$$\frac{(S_t - F_t) A}{[12/(T - t)] + S_t}$$

Forward Contracts

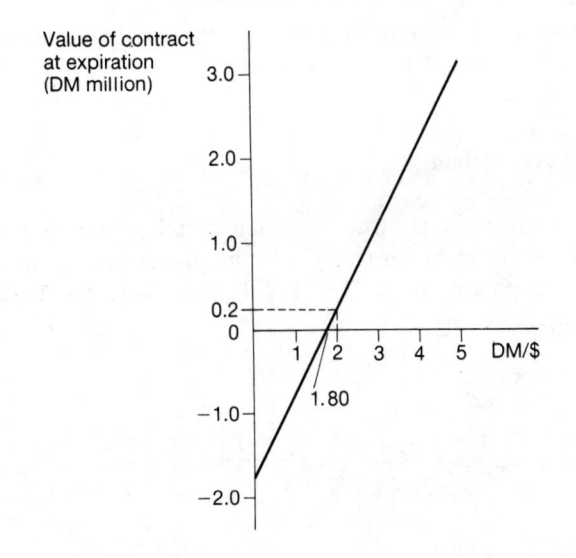

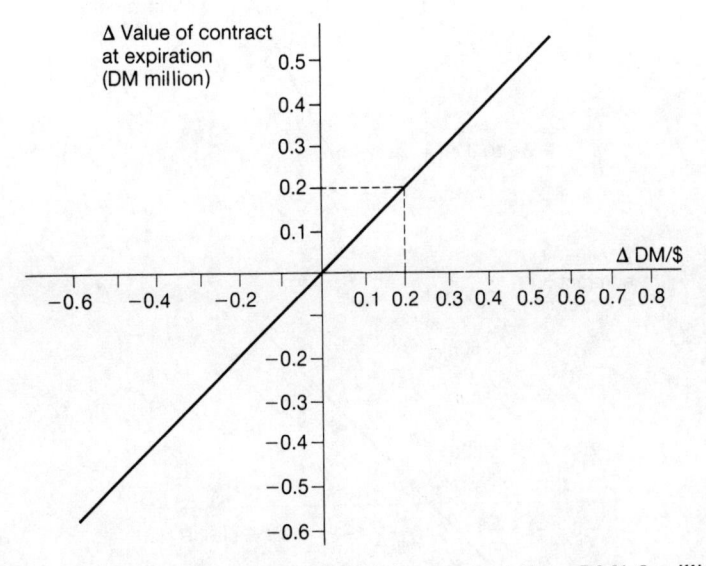

Figure 4.4 Payoff profiles to a forward contract to deliver DM1.8 million in return for $1.0 million

where T denotes the maturity period of the FRA, t denotes the starting period of the FRA, S_t denotes the spot interest rate (%) at the start of the FRA's period, F_t denotes the forward interest rate (%) embodied in the FRA contract, and A denotes the notional principal of the FRA.

The value of the FRA at maturity date – its payoff – is shown graphically in Figure 4.5

4.5 Contract Settlement

The currency forward contract is settled in full, by the exchange of the preagreed amounts of currency on the prearranged date. Thus we can show its payoff as in Figure 4.4. However, the lower part of

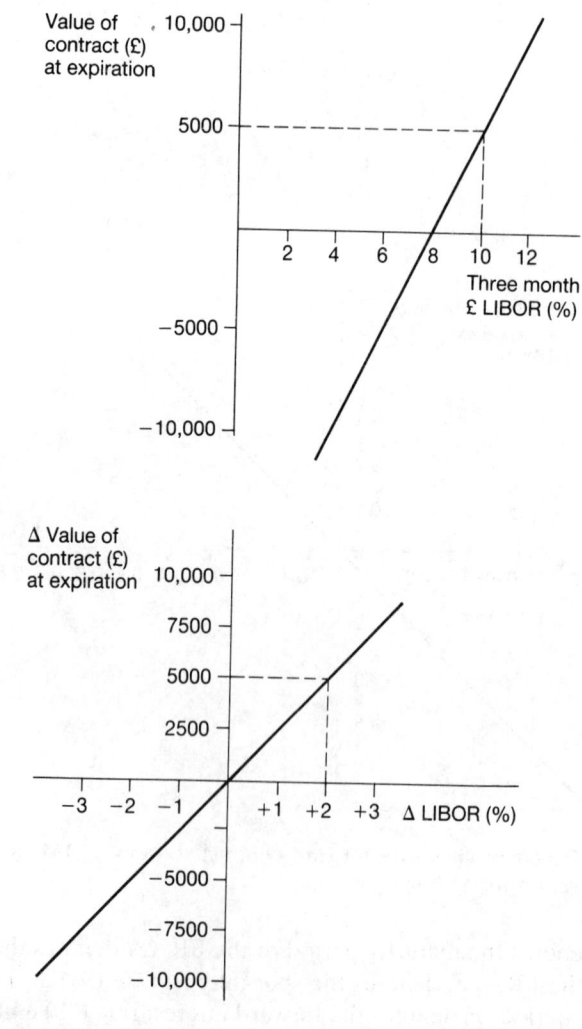

Figure 4.5 Payoff profiles to a three against six FRA on £1 million

Figure 4.4 suggests an alternative form of settlement. If it turns out that the spot rate in the future is equal to the forward rate in the contract, there is no particular advantage in the forward contract over an ordinary spot transaction. This suggests that two counterparties might agree to exchange only the difference in value between the forward contract and the then ruling spot rate, that is to exchange only the payoff to the contract. Hence if A agrees to pay to B a notional DM1.8 million in return for a notional $1 million from B, and if the spot rate turns out to be DM/$ 1.80, neither party pays anything. If it turns out that the spot rate at expiration is DM/$ 2.0, B pays DM200,000 to A; if it turns out that the spot rate is DM/$ 1.60, A pays DM200,000 to B; and so on. This type of contract is sometimes called an exchange rate agreement (ERA) or foreign exchange agreement (FXA). The settlement mechanism and the pricing of contracts are largely separate issues. The pricing of an ERA, that is the forward rate embodied in the contract and the bid–offer spread on the ERA to be made, is similar to that of an ordinary foreign exchange forward contract, even though the settlement process is different.[5]

A forward rate agreement can be thought of as a forward interest rate on a deposit or a loan and, as such, could be settled in this form. That is, the owner of an FRA could be given a loan covering the FRA period with an interest rate corresponding to the forward rate embodied in the contract. However, FRAs are usually settled in cash, the cash representing the payoff to the FRA. This suits many users of FRAs, who are often either traders who want to use FRAs independently of any loans or deposits, or corporations who have already made long term arrangements for loans or deposits and who want to use FRAs solely to protect themselves against adverse movements in interest rates without having to disturb those arrangements.

Consider, for example, a corporate treasurer who expects to borrow £1 million for a seven month period, starting in two months' time. Today's forward rate for the appropriate maturity is 9%, leading him to expect to have to pay £52,500 (7/12 of 9%) in nine months' time when his loan matures. If he buys an FRA, the FRA will guarantee him his expected interest charge, not by forcing him to borrow at 9% from the seller of the FRA, but by getting the seller's agreement to receive or pay an amount equal to the difference between the actual interest charge and the £52,500, should the rate turn out to be different from 9%. For example, if in two months' time the rate for a seven month maturity turns out to be 11%, the treasurer will have to pay £64,166.67. Under the FRA he will receive an amount compensating him for the difference. This amount will reduce his payment from £64,166.67 to £52,500.

One last complication. If FRAs were settled at the end of the period to which they apply, then, as we have already pointed out, the amount that the treasurer would receive would simply be the difference between £64,166.67 and £52,500, that is £11,666.67. However, they are usually settled once any uncertainty has been removed, that is once the relevant interest rates are known, which is at the start of the FRA period. Hence, instead of receiving £11,666.67 at the start of the seven month period, he receives £10,963.19 at the start of the period, that is £11,666.67 discounted by the seven month interest rate of 11%.

5
Futures Contracts

5.1 Introduction

In this chapter we discuss the second of the principal financial instruments – futures contracts. There are, in total, over 200 different types of futures contracts traded in over 40 exchanges worldwide, ranging from potato starch futures on the Hokkaido Grain Exchange to NZ crossbred wool futures on the New Zealand Futures Exchange. Of this total number of contracts, approximately 40% are financial futures, the balance being commodity futures.

Our interest here will very much be focused on financial futures, although the principles outlined below apply to all types of futures contracts. Also, we shall use examples taken from the London International Financial Futures Exchange (LIFFE), although the precise administrative details may vary a little from exchange to exchange.

LIFFE defines a financial futures contract as 'an agreement to buy or sell, on an organized exchange, a standard quantity of a specific financial instrument or foreign currency at a future date and at a price agreed between two parties'.

At first blush it might appear that futures contracts have a great deal in common with the forward contracts discussed in the previous chapter. For instance, both are contracts to buy/sell, both relate to a specific financial instrument and both have agreed prices embedded in them. However, there are four characteristics which are specific to futures contracts and distinguish them from forward agreements:

1 Futures contracts are openly traded on recognized exchanges.
2 Futures contracts are based on standardized amounts.
3 Futures contracts have standardized delivery rules and delivery dates.

4 Futures contracts use margining arrangements to help avoid credit risk problems.

Table 5.1 sets out details of four futures contracts traded on LIFFE that we will be discussing later in the chapter.

The financial futures traded on LIFFE fall into three categories:

- Currency futures
- Interest rate futures
- Stock market index futures.

We shall now look at these individual types of contract in turn.

5.2 Currency Futures

There are five currency futures contracts traded on LIFFE:

- Sterling currency futures
- Deutschmark currency futures
- Swiss franc currency futures
- Japanese yen currency futures
- Dollar–mark currency futures.

With the exception of the dollar–mark currency futures contract, all the contracts are traded against the US dollar. That is to say, holding a Swiss franc currency futures contract through to expiry obliges the owner to acquire, at some future date, a standard quantity of Swiss francs in return for an agreed number of US dollars. The dollar–mark currency futures contract entitles the holder to acquire a standard quantity of US dollars in return for an agreed number of Deutschmarks.

In this section we take as our example the sterling currency futures contract, and we consider the case of an individual deciding to buy, through a member of LIFFE, a single sterling currency futures contract. Referring to Table 5.1, note the characteristics of the sterling currency futures contract that we mentioned before: the standardized contract amounts (the units of trading), the standardized expiry months, the last trading days and the delivery dates. We assume that the contract expires in six months' time, in December, and that the contract is purchased with an embedded exchange rate of $/£ 1.70. We further assume that the forward exchange rate at the time of purchase is also $/£ 1.70.

Our individual is said to hold a long position in a December contract and is, in effect, contracting to receive £25,000 in December and to pay in return $42,500 (a rate of $/£ 1.70).

Table 5.1

	Sterling currency future	Three month sterling interest rate future	US Treasury bond future	FT-SE 100 future
Unit of trading	£25,000 traded against US $	£500,000	US $100,000 par value notional US Treasury bond with 8% coupon	£25 per full index point
Expiry months	March, June, September, December	March, June, September, December	March, June, September, December	March, June, September, December
Last trading day	Two business days prior to delivery day	Third Wednesday of expiry month	Seven working days prior to last business day in expiry month	Last business day in the expiry month
Delivery day	Third Wednesday of expiry month	First business day after last trading day	Any business day in expiry month (at seller's choice)	First business day after last trading day
Quotation	US $ per £	100 – rate of interest	Per $100 par value	FT-SE 100 index/10
Tick size	0.01 cents per £	0.01	$1/32	0.05
Tick value	$2.50	£12.50	$31.25	£12.50
Initial margin	$750	£500	$1250	£1250
Terms of settlement	Delivery of currencies	Cash	Any US Treasury bond maturing at least 15 years from the contract month if not callable; interest must be payable half-yearly	Cash

If our individual has bought a December futures contract, it follows that some other party has sold it. Following the ideas we outlined in the previous chapter, one party will lose and the other party will gain if the exchange rate on the last trading day in December (on which the December futures contract expires) actually turns out to be different from $/£ 1.70. However, in contrast to forwards, the chances of losses arising through one party defaulting in the six months to December are much lessened by the existence of the International Commodities Clearing House (ICCH), which acts as the counterparty in all transactions, looks after the administrative and settlement functions of LIFFE, and operates the daily marking-to-market system.

Upon buying the contract, our individual (as well as the party who sold the contract) will be required to lodge, with a clearing member of the ICCH, an initial margin of $750 which effectively provides a cash buffer against adverse exchange rate movements. The amount of the margin is determined by the ICCH and will reflect the past and expected volatility in the daily price movement of the futures contract.

Consider now what would happen if, on the day following the purchase of the futures contract, the price of the December futures contract moved to $/£ 1.7050. (This move represents 50 ticks; in the jargon of the futures markets, a tick is the minimum price movement. As noted in Table 5.1, a tick for this particular contract is 0.01 cents per £ ($0.0001 per £) and has a value of $2.50.) Based on just this one day's move, our individual is now better off by $125 (50 ticks at $2.50) in the sense that he has contracted to pay $42,500, whereas if the price stayed at $/£ 1.7050 he would have had to pay $42,625 on the spot market.

This amount of $125 would be paid into our individual's margin account by the ICCH (this is known as a variation margin). This payment would be made at the end of the day during which the forward exchange rate moved. At the end of the same day, the party who sold the contract would be obliged to make a payment of the same amount to the ICCH representing the amount by which the seller of the futures contract is worse off.

If, on the day following, the price of the December futures contract moved again from $/£ 1.7050 to $/£ 1.6900, the holder of the futures contract would now be required to deposit an additional $375 (150 ticks at $2.50) with the ICCH. The seller of the futures contract would now receive, from the ICCH, an equivalent amount in margin funds.

It should now be clear that the ICCH acts as the counterparty to both the holder and the seller of the futures contract. However, since both the buyer and the seller of the futures contract settle independently with the ICCH on a daily basis, the ICCH has no net position at the end of each day.

We noted above that the initial margin was a buffer against adverse movements; the initial margin of $750 per contract is equivalent here to 300 ticks. In the case of the sterling currency futures contract, funds with a minimum value of $750 per futures contract bought or sold must be maintained with the ICCH on a daily basis. These funds can be in the form of either cash or some easily liquidated instrument which the ICCH accepts in lieu of cash. However, the minimum balance is reduced for individuals simultaneously buying contracts and selling contracts with different expiry dates (straddle positions). The margins detailed in Table 5.1 are the minimum amounts required by the ICCH, and may well be increased by the member firms.

Contrast this daily marking-to-market and the maintenance of a margin with the forward contracts discussed in Chapter 4. For those contracts, no settlement would be made until the actual December exchange rate was known, with the associated risk that one of the parties to the contract might default in the meanwhile.

As we shall show more fully in Chapter 9, futures contracts can be considered as a string of successive daily forward contracts set up at the start of each business day and settled, in cash, at the close of each day. Thus, in the above example, the cash flow profile of holding a sterling currency futures contract which expires in six months' time could be replicated by: buying an exchange rate agreement to purchase £25,000 in return for dollars in six months' time; closing out the position (with the associated cash settlement) at the end of the day; the next morning, buying a new ERA to purchase £25,000 in six months minus one day; closing it out at the end of that day's business; and so on.

In our example above, we assumed that the exchange rate embedded in the futures contract was $/£ 1.70. We now further assume that, at the time that the futures contract was purchased at $/£ 1.70, the forward exchange rate was in fact $/£ 1.65 and not $/£ 1.70. This second assumption should appear rather unrealistic. Why should the rate in the futures contract be different from the forward exchange rate?

One reason is the different fee structure. The buying or selling of futures contracts involves a fixed commission per contract as well as a bid–offer spread, while the forward market usually involves only the bid–offer spread. Another reason is likely to be the uncertainty over the cost of the margining arrangements, which would reflect the amount and cost of funds that might be tied up in margin over the life of the futures contract.

A third possible reason is that one of the rates is out of line with the other. Let us assume that the observed difference of $/£ 0.05 exceeds the expected cost of margining. The next question is: what should happen now? The answer is unambiguous: arbitrage trading. As we have seen in Chapter 3, we would expect to see these arbitrage profits being rapidly exploited in competitive financial markets. In this case, an arbitrage profit could be made by buying a forward contract to receive £25,000 in return for a payment of $41,250 (forward rate $/£ 1.65) and at the same time selling the futures contract which would entitle the seller to receive $42,500 in return for a payment of £25,000 (futures rate $/£ 1.70). This would produce an arbitrage profit of $1250. The process of buying the cheaper forward contract and selling the expensive futures contract has the effect of bringing the two prices together, although the fact that they are slightly different in terms of margining arrangements means that the prices will not usually be exactly identical.

5.3 Interest Rate Futures

Ten interest rate futures contracts are traded on LIFFE:

- Three month sterling interest rate futures
- Three month Eurodollar interest rate futures
- Three month Euro-Deutschmark interest rate futures
- Three month ECU interest rate futures
- US Treasury bond futures
- Japanese Government bond futures
- German Government bond futures
- Short gilt futures
- Medium gilt futures
- Long gilt futures

We will use the three month sterling interest rate futures contract to illustrate the workings of these types of futures. Table 5.1 sets out the details of this contract. Holding such a contract assures the owner of receiving, at a specified future time, the interest at an agreed rate on an agreed principal sum embodied in the contract.

Assume then, for instance, that in June an individual bought a single three month sterling interest rate futures contract which was to expire six months later, that is in December. The unit of trading and the expiry date are both known. However, what will be the interest at an agreed rate that we referred to in the previous paragraph?

The answer is that it will be close to the expected three month interest rate starting in six months' time. In other words, in June it will be the

$_6R_9$ rate – exactly the same forward rate that we met in Chapter 4! Note though that we did say that the agreed rate embedded in the futures contract would only be *close* to the forward rate. The reason that the two rates may not be exactly the same in June is because, as already explained in Section 5.2, the interest rate embedded in the futures contract will reflect the uncertainty of the expected amount and cost of funds tied up in margin requirements over the life of the contract.

Let us assume that, in June, the three month interest rate starting in December (the $_6R_9$ rate) is in fact 12%. From Table 5.1 you will see that these types of contract are quoted as 100 minus the interest rate. We should therefore expect that, in June, the December three month sterling interest rate futures contract would be quoted in the region of 88. For simplicity we assume that the futures price in June is exactly 88.

You will also note from Table 5.1 that the tick size on this contract is 0.01. In other words, the smallest price movement around the purchase price would take it to either 88.01 or 87.99, corresponding to a 0.01% change in the interest rate. The tick value of £12.50 is calculated as the change in the amount of interest (0.01%) over the three month period (a quarter of a year) of the contract per tick movement, that is £500,000 × (0.01/100) × (1/4). Thus if, on the day following purchase, the forward interest rate for the three month period starting in December moved to 12.5% (with the futures price dropping to 87.5), the owner of the futures contract would be required to pay an additional amount of £625.00 (made up of 50 ticks at £12.50) into the margin account.

Before discussing the no-arbitrage opportunities in the pricing of interest rate futures, it is worth noting two slight differences across the contracts. While the units of trading for the four types of three month interest rate futures contract are straightforward in the sense that they are based on defined amounts of currency (£500,000, $1,000,000 and so on), this is not the case with the other six contracts. For instance, as noted in Table 5.1, the unit of trading for the US Treasury bond futures contract is based on $100,000 par value of a notional US Treasury bond with an 8% coupon with at least fifteen years remaining to maturity. The implications for the time of contract expiration and settlement are discussed further in Sections 5.4 and 5.5.

The other difference relates to the delivery days. In the case of the US Treasury bond futures contract, for example, LIFFE's regulations allow the delivery day to be any day within the expiry month at the discretion of the seller of the futures contract.

We now turn to arbitrage issues. If the interest rate embedded in any of the interest rate futures contracts, after allowing for differences in transaction costs and for the anticipated cost of the funds in the margin account, was too high or too low against the forward interest rate, arbitrage activity (buy the cheap, sell the expensive) would soon ensure that the two rates would align.

For instance, if the interest rate embedded in a three month sterling interest rate futures contract was too high relative to the forward rate, market traders would buy the lower interest rate and sell the higher rate. That is, they would buy forward contracts on the spot market and buy futures contracts.[1]

As we have already mentioned, holders of US Treasury bond futures contracts, at expiry, take delivery of defined amounts of specified long dated US Treasury bonds. On the expiry date the price of the futures contract and the spot price of the bond[2] must be equal (convergence). Otherwise, simply selling the futures contract and purchasing the cash instrument on that day would give rise to a riskless arbitrage profit.[3] On dates other than expiry, the arbitrage argument will still maintain the futures prices in a range defined by transaction costs and the potential uncertainties of the delivery process.

If a bond futures price deviated from the relevant synthetic forward price, arbitrage would again be profitable. For example, if the futures price was higher than the synthetic forward price, the arbitrage would involve selling the bond futures contract while simultaneously borrowing the money to purchase the bond in the cash market. If the futures price was below the synthetic forward price, bond holders would sell their bonds for cash, invest the proceeds, and buy bond futures contracts. Alternatively, potential investors would buy bonds through purchasing futures contracts rather than through the cash market.

A simplified example might help to illustrate the arbitrage opportunities. Consider a twenty year US Treasury bond with a 10% coupon payable semi-annually. Assuming that the relevant twenty year interest rate is 10%, this bond would trade at par. Further, suppose that the price of the futures contract on the bond with six months to expiry is 99.75 and that the six month interest rate is 8%. Under these assumptions an arbitrageur can make a profit by selling the futures contract at 99.75 today and by borrowing, at the same time, $100 cash which is used to buy the bond in the market at $100. After six months the arbitrageur delivers the bond for $99.75, receives a coupon of $5 (that is, $100 × (1/2) 10%) and repays the borrowing of $100 plus the interest of $4. This results in a profit of $0.75. In other words, the bond futures contract was initially overpriced. The theoretically correct price of the futures contract, given the above assumptions, would have been 99.00.

This example can also be described in terms of the cost of carry mentioned in Chapter 4. Here the cost of carry is negative, that is the money earned from holding the bond (the semi-annual coupon of $5) exceeds the borrowing cost of $4, resulting in an arbitrage-free futures price of 99.00 (today's price less the cost of carry). To satisfy the no-arbitrage condition, the capital loss (gain) on the bond has to be equal to the negative (positive) cost of carry. For bond futures prices we can generalize to say that, in an environment with an upward sloping yield curve, there is a negative cost of carry and the futures prices ought to be below the cash prices. Conversely, in an environment with a downward sloping yield curve, the positive cost of carry implies a bond futures price above the price of the equivalent cash instrument.

5.4 Stock Market Index Futures

Stock market index futures are somewhat different from the other categories of futures in the sense that we cannot appeal to a yield curve to extract a forward interest or exchange rate in the way that we were able to do for the other types of contract.

The contract still has the standardized expiry dates, but the tick size and tick value are arbitrarily determined as one-half of one index point and £12.50 respectively. The daily margining arrangements are similar to those we have already discussed. Thus if an individual buys an FT-SE futures contract, and the price of the contract drops by two points the following day, he would be obliged to pay an additional £50 in margin funds.

At the time of writing, the FT-SE 100 futures contract which is due to expire in just over six months' time is nearly 4% above the current index level of 2350.

There is no forward rate for share prices. However, in the event of say the six month FT-SE futures price being thought too high, traders would act quickly to arbitrage away the overvaluation. One way of doing this would be to construct a synthetic forward by borrowing funds today for just over the six months, investing the proceeds in a portfolio of securities that mirrored the composition of the FT-SE index and at the same time selling FT-SE futures contracts which would expire when the borrowing was due to be repaid. This process of extracting arbitrage profits would tend to raise current share price levels and to lower the futures price, thus bringing about an equilibrium between the spot and futures price levels.[4]

5.5 The Value of a Futures Contract at Expiration

We consider first the case of the currency future that we discussed in Section 5.2. Recall that our individual bought the sterling currency

80   *Futures Contracts*

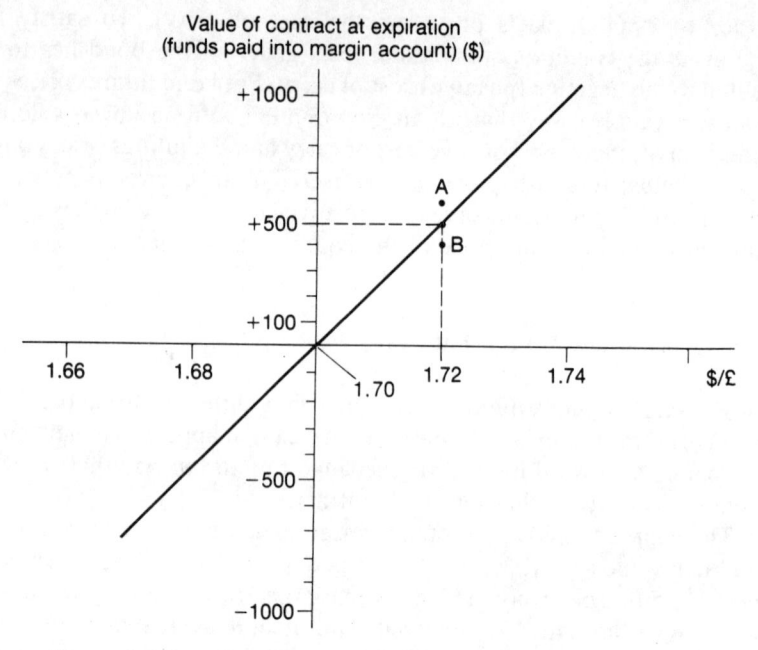

Figure 5.1 Payoff profile to a sterling currency futures contract

futures contract with a December expiry, which at the time of purchase was six months hence. At that time the $/£ 1.70 exchange rate embedded in the futures contract was the same as the December forward exchange rate. When sterling strengthened (the forward exchange rate moved to $/£ 1.7050), our individual received margin funds but was obliged to pay in additional margin funds when sterling weakened (the forward rate moved to $/£ 1.69).

We now consider what would happen when the futures contract closes two days before the third Wednesday in December. If the spot exchange rate on that day is $/£ 1.70, and if for the moment we ignore interest on margin funds, the contract will expire with a zero value both to our individual and to the party who sold the contract. This is because however many movements there might have been over the life of the contract, the inflows into the margin account will have been exactly matched by the outflows.

Let us assume that the December sterling currency futures contract actually closes at a rate of $/£ 1.72. Figure 5.1 illustrates possible values of the contract at expiry and is drawn in terms of deviations from the forward exchange rate embedded in the futures contract.

The dashed line from $/£ 1.72 on the horizontal axis to the contract line corresponds to $500 on the vertical axis, indicating that the holder of the contract should have margin funds of that amount at the expiry of the contract (assuming that the contract is held to expiry). This amount can be seen to be made up of 200 ticks at $2.50 per tick. However, this calculation does not take into account the interest earned on margin funds. Nor does it take into account the possible external opportunity cost of the funds tied up in the margin account when the dollar strengthened above the $/£ 1.70 rate.

The points marked A and B allow for these adjustments. Point A might be compatible with a case where sterling has strengthened over the six month life of the futures contract, and as a result the holder of the futures contract has enjoyed the benefit of earning interest on his margin funds. Point B, on the other hand, might be a case where sterling had weakened below the $/£ 1.70 rate for long periods within the six months to expiry (with the consequent requirement for the holder of the contract to pay more funds into the margin account) and had only recently strengthened against the dollar to end at $/£ 1.72.

In the case of the interest rate futures contracts, the same principles apply. In our example in Section 5.3, the three month sterling interest rate futures contract was bought at a price of 88. If the spot three month interest rate on the third Wednesday in December actually turned out to be 12%, the value of the futures contract, again ignoring the interest on margin funds, would turn out to be zero.

If we assume instead that the three month spot rate at the time of expiry actually turned out to be 14%, the futures contract would close at 86. In total, the holder of the futures contract would sustain a loss of 200 ticks at £12.50, that is £2500. The payoff profile, again drawn in terms of deviations from the forward rate embedded in the futures contract, is shown in Figure 5.2. As we have already discussed in the case of the currency future, the total loss sustained by the holder of this futures contract might in fact be more or less than the £2500 indicated, depending on the movement of funds into and out of the margin account over the holding period of the contract.

5.6 Contract Settlement

In the case of the settlement of the sterling currency futures contract, the actual currencies will be delivered at the spot rates ruling on the last trading day when the contract expired. In our example, the holder of the sterling currency futures contract will receive the £25,000 and pay in return $43,000 (that is, £25,000 × $/£ 1.72). Remember, however, that he bought the contract originally at $/£ 1.70 and will have received, as we have indicated in Section 5.5, an amount of $500 in margin funds.

82 *Futures Contracts*

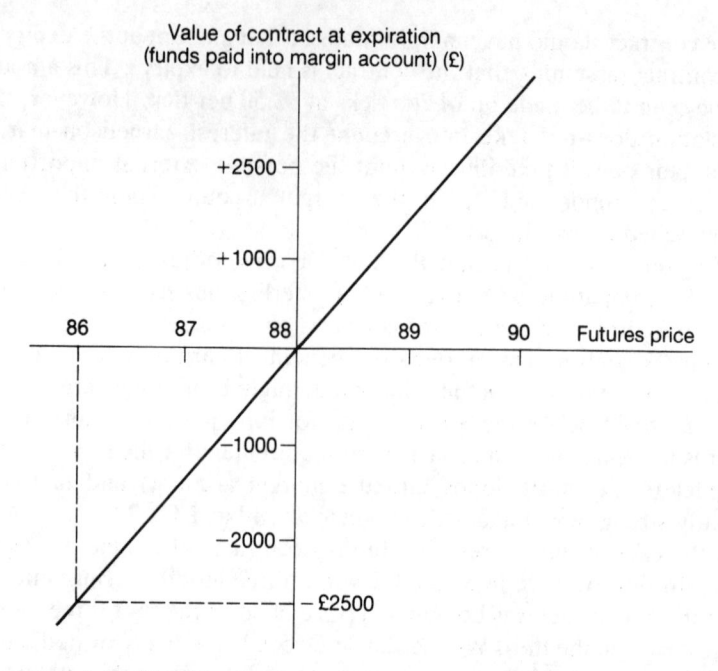

Figure 5.2 Payoff profile to a three month sterling interest rate futures contract

The net cost of acquiring the £25,000 is $42,500, thus achieving the locking in of the rate of $/£ 1.70.

In the case of the four types of three month interest rate futures, the Japanese Government bond futures contract and the FT-SE 100 futures contract, the settlements are all in cash. No exchange of principal amounts, or transfer of shares in the case of the FT-SE 100 contracts, is involved. These contracts expire at the spot price ruling on the last trading day, and the only change on that day will be the movement of funds through the margin account if the price has changed over the previous day's closing price. Any balance on margin funds will be settled on the delivery day, which will normally be within 24 hours of the last trading day.

In our three month sterling interest rate futures contract example, we indicated that the futures contract would entitle the holder to receive interest at an agreed rate on an agreed principal sum. The interest rate embedded in the contract was 12%. In other words the holder of the futures contract could be assured of earning interest of £15,000 in the three month period following December, that is £500,000 × (1/4) × 12%. In the event, the spot rate at the expiry of the futures contract was 14%. It is important to note that ownership of this contract did not oblige the seller of the contract to provide the principal sum of £500,000.

In December the owner of the contract was in fact able to invest the money at the spot rate of 14% to give an interest income of £17,500, that is £500,000 × (1/4) × 14%. However, the bad news is that the holder loses, as we have already indicated, £2500 on his long futures position. His net interest income was indeed £15,000, which was what ownership of the futures contract ensured.

In the case of the five other interest rate futures contracts whose units of trading are based on notional securities, ownership of a futures contract at expiry actually entitles the holder to receive certain designated securities. For example, the owner of a US Treasury bond futures contract would receive, at delivery, any US Treasury bond which meets certain maturity, interest and transferability criteria set down by LIFFE. Given that various US Treasury bonds can be used in settlement, standardization is resolved by having the units of trading quoted in terms of different par values for the different Treasury bonds that can be offered in settlement.

6
Swap Contracts

6.1 Currency Swaps

The ordinary currency swap involves the exchange of currencies between two counterparties.

Imagine a situation in which the counterparties exchange at the spot and forward rates. For example, party A might today give party B DM180 while B gives A $100, the exchange taking place at today's spot rate of DM/$ 1.80. If one year interest rates in Germany and America are 5% and 10% respectively, the one year forward rate is DM/$ 1.7182. The two parties will thus agree today that, in one year's time, A will give B $100 while B will give A DM171.82.

This type of exchange shows clearly the relation between a swap and some of the other instruments which we have discussed so far, because the swap can be seen as the combination of a spot contract and a forward contract. It also shows another important general principle: namely that, for a swap to take place, the two counterparties must exchange equal values. More exactly, each party must exchange payments with equal present value as determined by the market at the time the swap is agreed.

Let us briefly verify that the exchange described above meets this condition. We can show the swap as follows:

	A pays to B	B pays to A
Today	DM180	$100
One year's time	$100	DM171.82

It is common practice to show a swap in the form of a flow diagram, as in Figure 6.1. The present value of A's payments to B is DM180 + $100/1.1 which, using today's exchange rate of DM/$ 1.80, can be expressed either as $190.91 or as DM343.64. The present value of B's

Swap Contracts

Today

```
┌──────────────┐    DM180    ┌──────────────┐
│ Counterparty A│ ──────────▶│ Counterparty B│
│              │◀────────────│              │
└──────────────┘    $100     └──────────────┘
```

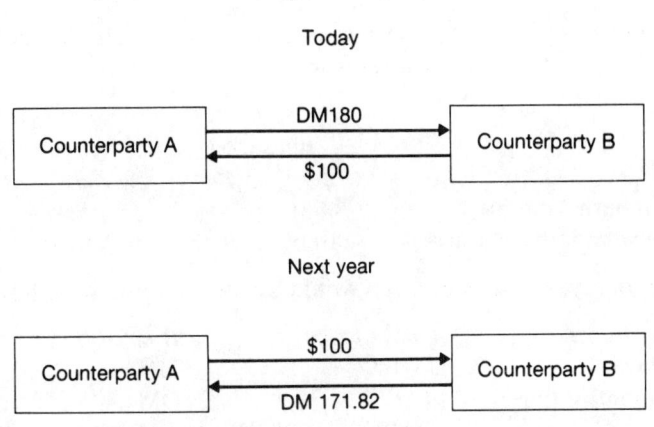

Next year

```
┌──────────────┐    $100     ┌──────────────┐
│ Counterparty A│ ──────────▶│ Counterparty B│
│              │◀────────────│              │
└──────────────┘  DM 171.82  └──────────────┘
```

Figure 6.1 Flows involved in a swap

payments to A is $100 + DM171.82/1.05, which can be expressed either as $190.91 or as DM343.64.

If a swap is proposed under which the present values of the two payment streams are unequal, it will not be possible to find two counterparties for it. While the intended recipient of the higher of the two values will be keen to enter into the swap, the intended payer will be correspondingly reluctant![1]

In fact, the type of swap which we have just discussed is rare. Partly because of its beginnings in the form of the back-to-back loan, the typical swap involves two exchanges of principals, both at the initial spot rate. Hence at the start of the swap period A gives B DM180 in return for $100, and at the end of the period the opposite exchange takes place. This is not the end of the story, though, because the present value of each counterparty's payments is not the same. Return to our example and consider the one year swap just outlined. The forward rate is DM/$ 1.7182, so the swap would have a positive present value for A and a negative present value for B, because B is agreeing to give A more Deutschmarks than the market rate justifies. Hence, in order to give the swap an initial value of zero, A must give something more to B. As we have seen, the forward exchange rate reflects the interest rate differentials between the two currencies. Hence, if B and A exchange interest payments in addition to the currencies, the swap in which each currency exchange takes place at the spot rate will have an initial value of zero. It is usual to exchange interest payments at six monthly intervals, in which case the appropriate interest rate to use is the par or swap rate with the same maturity as the currency swap.

Swap Contracts

A simple example might be helpful here. Suppose that the spot DM/$ rate is 1.80 and that interest rates are as follows:

	Spot $ interest rates (%)		Spot DM interest rates (%)	
	Zero	Par	Zero	Par
Six months' maturity	8.0		4.5	
Twelve months' maturity	10.0	9.72	5.0	4.93

Then a one year currency swap would involve the following flows:

	A pays to B	B pays to A
Today	DM180	$100
Six months' time	$4.86	DM4.44
	($100 × 9.72%/2)	(DM180 × 4.93%/2)
One year's time	$4.86 + $100	DM4.44 + DM180

Each of these flows has an equal present value (of $200 or DM360), thus giving the swap the required net value of zero when the swap terms are first arranged.

Figure 6.2 illustrates the documentation for a currency swap. As with Figures 4.2 and 4.3, only the essentials of the agreement are shown.

Currency swap agreement

This document records an agreement between A Company and B Bank. Under the agreement

(i) A makes the following payments to B:
  14 March 1990 (today)   DM180
  14 September 1990 $4.86
  14 March 1991 $104.86

and

(ii) B makes the following payments to A:
  14 March 1990 (today) $100
  14 September 1990   DM4.44
  14 March 1991   DM184.44

Figure 6.2

6.2 Interest Rate Swaps

The ordinary interest rate swap involves the exchange of interest payments (in one currency) without any exchange of principal. A notional principal is agreed upon to determine the sizes of the cash flows which result from any interest rate movements.

To illustrate this, consider a swap arranged at the time at which the interest rates shown in Section 3.4.3 were seen in the market. The zero and the par yield curves shown in Tables 3.3 and 3.4 contained the figures given in Table 6.1.

Table 6.1

Time to maturity (months)	Zero yield curve (%)	Par yield curve (%)
6	12.1944	—
12	12.3438	11.9805
18	12.5000	12.1205
24	12.7500	12.3378

Let us look at two possible swaps, which, although not very useful and therefore untypical, satisfy the condition that, at the moment of signing, each counterparty's payments should have an equal present value, with the result that the net market value of the swap is zero. One such swap would involve A paying B £123,438 at the end of one year, and B paying A £59,902.50 after six months followed by a further £59,902.50 at the end of one year. We can see that this swap, which is based upon a notional principal of £1 million, satisfies the condition of equal present value. A's single payment is determined by the zero yield curve, showing a rate of 12.3438%. Each of B's payments is determined by the corresponding par yield curve, showing a rate of 11.9805% and so warranting two six-monthly payments, each of half that figure. This is illustrated in Table 6.2. A's cash flows are shown as (i), while B's are shown as (ii). The present values of these two flows are equal.

Table 6.2 Example swap cash flows

	Now	Six months hence	Twelve months hence
(i)	—	—	→ 12.3438%
(ii)	—	→ ½ (11.9805%)	→ ½ (11.9805%)
(iii)	—	→ $100[(1.121944)^{0.5} - 1]$	→ $100[(1.124934)^{0.5} - 1]$
(iv)	—	→ $100[(1.121944)^{0.5} - 1]$	→ $100[(1 + {}_6R_{12})^{0.5} - 1]$

88   *Swap Contracts*

Another possible swap would involve A paying B in six months' time an amount determined by today's six month interest rate ($_0R_6$), which in our example is 12.1944%, followed by a further payment in one year's time determined by today's foward rate ($_6R_{12}$), which in our example is 12.4934%. B makes payments in the same way as in the swap just discussed. How do we know that the swap satisfies the condition of equal present value? Because, as explained in Section 4.2, today's forward rate $_6R_{12}$ is calculated so that the payments determined by $_0R_6$ and $_6R_{12}$ (made by A) have the same present value as a single payment determined by $_0R_{12}$. Furthermore, two payments determined by the par rate $_0R_{12}$ (made by B) have the same present value as a single payment determined by $_0R_{12}$. QED! This swap is illustrated by the flows (ii) and (iii) in Table 6.2.

However, for reasons that will become apparent later – if they are not already apparent – the typical swap seen in the market involves some interest payments whose size will not be known at the moment the swap contract is signed.

A much more realistic swap, which follows from the example just discussed, would involve A paying amounts to B which are determined by the apropriate spot six month rate rather than today's forward rate. Thus in six months' time A pays an amount determined by today's six month rate and in one year's time A pays an amount determined by the actual spot rate seen in six months' time. As before, B pays a fixed rate determined by today's par yield curve. This swap is illustrated by the flows (ii) and (iv) in Table 6.2. Now we have a swap which is much closer to those seen in the market. Indeed, simple as it is, this swap is untypical only because it has a one year maturity while most swaps involving payments at six monthly intervals have longer maturities. A swap of this kind is described as a fixed versus floating swap.

Figure 6.3 illustrates the documentation for an interest rate swap. As before, only the essentials of the agreement are shown.

What is the value[2] of such a swap at the moment of its signing? In one sense, its value is unknown at the time of signing because the actual six month rate in six months' time is unknown. It should be apparent that if this rate turns out to be equal to today's forward rate, the swap's present value on signing was zero. For valuation purposes it is usual to take today's forward rate as the estimate of the future spot[3] and so to calculate the expected net present value of the swap as zero.[4]

To finish this section we shall look in a little more detail at the valuation of a real-life swap, again using the interest rates in Table 6.1. Consider a two year swap (that is, a swap with a two year maturity) with a notional principal of £100, under which one counterparty pays a semi-annual fixed rate while the other makes semi-annual payments

Swap Contracts

Interest rate swap agreement

This document records an agreement between A Company and B Bank. Under the agreement, A and B agree to exchange interest payments based on a notional principal of £100 for a period of two years. Under the agreement, A will pay to B six monthly in arrears an interest rate of 12.3378%, payable six monthly as 6.1689%, while B will pay to A six monthly in arrears an amount determined by the six month rate in market X. In market X the payment amounts are determined exponentially, that is a rate of $R\%$ leads to an interest payment in six months' time of $£[(1+R/100)^{\frac{1}{2}}-1]$ per £1 principal.

Figure 6.3

according to the relevant spot six month interest rate. Suppose A pays fixed while B pays floating. A will therefore pay at the rate of 12.3378%, this being the par rate for a two year maturity. B will make the first interest payment at the rate of 12.1944%. The remaining payments made by B will depend upon the future course of interest rates.

To value the swap today we must use the forward rates ($_6R_{12}$, $_{12}R_{18}$, $_{18}R_{24}$), which can be calculated from today's spot zero yield curve. Using the formula shown in Chapter 4, note 2, namely

$$(1 + {}_0R_t)^{t/12} (1 + {}_tR_T)^{(T-t)/12} = (1 + {}_0R_T)^{T/12}$$

these rates can be calculated as 12.4934%, 12.8130% and 13.5033%. On the day on which the swap is arranged, its cash flows can be shown as in Table 6.3.

Table 6.3

Months hence	A pays to B (£)	B pays or can be expected to pay to A (£)
6	0.5 (12.3378) = 6.1689	100 [(1.121944)$^{0.5}$ − 1] = 5.9218
12	0.5 (12.3378) = 6.1689	100 [(1.124934)$^{0.5}$ − 1] = 6.0629
18	0.5 (12.3378) = 6.1689	100 [(1.128130)$^{0.5}$ − 1] = 6.2135
24	0.5 (12.3378) = 6.1689	100 [(1.135033)$^{0.5}$ − 1] = 6.5379

The present value of A's payments to B is

$$\frac{6.1689}{(1.121944)^{0.5}} + \frac{6.1689}{(1.123438)^{1.0}} + \frac{6.1689}{(1.125)^{1.5}} + \frac{6.1689}{(1.1275)^{2.0}}$$

The present value of B's payments to A is

$$\frac{5.9218}{(1.121944)^{0.5}} + \frac{6.0629}{(1.123438)^{1.0}} + \frac{6.2135}{(1.125)^{1.5}} + \frac{6.5379}{(1.1275)^{2.0}}$$

Each is equal to £21.3376, giving the swap a net present value of zero.

6.3 The Value of a Swap Contract at Expiration

As with forwards and futures, swaps can be valued at expiration. Consider first the interest rate swap which we have just discussed. If each of the spot interest rates in the future turns out to be equal to the forward rates anticipated at the start of the swap, the present (and terminal) value of A's and B's cash flows will turn out to be equal and the swap's terminal value will be zero. To the extent that the spot rates turn out to be higher than the forward rates, A will have gained from the swap while B will have lost. To the extent that the spot rates turn out to be lower than the forwards, A will have lost and B will have gained.

It is clear that the more the future spot interest rates move above the forward rates, the greater is the value of the swap to A (who pays the fixed rate) and the lower the value to B. However, the calculation of the payoff or net terminal value is not always easy because, in general, both the numerators and the denominators of the calculations will change if the yield curve changes. Thus, in place of a single diagram showing the payoff of the swap, we should draw a series of pictures, one for each of the interest payment dates. Hence there would be three pictures for our example: the first showing the impact of a deviation between the expectation of the rate in six months' time and the actual rate on that date; the second showing the impact of a deviation in twelve months' time; and the third showing the impact of a deviation in eighteen months' time. The overall impact on the swap would be the appropriately discounted average of each of these three deviations.[5] In some circumstances there might be a deviation at each of the three dates in question but, given a mixture of positive and negative deviations, the swap might still expire with a net terminal value of zero.

Hence, if the payoff to the swap is to be shown in a single picture with a single interest rate, such as $_{12}R_{18}$, on the horizontal axis, it will look a little like Figures 5.1 and 5.2, which showed the payoff to a futures contract. Now the points A, B and so on correspond to differences between the three interest rates making up the uncertain (at the outset) part of the swap, namely $_6R_{12}$, $_{12}R_{18}$ and $_{18}R_{24}$.

If instead we want to show the payoff to the swap as a single line, the horizontal axis must be defined as an appropriately weighted combination of $_6R_{12}$, $_{12}R_{18}$ and $_{18}R_{24}$.

The same principles apply to a currency swap. If all future spot rates turn out to be equal to the rates embodied in the swap, the swap will have a net terminal value of zero to each of the counterparties. Deviations in one (or more) rates will (usually) lead to non-zero outcomes.

6.4 Contract Settlement

A currency swap involves an exchange of principals at beginning and end, together with regular interest payments during the life of the swap. As the interest payments are expressed in different currencies it is usual for each counterparty to make payments to the other, although, by converting at the then prevailing spot rate, some netting is possible.[6]

As interest rate swaps involve only one currency, netting of payments is the norm. That is, although the rules of the swap say that A pays B while B pays A, the two payments are netted. Each time a pair of payments becomes due, a single payment is made from A to B or from B to A which is equal to the difference between the two payments. This payment is usually described as the difference cheque. Referring back to the two year swap which we priced in Section 6.2, we can say that, should interest rates turn out to be equal to the forward rates seen when the swap was signed, the first difference cheque will be for £0.2471 (6.1689 − 5.9218) and will pass from A to B (see Table 6.3). The second, for £0.1060, will also pass from A to B. The third and fourth, for £0.0446 and £0.3690 respectively, will pass from B to A.[7]

6.5 A Brief Note on Commodity-Indexed Swaps

It should be clear to the reader by now that, although there are some minor differences – often based on the settlement arrangements – between them, a currency forward contract is essentially the same instrument as an interest rate forward contract. Each allows the fixing today of a rate to become applicable at a future date. The different names identify the market to which the instruments belong rather than any important difference between them. The same is true of the various futures, swaps and options contracts. Thus making 'new' forwards, futures, swaps or options applying to different markets is relatively easy. One fast growing area of activity in the swaps market is the use of commodity-indexed swaps.

Consider, for example, a user of jet kerosene, such as an airline. Fluctuations in the price of kerosene may be just as important, or even more important, than fluctuations in exchange rates or interest rates. Such a company may want an instrument to remove its exposure to kerosene prices. A kerosene-indexed swap could do the job. Such a swap mirrors almost exactly an interest rate swap, which can be described as a swap whose payments are indexed to interest rates.

Under a kerosene-indexed swap the airline would decide on a notional principal of x tonnes. To remove all exposure, x would be set equal to the airline's requirements. The airline would agree to pay a fixed rate and to receive a floating rate. Suppose current market conditions dictate a fixed rate of $200 per tonne. Then, at six monthly intervals, the spot kerosene price would be compared with the fixed rate. A spot price of $200 per tonne would trigger no payment by either counterparty. A spot price of $210 per tonne would lead to a difference cheque of 10x$ being paid to the airline. A spot price of $190 per tonne would lead to the airline's paying 10x$; and so on. As can be seen, such arrangements would lock in a price (via the spot payment taken together with the difference cheque) of $200 per tonne throughout the life of the swap.

Despite the name 'kerosene-indexed swap' – or even, as the instrument is sometimes called, 'kerosene swap' – no kerosene changes hands, just as the notional principal in an interest rate swap does not change hands. The airline continues with its chosen arrangements for buying kerosene but enjoys the guarantee that, whatever the spot price, it will face an effective price of $200 per tonne.

Indexation to oil-based products such as kerosene, naptha and crude oil is often classed under the general heading of oil indexation. Similar arrangements can be made with gold indexation, silver indexation, copper indexation and so on. The market for commodity indexation seems to be developing very rapidly at present.

6.6 Variations on the Swap Theme

We have already seen that swaps can be constructed around many different indices and that different types of payment pattern can be agreed. In this final section we look at two quite common variants on the basic swap.

6.1.1 Delayed or Forward Swaps

Some users like to arrange all the details of a swap in advance of the swap's coming into operation. Thus, for example, they may choose today to enter into a swap agreement with a two year maturity which does not begin to come into operation until one year's time. For the sake of illustration, let us assume that an individual enters into such a swap under which he agrees to pay six monthly floating payments in return for the receipt of six monthly fixed payments. There will therefore be four net payments made under the swap, the first at 18 months and the last at 36 months from the time of signing. The size of these payments will not be known at the time of signing. The question we now want to answer is: what will be the fixed rate on the other side of the swap which will be agreed at the time of signing?

Using the spot zero interest rates given in Table 3.4, and calculating today's forward rates as in Section 6.2, we can show the expected flows on the two sides of the swap as follows:

Months from signing	18	24	30	36
Floating payments	£6.2135	£6.5379	£6.7734	£7.0086
Fixed payments	£x	£x	£x	£x

where x denotes the fixed rate which is to be calculated. Again using the spot zero interest rates in Table 3.4 we find that, in order to make the two sides of the swap have equal present value (£20.1654), x must be set at £6.6119. That is, the fixed rate will be quoted as 13.2238% annually.

It is worth noting that, although the delayed swap may seem complicated, it is a little more simple in its construction than might meet the eye. This is because the delayed swap can be thought of as the combination of two ordinary swaps. For example our swap (pay floating, receive fixed for two years, starting next year) can be made up from one ordinary three year swap (pay floating, receive fixed) and one ordinary one year swap (receive floating, pay fixed). During the first year of this combination the payments counterbalance each other. The swap is a little more difficult to price than this intuitive approach suggests because the payments, while counterbalancing in a conceptual sense, do not offset each other in an exact numerical sense. That is, in general, the three year swap rate will differ from the one year swap rate, so that the simple combination of the two swaps would still leave two equal (known) payments to be made at 6 and 12 months. The pricing process effectively shifts these payments into the swap payment period (from 18 to 36 months) in such a way that the net present value of the delayed swap is, like other swaps, zero at origination. This explains why the fixed rate which we calculated above differed from the ordinary swap rates taken from the interest rates seen in the par yield curve at the time of signing (Table 3.3).

6.6.2 Amortizing Swaps

Many swaps are used as instruments to hedge an outstanding loan, and many loans are amortized over their life rather than repaid in a single lump sum at maturity. Thus there is a demand for swaps whose notional principal declines during their life; these are known as amortizing swaps.

To give an example, consider the pricing of a three year amortizing swap with notional principals of £150, £100 and £50 in the three successive years of the swap. Using the forward rates shown in Sections 6.2 and 6.6.1, we can see that the expected flows on the floating side of the swap will be as in Table 6.4. The present value of these flows is £31.7391, indicating that the six payments based on the fixed rate must be quoted as 12.4746% anually to give equal present value.

Table 6.4

Months	Floating payments
6	£150 × 5.9218% = £8.8827
12	£150 × 6.0629% = £9.0944
18	£100 × 6.2135% = £6.2135
24	£100 × 6.5379% = £6.5379
30	£50 × 6.7734% = £3.3867
36	£50 × 7.0086% = £3.5043

As with the delayed swap, the amortizing swap can be thought of as a combination of ordinary swaps. Our example could be constructed from three ordinary swaps, each with a notional principal of £50, one spanning three years, one spanning two years, and one spanning one year. Again the complications of pricing result from the need to quote a single fixed interest rate applicable over the whole life of the amortizing swap.

7
Share Options

7.1 Introduction

In this chapter we will be considering options on shares. Options on interest rates and currencies will be dealt with in the next chapter.

To show the characteristics of share options, Figure 7.1 sets out illustrative and simplified examples of four different types of option contract. Let's look initially at the general characteristics of these documents.

First, in all cases the ownership of the option carries a right, but not an obligation. In the case of call options, ownership carries the right, but not the obligation, to purchase shares in ABC PLC. In the case of the put options, ownership of the option carries the right, but not the obligation, to sell the shares of XYZ PLC.

Secondly, all of the options carry a price at which they can be exercised, known as the exercise (or strike) price. Thus the holders of the two call options illustrated have the right, but not the obligation, each to purchase one share in ABC PLC at a price of £1.50 per share. Similarly, the holders of the put options have the right, but not the obligation, each to sell one XYZ PLC share at a price of £2.25 per share.[1]

Finally, all the options expire by or on a specified date. European options have a single specified expiry date, given in the examples in Figure 7.1 as 22 September 19X9 for the call option and 24 June 19X7 for the put option. In contrast, the holders of American options have the right to exercise the options at any time on or before a specified date.

96   Share Options

European call option	European put option
The owner of this option has the right, but not the obligation, to purchase 1 share of ABC PLC at a price of £1.50. This option can only be exercised on 22 September 19×9.	The owner of this option has the right, but not the obligation, to sell 1 share of XYZ PLC at a price of £2.25. This option can only be exercised on 24 June 19×7.

American call option	American put option
The owner of this option has the right, but not the obligation, to purchase 1 share of ABC PLC at a price of £1.50. This option can be exercised on or at any time before 22 September 19×9.	The owner of this option has the right, but not the obligation, to sell 1 share of XYZ PLC at a price of £2.25. This option can be exercised on or at any time before 24 June 19×7.

Figure 7.1

7.2 Expiration Values

Having dealt with these introductory issues, we can now go on to outline the ideas underlying option pricing.

7.2.1 European Call Options

We start by considering the possible values of a European call option at expiry. If, for example, on 22 September 19X9 (the expiry date for the call options in Figure 7.1) the ABC PLC share price is £1.45, the option will expire with a value of zero and so will expire unexercised. Nobody would wish to exercise the option and pay £1.50 for the share when they could buy it in the open market for £1.45!

However, if on the expiry date the ABC PLC share price was £1.65, the call option would expire with a value of 15p. In this instance the

Share Options

holder of the call could exercise the option, buy the share for £1.50, then sell it in the market for £1.65 and immediately be 15p better off.[2]

Thus the call option will take a positive value at expiry if the share price at that time is higher than the exercise price of the option. This option value will be a linear function of the excess of the share price at expiry over the exercise price. The expiry value to the holder of this type of European call option is illustrated in Figure 7.2.

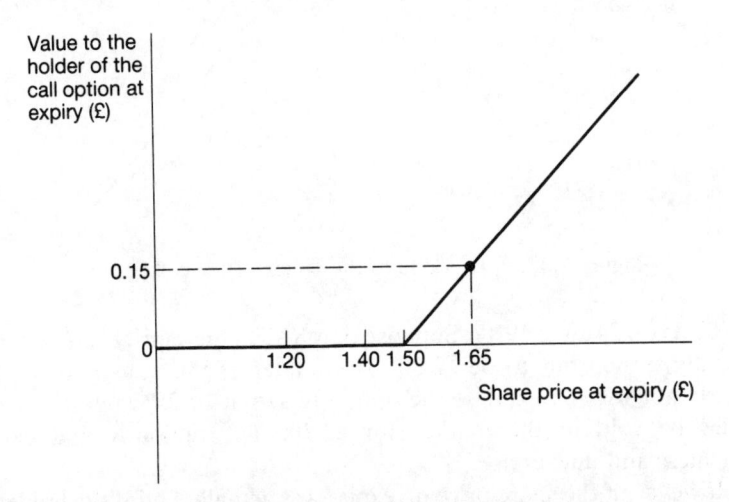

Figure 7.2 Expiry value to the holder of the call option

Up to now we have only considered the expiry value of the option to the holder of the option contract. We need now to consider the position of the party who has provided the holder with the option: in other words, the position of the party that has sold (or written) the call option.

If the share price at expiry is £1.65, the writer of the call option would be obliged to provide the holder of the call with a share at a price of £1.50 when the share is available in the market at £1.65. The writer of the call suffers a loss of 15p. This would be a real cash loss if the writer has to go out and buy the share on the market. If the writer already owned the share,[3] he would have to give up the share for less than the market price and would therefore incur an opportunity loss. The expiry value to the writer of this European call option is drawn in Figure 7.3.

7.2.2 European Put Options

We now turn our attention to the expiry value of an European put option using the details set out in Figure 7.1. The holder of that put option has the right, but not the obligation, to sell a share in XYZ PLC

98   *Share Options*

```
Value to the
writer of the
call option
at expiry (£)
                     1·40 1·50  1·65
            0 ─────────┼────┼───┼──────────────
                                │  Share price at expiry (£)
         -0·15 ├─ ─ ─ ─ ─ ─ ─ ─┤
                                 \
                                  \
                                   \
```

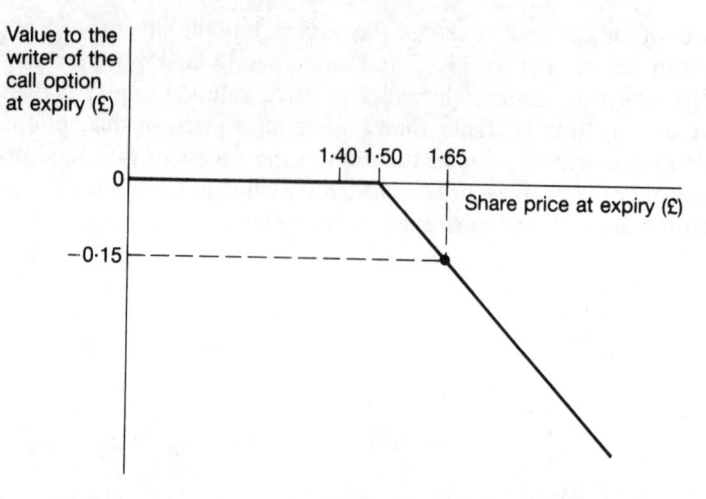

Figure 7.3 Expiry value to the writer of the call option

for £2.25 on 24 June 19X7. Suppose that XYZ's share price, on that day, actually turned out to be £2.30. The holder of the put option would clearly not wish to exercise the option to sell at £2.25 when the shares could be sold in the market for £2.30. The option would expire worthless and unexercised.

However, if the share price on expiry was actually £1.15, the holder of the put would buy the share in the market for £1.15, exercise the option to sell the share at £2.25 and £1.10 better off. So, for the holder of a put option, the option will have a value at expiry if the share price on that date is lower than the exercise price of the option. The expiry value to the holder of the European put option in Figure 7.1 is plotted in Figure 7.4.

For completeness, the expiry value to the writer of the put option is plotted in Figure 7.5.

Note though that these profiles have simply graphed the value of the options at expiry. We have not yet considered the net payoff to buying or writing an option, taking into account the fact that the option holder would have to pay for the ownership of the option and that this money would be received by the option writer.

7.3 Pricing Call Options

7.3.1 *Introduction to the Black and Scholes Method*

The previous sections have concerned themselves with the option value at expiry. In this and the following sections, we will be looking at ways

Share Options 99

Value to the holder of the put option at expiry (£)

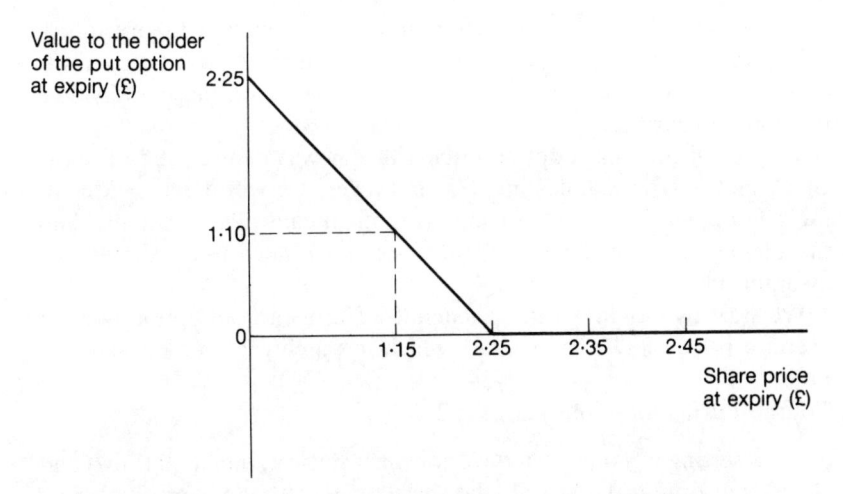

2·25

1·10

0   1·15   2·25   2·35   2·45
Share price at expiry (£)

Figure 7.4 Expiry value to the holder of the put option

of pricing options with some time to run before expiry. We have already considered the expiry value of the call option on ABC PLC shares with an exercise price of £1.50 and an expiry date of 22 September 19X9. But what might the market value of such a call option be, say, two months before expiry, in July 19X9? This clearly introduces the problem of uncertainty, as no one can be certain today of what the future share price will be in September. Intuitively, one would think that the market value of the option in July would reflect the probability of the different possible share prices at expiry in September. That approach was indeed

Value to the writer of the put option at expiry (£)

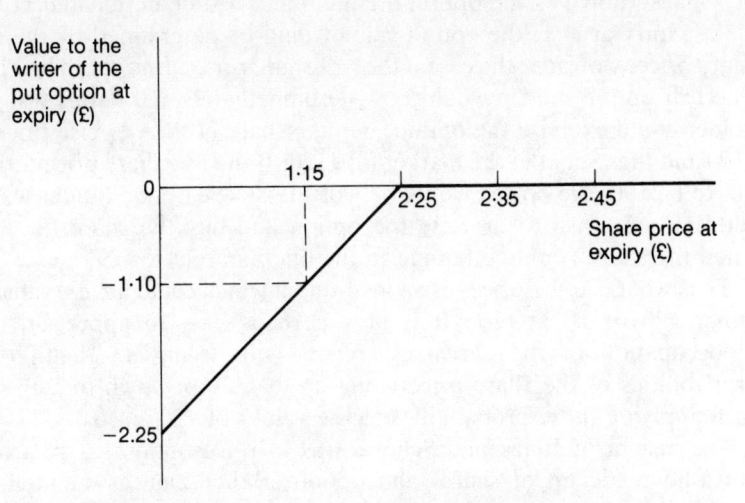

0   1·15   2·25   2·35   2·45
Share price at expiry (£)

−1·10

−2·25

Figure 7.5 Expiry value to the writer of the put option

the one taken by early researchers in option valuation theory; much effort was put into trying to identify the possible share price outcomes at expiry, together with the associated probability of those individual outcomes occurring.

The breakthrough in option pricing theory was pioneered by Fischer Black and Myron Scholes in 1973. However, we will defer looking at their model until later in this chapter. In the meanwhile we will build up the elements of option pricing in a series of steps using simplifying assumptions.

We start by looking at the pricing of a European call option with an exercise price of £100 on a share which has a current market value of £100.

First, our assumptions are as follows:

- The setting is a one period world which starts at time $t=0$ (now) and ends at time $t=1$. At $t=1$, the share price can take one of only two possible values.
- The share price jumps once during the period, and the possible values that the share price could take at $t=1$ are limited to either £120 or £90.[4]
- The appropriate risk-free rate of interest over the period $t=0$ to $t=1$ is 4%.

Our task is to calculate the $t=0$ price of such a call option in the face of the uncertainty over the outcome for the share price.

Let's consider the cash flows associated with holding a call on the share. At $t=0$, the holder of the call option would be required to pay for it. This is known as the option premium and will be designated £C.

At expiry at $t=1$, the option value would be determined by the $t=1$ share price. Consider the case if the $t=1$ share price turns out to be £120. The call option holder would now be immediately £20 better off: the holder could exercise the option, buy the share at the exercise price of £100 and then sell it in the market for £120. If the $t=1$ share price turned out to be £90, the option would be worthless. The option holder would certainly not wish to exercise the option and buy the share for £100 when the share could be bought in the open market for £90.

Thus what is to be priced is an instrument which could have a value of either £20 or £0 at $t=1$. It is now perhaps easy to appreciate the preoccupation of the early researchers with trying to identify the probabilities of the share price going up to £120 or down to £90, and then applying those probabilities to the values of £20 and £0.

The insight of Black and Scholes was to price options as part of a portfolio made up of shares and options rather than as stand-alone instruments. Let us now consider the construction of such a portfolio.

Share Options

First, consider the cash flows associated with buying the share (known as being long in the share) at $t=0$ and selling it at $t=1$. These flows are shown in Figure 7.6.

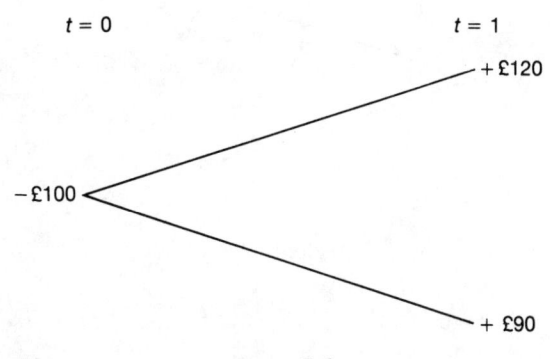

```
        t = 0                           t = 1
                                  ╱ + £120
                                 ╱
                                ╱
        −£100 ◄─────────────────
                                ╲
                                 ╲
                                  ╲ + £90
```

Figure 7.6

Secondly, consider the cash flows associated with buying a call option at $t=0$ (known as being long in the option) and exercising it when appropriate at $t=1$. The cash flows for the holder are as in Figure 7.7.

```
        t = 0                           t = 1
                                  ╱ + £20 (if the t = 1 share
                                 ╱       price is £120)
                                ╱
        −£C ◄───────────────────
                                ╲
                                 ╲
                                  ╲ £0 (if the t = 1 share
                                        price is £90)
```

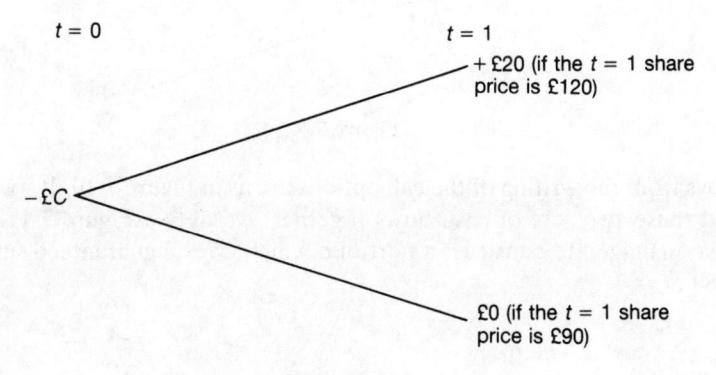

Figure 7.7

The writer of the call option will receive the option premium of £C at $t=0$ but will, if the $t=1$ share price is £120, have to provide the holder of the call option with the share at the exercise price of £100 and thus be worse off by the £20. Hence the writer's cash flows are of opposite sign, and are shown in Figure 7.8.

Consider the cash flows associated with buying two shares and writing three call options. You will see in a moment why we have chosen this particular portfolio mix. The cash flows associated with the purchase of the shares at $t=0$ and their sale at $t=1$ are as in Figure 7.9. The cash

102   *Share Options*

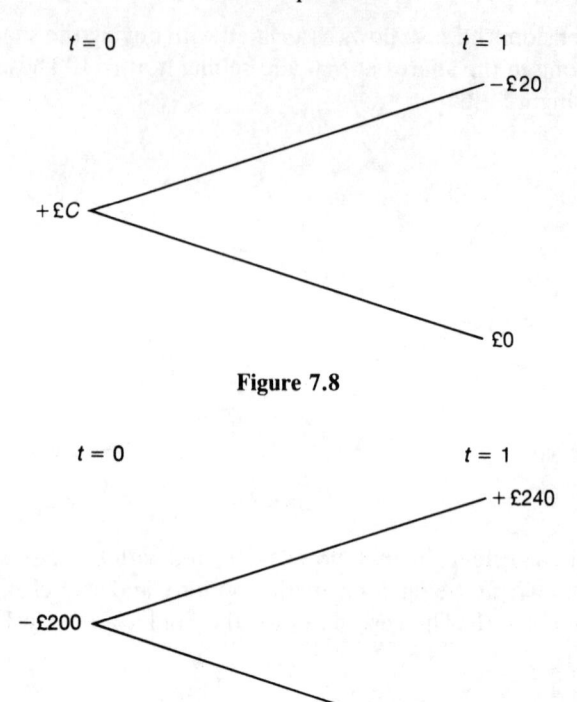

```
            t = 0                          t = 1
                                             −£20
             +£C  <
                                             £0
```
Figure 7.8

```
            t = 0                          t = 1
                                             +£240
            −£200  <
                                             +£180
```
Figure 7.9

flows from the writing of the call options are as in Figure 7.10. If we now add these two sets of cash flows together, we obtain Figure 7.11. We have managed to construct a portfolio which gives a guaranteed sum of £180 at $t=1$!

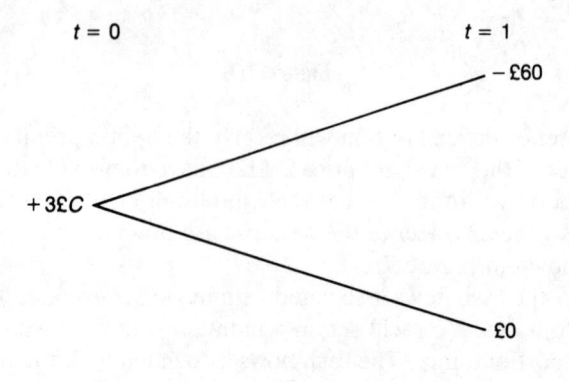

```
            t = 0                          t = 1
                                             −£60
            +3£C  <
                                             £0
```
Figure 7.10

Share Options

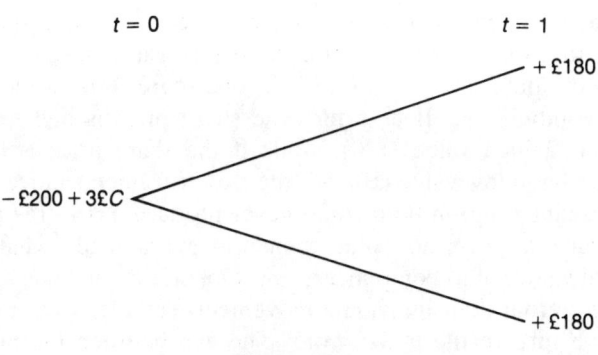

```
       t = 0                      t = 1
                               ╱ +£180
                              ╱
                             ╱
   -£200 + 3£C  ◄───────────
                             ╲
                              ╲
                               ╲ +£180
```

Figure 7.11

We can now turn our attention to $t=0$, and ask ourselves how much one would pay at $t=0$ for the right to receive a guaranteed sum of £180 at $t=1$. The amount one would be willing to pay must reflect the time value of money. In other words, we need to discount the £180 at an appropriate rate of interest for the period. And since we know that the £180 is guaranteed, the appropriate interest rate is the risk-free rate of interest for the period. Here we assume that the risk-free of interest is 4%. One would therefore be willing to pay £180/1.04 = £173.0769 for the right to receive £180 at $t=1$. Thus the $t=0$ cost of the portfolio of shares and written calls will be equal to that amount.

If the $t=0$ cost of the portfolio was say £175, nobody would wish to hold it. The return on holding the portfolio bought at that price would only be 2.8571% (£5/£175). Conversely, if the price was less than £173.0769, there would be huge demand for the portfolio; holders would be obtaining a rate of return greater than the 4% risk-free rate of interest.

Priced at £173.0769, the portfolio of shares and options provides exactly the required risk-free rate of return and is therefore a zero net present value investment. The discounted $t=1$ cash inflows exactly equal the $t=0$ cash outflows.

We now know that the $t=0$ cost of the portfolio of shares and written call options is £173.0769, and we also know that the $t=0$ cost of the shares was £200. It then follows that the proceeds of writing the three call options must be equal to £26.9231 (£200 − £173.0769). The $t=0$ price of the call option £C will be £8.9744 (£26.9231/3).

Notice that we have priced the call in our one period, one jump world without any reference whatsoever to the probabilities of the share price either going up to £120 or falling back to £90 at $t=1$.

The time has now come to explain how we knew that the risk-free portfolio could be constructed by buying two shares and selling three

104   Share Options

calls (that is, by choosing a ratio of two-thirds of a share to each call) and also that the way to replicate the expiry value of one call option involved the purchase of two-thirds of one share. First we look at the buy/sell combination. If at expiry the share price is high (£120) the option has a high value (£20), while if the share price is low (£90) the option has a low value (£0). As the two instruments move together, holding (being long) in both could never produce a risk-free portfolio. To produce a portfolio value which is guaranteed, whatever the individual values of its components, must involve buying one and selling the other so that their individual movements can offset each other.[5]

Now we turn to the hedge ratio. The gap between the higher and lower share prices at $t=1$ is £30 (£120 − £90), while the gap for the option prices is £20 (£20 − £0). To balance the smaller gap with respect to each option we need less than one share. Hence we obtain the ratio 2:3 in the risk-free portfolio.

7.3.2 Introduction to Option Replication

Perhaps it is appropriate here, having priced the option in our one period, one jump world, to examine whether there is anything unique about the $t=1$ option values that we were able to achieve above or whether indeed these values can be replicated using other means. In other words, is it possible by other means to achieve the same $t=1$ values as those associated with holding the call option, that is £20 and £0?

Recall that we created our risk-free portfolio by buying two shares and writing three calls. The ratio of shares to options in the portfolio is known as the hedge ratio, and is more usually written in terms of unit options. In our portfolio, two-thirds of a share are bought for each option written;[6] that is, the hedge ratio is 2/3:1. The cash flows from buying two thirds of a share are shown in Figure 7.12; these flows are one-third those of Figure 7.9.

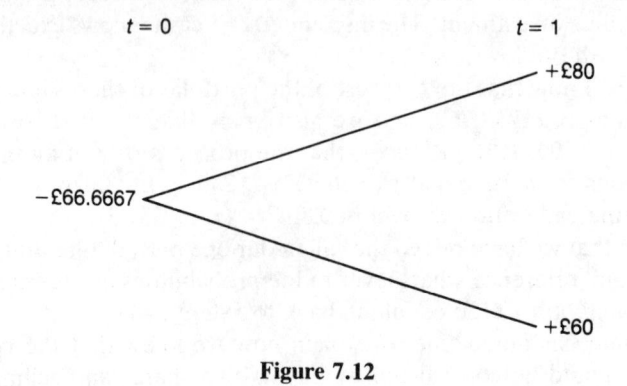

```
       t = 0                         t = 1
                                     ↗ +£80
   −£66.6667 ⟨
                                     ↘ +£60
```

Figure 7.12

Share Options

Consider now borrowing an amount at $t=0$ to finance our purchase of two-thirds of a share. The minimum $t=1$ value of this holding of two-thirds of a share is £60, and therefore we could afford to borrow up to a maximum of the present value of that amount, that is £60/1.04 = £57.6923 (the risk-free rate of interest being 4%). We would therefore receive £57.6923 at $t=0$ and agree to repay £60 at $t=1$. Our borrowing cash flows would thus be as in Figure 7.13.

If we add the cash flows in Figures 7.12 and 7.13 together, we obtain the net cash flow at $t=1$ shown in Figure 7.14. This net cash flow replicates exactly the realizable cash flows from holding a call option (Figure 7.7).

Let's now look at the cost of the replication strategy. The cost of the share was £66.6667 but £57.6923 of this came from money that we borrowed, so the only amount that we would have had to find was

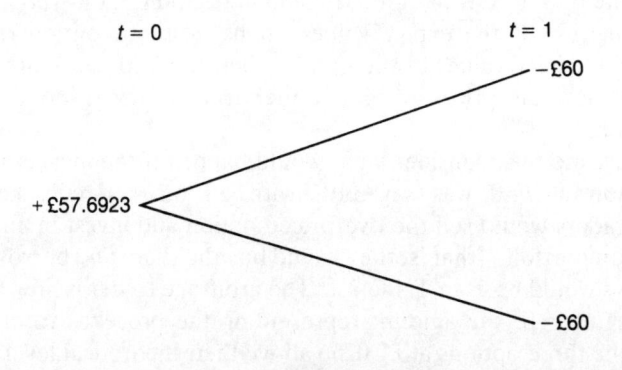

Figure 7.13

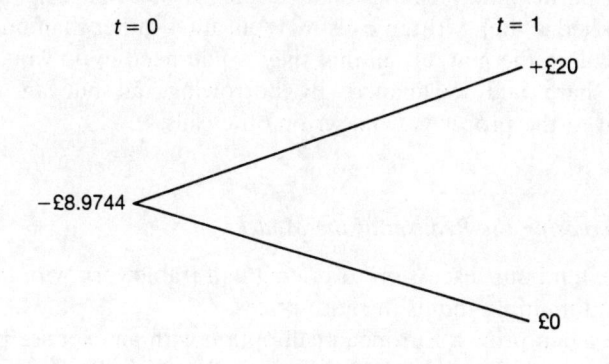

Figure 7.14

Table 7.1

	At t = 0 (£)	At t = 1 If the share price is £120 (£)	At t = 1 If the share price is £90 (£)
Sell 3 call options	+30	−60	0
Buy 2 shares	−200	+240	+180
Borrow the present value of £180	+173.0768	−180	−180
	+3.0768	0	0

£8.9744. In other words, our net investment was £8.9744. Recall that this is exactly the same amount that we would have had to spend had we bought the option. Given our discussion in Chapter 3, this should come as no surprise. If the expiry values of the synthetic option replicate exactly the expiry values of the option, their initial prices must also be identical. If their prices were not identical, arbitrage opportunities would arise.

To illustrate this, consider what would happen if the market price of the option at $t=0$ was say £10, with all other details kept the same. Traders would sell the overpriced option and invest in an option replication portfolio (that is, they would buy the share and borrow). The cash flows would be as in Table 7.1. The arbitrage trader is now £3.0768 better off at $t=0$, the amount representing the proceeds from selling each of the three options at £1.0256 above their theoretical level (£10 − £8.9744).

The ability to replicate option-type payoffs is particularly important to market participants wishing to write calls. If those participants then wished to hedge their written calls by replication rather than buying an identical call in the market, all that they would need to do would be to buy the share and to finance, by borrowing, all but an amount equivalent to the proceeds from writing the calls.

7.3.3 Increasing the Realism of the Model

We now extend our discussion to pricing in a framework with multiple periods and multiple jumps in share prices.

We will again price a European call option with an exercise price of £100, but this time in a two period scenario in which the share price is allowed to jump twice. The option is only exercisable at the end of the

Share Options

second period ($t=2$). The share price pattern for the next two periods starting at $t=0$ and now going through to $t=2$ is as in Figure 7.15.

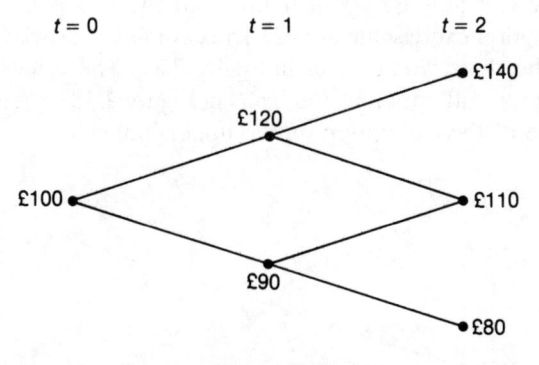

Figure 7.15

The appropriate risk-free rate of interest over the period $t=0$ to $t=1$ is kept at 4%, while the appropriate risk-free rate of interest for the period $t=1$ to $t=2$ (the forward rate) is assumed to be 6%.

Depending on the share price at expiration, ownership of the call option with an exercise price of £100 would give entitlement to one of the following cash flows at expiry (see Figure 7.16):

- £40, given that the above price at expiry is £140
- £10, given that the share price at expiry is £110
- £0, given that the share price at expiry is £80.

In this case, we work out the $t=0$ price of the call option by working back from the $t=2$ payoffs in Figure 7.16.

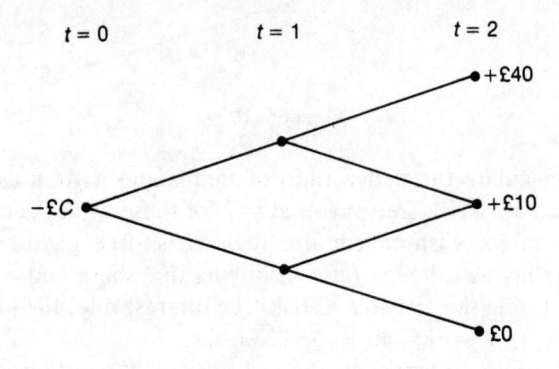

Figure 7.16

108 *Share Options*

Consider first the top two branches over the period $t=1$ to $t=2$ and the relevant cash flows if we bought, at $t=1$, the share and a call option exercisable at $t=2$. We know that the price of the share at $t=1$ would be £120 and we can now go about finding out the $t=1$ price of the one period call option exercisable at $t=2$. The cash flows associated with the holding of the share would be as in Figure 7.17. The values associated with holding the call option would be as in Figure 7.18, where $-£C_{1,u}$ is the $t=1$ price of the call option on the upper branch.

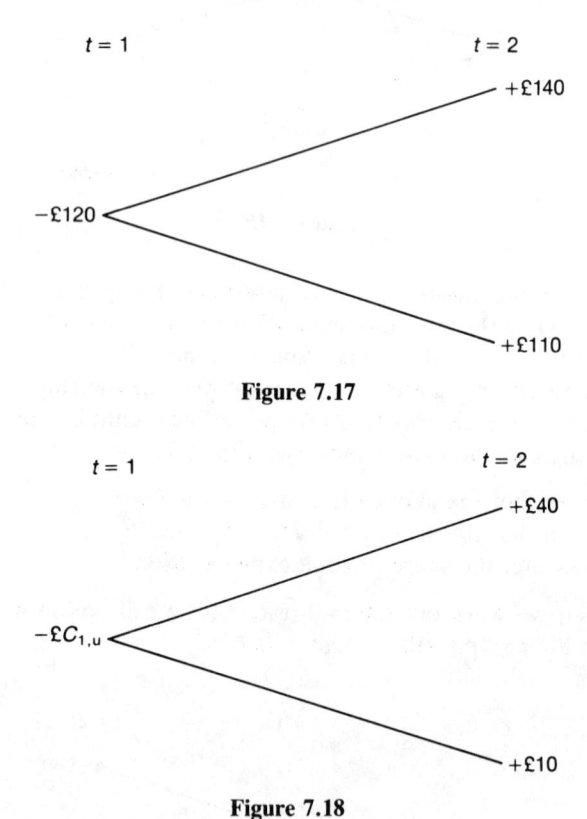

```
         t = 1                    t = 2
                               ┌─ +£140
                              ╱
              -£120 ◁
                              ╲
                               └─ +£110
```
Figure 7.17

```
         t = 1                    t = 2
                               ┌─ +£40
                              ╱
              -£C₁,u ◁
                              ╲
                               └─ +£10
```
Figure 7.18

We can calculate the hedge ratio of shares and written call options that would create a risk-free payoff at $t=2$ for these two upper branches. The reader might wish to confirm that a risk-free payoff at $t=2$ is achieved by having a hedge ratio of buying one share and writing one call option. Using the $t=1$ to $t=2$ risk-free interest rate, the price of the call option at $t=1$ works out to be £25.6604.

The next step is to work out the $t=1$ price of the option on the two lower branches in Figure 7.16. The hedge ratio shows that the risk-free

Share Options

portfolio involves the purchase of one-third of a share and the writing of one call option. The $t=1$ price of the one period option, exercisable at $t=2$, on the lower branch is £4.8428.

It should be clear now that the problem reduces to one over the single period $t=0$ to $t=1$, seeing that we know what the price of the call option would be at each of the two $t=1$ nodes.

We are now in a position to calculate the $t=0$ price of the call option £C_0. The cash flows from buying the share at $t=0$ and selling it at $t=1$ are as in Figure 7.19, and the $t=1$ values associated with buying the call option at $t=0$ are as in Figure 7.20. Given these data, the risk-free payoff at $t=1$ can be constructed by holding 0.6939 shares and writing one call option. Using the 4% risk-free rate of interest, the $t=0$ price of the call option £C_0 is £13.9978.

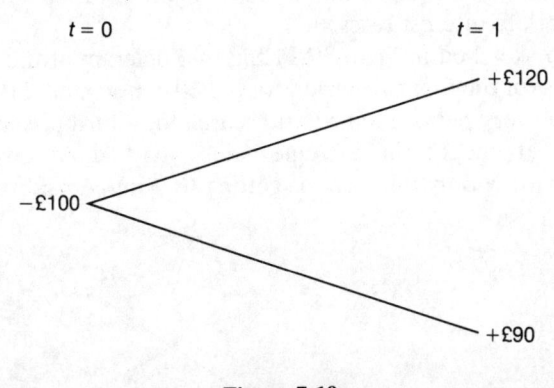

Figure 7.19

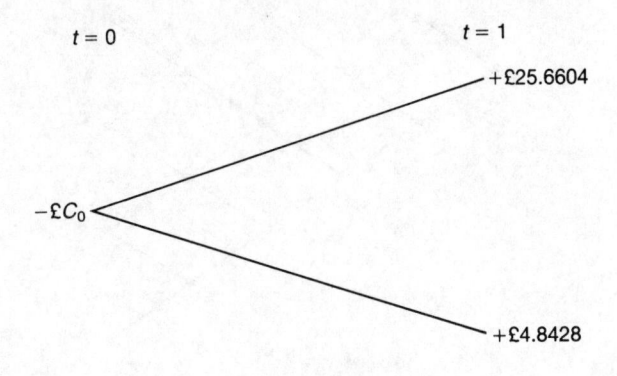

Figure 7.20

7.3.4 Still More Realism

Given that we have solved for a call option price in this two jump, two period scenario, it follows that we would now be able to price a call option with any number of periods or jumps in the share price before expiry. If we were to consider the $t=0$ price of a call option on a share with, say, 30 periods to expiry with a price jump every period, the problem is no more complex. However, it would certainly take time (and space) to sketch the tree diagram over the 30 periods – and a much longer time still to work back through the tree evaluating the price of the call option at each of the 465 nodes!

This sort of problem requires repetitive number crunching and is ideal for computerization. All that we would need would be an indication of the expected pattern of the share price movements (in our one period, one jump model, the return on the share was either 20% or -10%) and the appropriate interest rates.

We have sketched in Figure 7.21 the tree diagram of the share price movements for the first five periods of our 30 period model (with a share price jump every period) in order to search for a further simplification. Let's look at one of the extreme values marked A. Over the five periods, there is only one way of getting to point A and that is if the

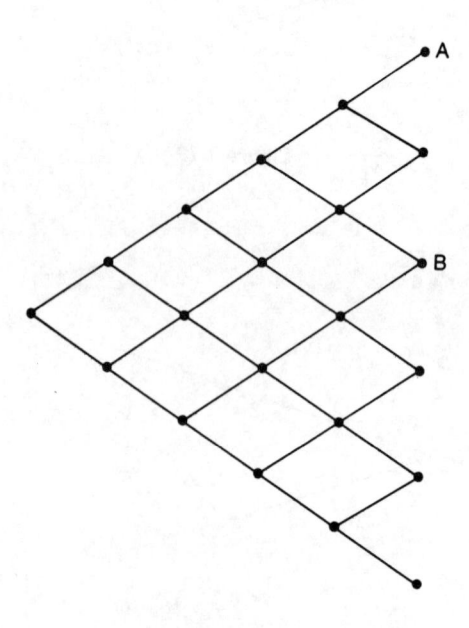

Figure 7.21

share price increases in each of the periods. Contrast this with the ten possible ways of getting to the value marked B. Unless there are extreme probabilities attaching to share price movements it is clear that, given there are so many ways of getting to point B and only one way of getting to point A, the probability of the value at A occurring is less than that of the value at point B occurring. Even after only five periods it should be apparent that there will be a range of value outcomes, but with more occurrences of the central values, and with less likelihood of the more extreme values.

Figure 7.22 repeats the tree diagram of Figure 7.21, but now indicates the number of possible ways of getting to a particular outcome value. The distribution of the values at expiry that we have now added can be used, as we shall see, to describe the possible outcomes in the Black and Scholes model.

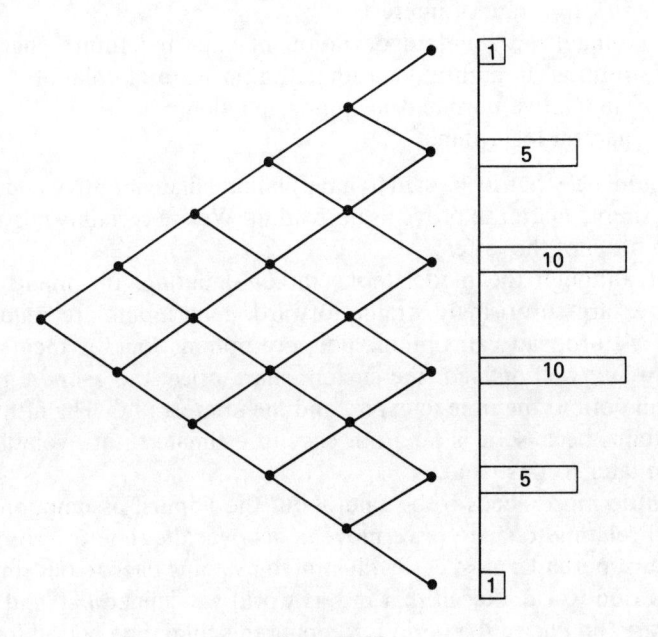

Figure 7.22

7.3.5 The Black and Scholes Formula

Having covered the multiperiod, multijump case and the idea of a distribution to describe future outcomes, it is now appropriate to move on to the Black and Scholes model, which is set in a world with continuous share price movement.

The Black and Scholes model for determining the price C of a European call option is written as follows:

$$C = S\,N(d_1) - X\,e^{-RT}\,N(d_2)$$

where

$$d_1 = \frac{\ln(S/X) + [R + (\sigma^2/2)]\,T}{\sigma\sqrt{T}}$$

$$d_2 = \frac{\ln(S/X) + [R - (\sigma^2/2)]\,T}{\sigma\sqrt{T}}$$

and the notation is as follows:

S	current share price
X	exercise price
T	time to expiry
R	risk-free rate of interest
σ	annualized standard deviation of expected future share price returns (in natural logarithms), a measure of volatility
N	cumulative normal distribution function
ln	natural logarithm.

The model can hardly be said to have an immediate intuitive appeal; nor is it a simple matter to prove its derivation. We are certainly not going to try to attempt the latter!

But although the model looks rather daunting, the inputs that it requires are surprisingly straightforward. Five inputs are required to price a European call option. For any option, four of them will be known and well defined: the current share price, the exercise price of the call option, the time to expiry and the interest rate. The fifth will be uncertain, because it is far from easy to estimate future volatility; we return later to this issue.

A little more needs to be said about the implicit assumption in the model relating to share price movements over the time to expiry. This aspect is, perhaps, most easily illustrated by going back to our simplified one period world. Recall that in this world we defined $t=0$ and $t=1$ as the start and end of the period. Keeping this total time period fixed, we now slice the time between $t=0$ and $t=1$ into infinitely small time intervals and allow the share price to move in each of these intervals. So whereas we initially had the share price jumping only once (from £100 to either £120 or £90) in our one period world, the Black and Scholes model assumes that the share price will move an infinitely great number of times over the period. The model further assumes that consecutive share price changes are random and that the share price drifts upwards over time as in our one period example, where the jump was either £20

Share Options

(from £100 to £120) or −£10 (from £100 to £90). This last assumption is reasonable given that risky assets should earn a positive rate of return and thus share prices should exhibit positive drift over time.

Diagrammatically, the share movements over the period $t=0$ to $t=1$, given these small slices of time, would now appear as in Figure 7.23. Of course what we have just done is to create a large number of consecutive one period worlds, each with a very short time span. If we were able to attach values to each of the share outcomes at $t=1$, we could still price the call at $t=0$ by working backwards from $t=1$ through each of the branches of the tree to $t=0$ – but it would be a rather laborious task!

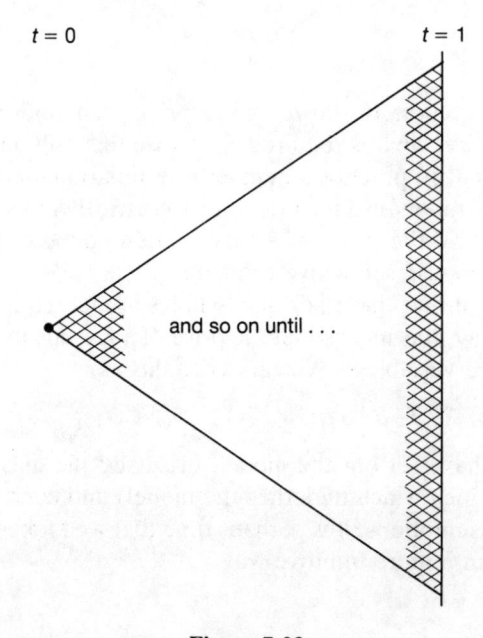

Figure 7.23

The effect of the positive drift in share prices is illustrated in Figure 7.24. The skewed distribution of share prices at $t=1$ approximates to what is known as the log-normal distribution. It follows from this (although it is not proved here) that the natural logarithms of the share price returns (price relatives), measured as share price changes, will be normally distributed. That is to say, the distribution at $t=1$ will be the familiar bell-shaped curve. Given this normality, the standard deviation used in the Black and Scholes model is the appropriate statistic to measure the range of outcomes.

In pricing options in practice, the input figure for volatility usually poses the greatest problem. Of course with hindsight the volatility can

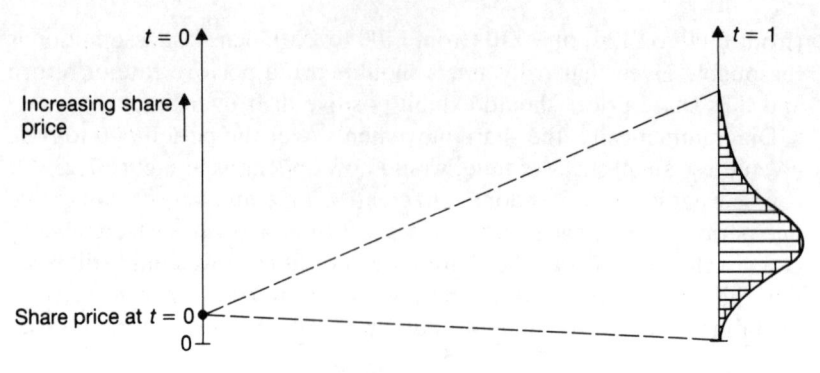

```
                    t = 0                              t = 1

Increasing share
price


Share price at t = 0
                 0
```
Figure 7.24

be measured accurately; however, in pricing an option with say six months to expiry, what is required is a figure that will decribe what the volatility will be! In practice a number of estimation methods are used. Some market traders use historical measures; others use the volatility figure implied by the price of similar options quoted in the market; whilst yet others use subjective estimates.

We have seen that the Black and Scholes model requires five inputs. Put another way, this means that the price of a European call option is a function of five variables.[7] We can write this as

$$C = C(S, X, T, R, \sigma)$$

Now that we have set out the model, discussed the idea of a risk-free portfolio (the idea which underlies the model) and considered some of the model's assumptions, it is perhaps time that we look at some aspects of the model in a more intuitive way.

7.4 Sensitivity of European Call Option Values

7.4.1 Sensitivity in a One Period, One Jump Model

In this section we provide an intuitive explanation for the direction of the change in call option prices following a change in the value of each of the five input variables.

Recall that the exercise price and time to expiry of any one particular European option are defined as part of that option's documentation. The other three variables which determine option values can and do change over the life of the option. We have, however, included a discussion of sensitivity of call option prices to changes in exercise price and time to expiry even though, as we have just noted, these variables

Share Options

are fixed for any one option. Such sensitivities are still useful in comparing two options alike in every respect apart from exercise price or time to expiry.

Recall the data that we used initially in pricing a European call (Section 7.3.1):

- The current share price and the exercise price were both £100.
- The share price at expiry ($t=1$) was either £120 or £90.
- The risk-free rate of interest was 4%.

The $t=0$ price of the call was calculated as £8.9744.

We start by examining the impact of a change in the exercise price. Suppose the exercise price is raised to £105; no other variable is changed. The possible $t=1$ option values (given the same end of period share prices of £120 and £90) will now be £15 and £0 rather than the original £20 and £0. Given that the possible $t=0$ option values decline, the $t=0$ cost of acquiring these values will decline also, in this instance to £6.7308. The higher its exercise price, the cheaper the call option will be. Conversely, the lower the exercise price, relative to the current share price, the more the $t=0$ price of the call option will be.

Consider now changing the current share price and keeping the exercise price constant. Let us assume that the share price at $t=0$ is now £105 while the exercise price is retained at £100. Although the possible $t=1$ option values remain the same (at £20 and £0), the option already has a potential value of £5 locked in, and this is reflected in the $t=0$ cost of the option which increases to £12.3077. Thus the higher the current share price relative to the option exercise price, the higher the price of the call option.

The impact of changing the risk-free rate of interest can be seen if we use 7% instead of the original 4%. Such a change does not affect the possible $t=1$ option values and therefore does not affect the hedge ratio. The $t=0$ cost of the call option, however, increases to £10.5919. In terms of explanation it is perhaps clearer to consider the impact of such a change through the option replicating strategy of investing in the share and borrowing. Although the investment in the share does not change when the interest rate changes, the increased interest rate will reduce the amount of funds that can be borrowed. The investment in the share (net of the borrowed funds) will therefore increase; and since this amount is the same as the $t=0$ cost of the call, it follows that increasing the interest rate raises the $t=0$ price of the call option.

The next variable is volatility, which in this context is taken to be shown by the range of outcomes at expiry. We can demonstrate its effect by changing the range of the $t=1$ expected share prices. Changing the $t=1$ share prices to £140 and £90 (rather than £120 and £90) and so making the range of outcomes £50 leads to a change in the cost of replicating the option. In this case, the $t=0$ price of the call option increases to £10.7692. It is worth noting that a change to £120 and £70 also increases the price of the call option, this time to £13.0769.

Given our assumption about a fixed one period world, it becomes difficult to examine the effect of changing the time to expiry using our example! Instead, consider holding a call option on a share with an exercise price of £100. The option is due to expire tomorrow. The current market price of the share is £98. Today's price of the option is going to be very close to zero, given that it is most unlikely to be worth exercising. If however the option still had six months to expiry, it is almost certain that the price of the option would be positive. There would now be more time in which the share price might drift up to and beyond the exercise price and thus for the option to take on value at expiry. Thus the longer the time to expiry, the more costly the call will be.

We have summarized in Table 7.2 the direction of movements in European call option prices to changes in the determining variables.

Table 7.2

Changes	Impact on call price
Increase in current share price	↑
Increase in exercise price	↓
Increase in time to expiry	↑
Increase in risk-free rate of interest	↑
Increase in volatility	↑

7.4.2 Sensitivity in the Black and Scholes Model

We start by defining some arbitrary values as follows:

Current share price	£60
Exercise price of the call option	£60
Time to expiry	200 days
Risk-free rate of interest	8%
Volatility	20%

The Black and Scholes determined price for the European call option is £4.9017.

In Figure 7.25 we have graphed the Black and Scholes call prices as we have altered each of the five variables in turn, while keeping the other four constant at the above values.

It is, of course, also possible to graph the option price for various

Share Options

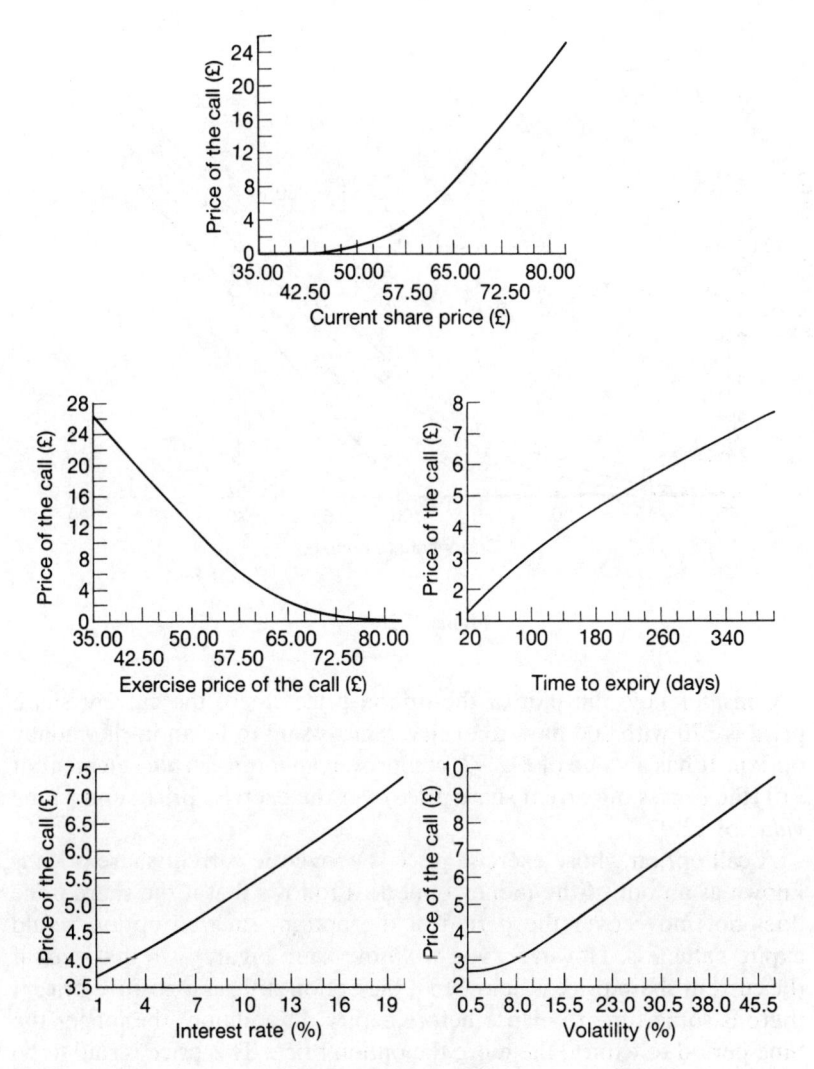

Figure 7.25

pairings of determining variables. Figure 7.26 plots the call prices generated by the Black and Scholes model for various current share prices and various times to expiry. Call option prices are quoted for a range of current share prices (£40 to £80) and for periods of 300, 200, 100 and 0.1 days to expiry. This is an important diagram and we shall come back to it in the next section. Before that, we shall use it to introduce some more options market terminology.

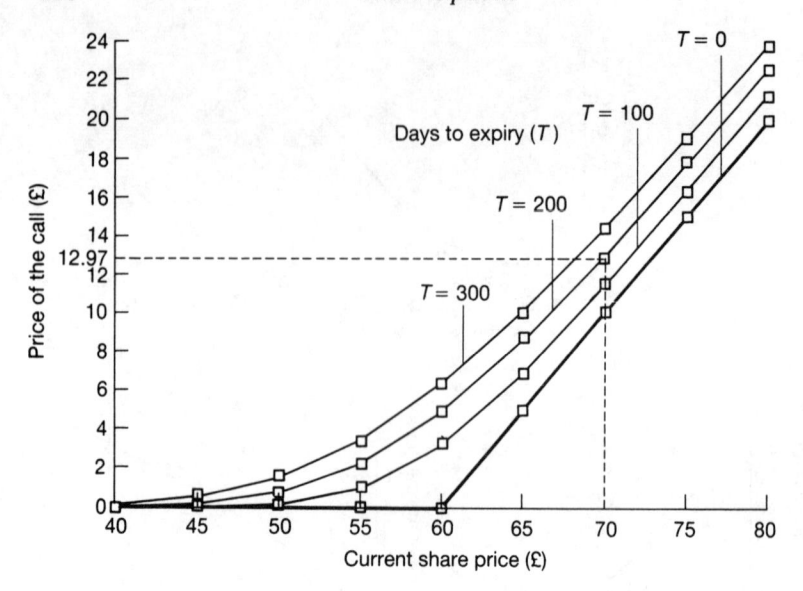

Figure 7.26

Consider now the plot of the option price where the current share price is £70 with 200 days to expiry. This is said to be an in-the-money option. It has a value of £12.97, comprising an *intrinsic value* element of £10 (the excess of current share price over the exercise price) and a *time value* of £2.97.[8]

A call option whose exercise price is above the current share price is known as an out-of-the-money option. It follows that if the share price does not move over the period of the option, such an option would expire valueless. However, you will note from Figure 7.26 that even if the current share price is below £60, the option still has a positive price if there is some time to elapse before expiry; in addition, the longer the time period to expiry, the more the option price. This price is said to be the time value of the option, and reflects the time to expiry and the volatility of the price of the underlying share.

In the case of a call option which expires as an at-the-money option (where the exercise price is equal to the share price at expiry), the value of the option will be zero. It is clear, though, from Figure 7.26 that call options which are at-the-money (the current share price is £60), and which still have time to run, also have a positive time value.

Share Options

7.4.3 Sensitivities: a Bit of Greek

A more formal approach is to differentiate the Black and Scholes formula with respect to each of the five input variables. In other words, taking the first derivative allows us to see the direction of the change in the call option price consequent upon a change in the value of each of the input variables in turn. These derivatives provide us with option sensitivities to changes in input variables, as well as being the basis of other measures used to gauge changes in the option price resulting from changes in, for example, the time to expiry, the current price of the share and so on during the life of the option.

Most of these measures would be required by traders holding option positions wishing to hedge them. Suppose a trader has written call options and is hedging his position by an investment in the shares and borrowing. It is obvious that if the hedge is to be efficient the trader has to know the sensitivity of the written options position to the passing of time towards the expiry date in order to adjust the hedge position accordingly.

We now briefly discuss each of the main six measures of sensitivity.

Option delta

The option delta measures the sensitivity of the option price to a unit change in the price of the underlying security, the share. This is the first derivative of the Black and Scholes formula with respect to S.

In Figure 7.27 we have repeated Figure 7.26 but have sketched in only two contours of call option prices. One is the price of the call option at expiry ($T=0$), the other is the option price with 200 days to expiry ($T=200$).

We consider the call option price when the current share price is £50 and the option has 200 days to expiry. The option price is marked as C_1 on the vertical axis. Now consider a small move in the current share price around £50. The option price will change but the slope of the contour makes it clear that it will be less than the movement in the share price. The delta is the slope of the contour at one particular point and will, at £50, be much less than 1.

On the other hand, it is clear that a small change in the current share price around £70 will lead to an almost corresponding change in the option price. Given the 45° line drawn from the exercise price (which has a slope of 1), the option when the current share price is around £70 will have a delta close to 1.

Figure 7.28 shows delta as a function of the current share price, for

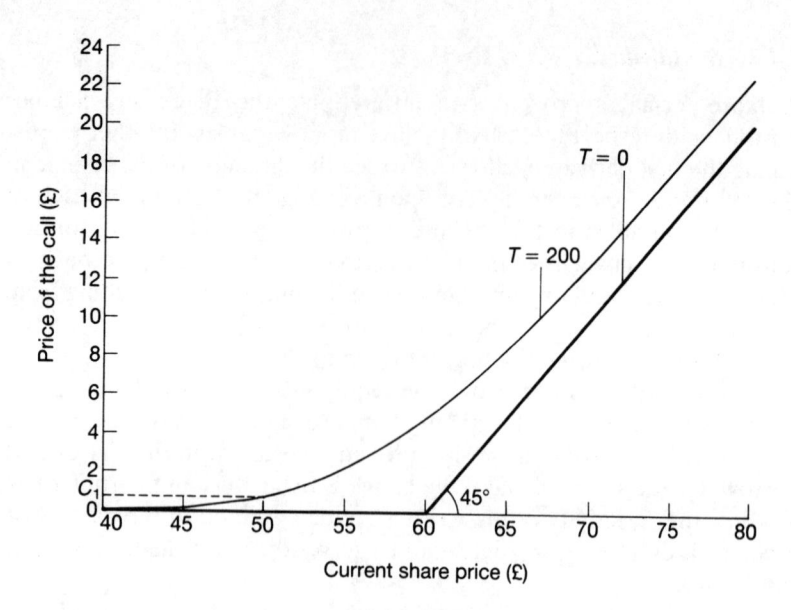

Figure 7.27

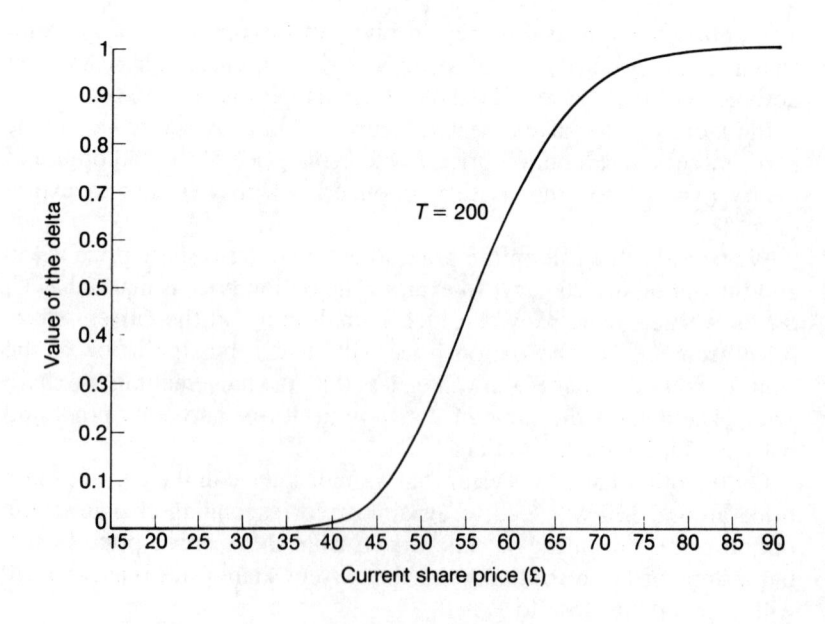

Figure 7.28

the same call option as we have been discussing so far, with 200 days to expiry.

Option gamma

The option gamma measures the change in the option delta value resulting from a unit change in the current share price. This is the second derivative of the Black and Scholes formula with respect to S. Figure 7.29 illustrates the behaviour of option gamma.

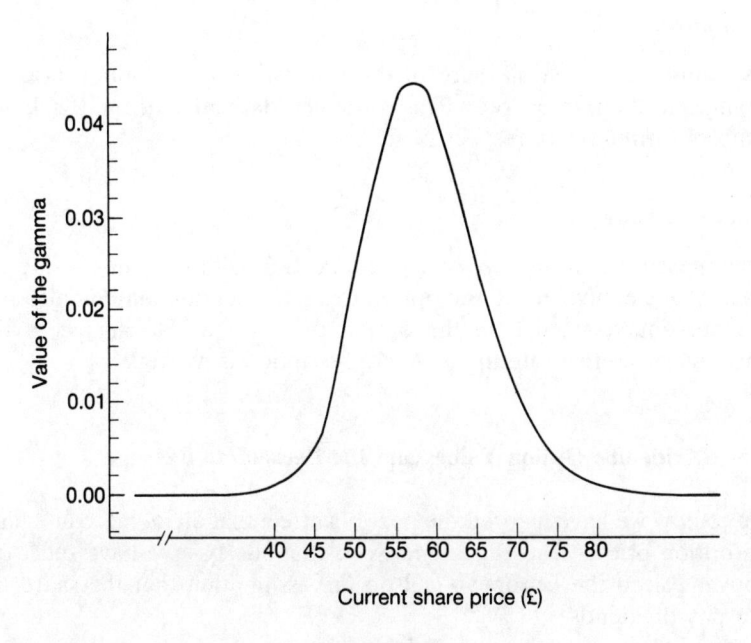

Figure 7.29

Option Theta

The option theta measures the change in the option price as the time to expiry elapses. This is the first derivative of the Black and Scholes formula with respect to T.

In Figure 7.27 we saw that the call price would be C_1 given 200 days to expiry and a current share price of £50. If at expiry the share price had not moved, the option would expire worthless. That drop in option price from C_1 to zero is not a linear function of time. That is to say, the option would not drop in price by 1/200 each day. It will drop less in price between, say, the 200th and 199th day to expiry than between, say, the 10th and 9th day to expiry. The process of declining value with respect to time is known as time decay.

Option kappa (or option vega)

The option kappa is a measure of the sensitivity of the option price to changes in volatility. This is the first derivative of the Black and Scholes formula with respect to σ.

Option rho

The option rho is a measure of the sensitivity of the option price to changes in the interest rate. This is the first derivative of the Black and Scholes formula with respect to R.

Option lambda

This measure is normally used in connection with options on interest rates and is equivalent to the option delta. The option lambda meaures the percentage change in the option price for a 1% change in the underlying interest rate upon which the option is written.

7.5 Dividends: Option Values and the Decision to Exercise

Up to now we have ignored the possible effect that dividends could have on option prices. The Black and Scholes model, as we have set it out above, priced the European call on the assumption that the share did not pay dividends.

A number of pricing models incorporating dividends have been suggested, some based on the original Black and Scholes model, others based on the binomial model illustrated in Figure 7.22.

Dividends are paid to the owners of the shares, and in general when the dividends are paid (or more strictly when the share goes ex-dividend) the share price falls. To see the impact that the payment of a dividend could have on call prices, we return to our world with one period and one jump in share price. As in Figure 7.6, the values that the share price can take at expiry ($t=1$) are £120 and £90. The associated $t=1$ values of the call option (given the £100 exercise price) are £20 and £0, as in Figure 7.7.

Now consider if a dividend of £5 was paid to the shareholders just before the expiry date of the option. The share price would drop to £115 or £85, and the two possible $t=1$ values of the call would fall from £20 and £0 to £15 and £0. The $t=0$ price of the call would drop from £8.9744 to £6.7308.

Having seen how dividends impact on the price of calls in this scenario, the idea can be generalized to the multiperiod, multijump world that we met in Section 7.3.3. The problem is now first to identify the points in our tree diagram at which the share will go ex-dividend (and so reduce the option values at those times), and secondly to predict what the future dividend amounts will be.

Other researchers have adapted the original Black and Scholes model to allow for dividends. One of the earliest models was suggested by Robert Merton in 1973. Although there have been a number of subsequent models, we discuss the Merton model here because there are parallels between this model and the models for pricing foreign exchange options that we will cover in the next chapter.

Merton's model for the valuation of a European call option on a dividend paying share is of the following form:

$$C = e^{-\delta T} S N(d_1) - e^{-RT} X N(d_2)$$

where

$$d_1 = \frac{\ln(S/X) + [R - \delta + (\sigma^2/2)] T}{\sigma \sqrt{T}}$$

$$d_2 = \frac{\ln(S/X) + [R - \delta - (\sigma^2/2)] T}{\sigma \sqrt{T}}$$

The only new variable here is the constant dividend yield δ; the other variables are as in Section 7.3.5. The share is assumed to pay dividends on a continuous basis.

The two revisions to the original model have an intuitive appeal. The first – the $R - \delta$ term – is most easily seen if we consider the option replication portfolio of buying the share and borrowing. The holder of the share will now receive dividends and this, in turn, will offset the principal that the option replicator will need to borrow during the period to the expiry of the option. The cost of funding the position will fall as a result; hence the $R - \delta$ term. The second – the discounting of the current share price by the dividend yield $e^{-\delta T}$ – reflects the fact that the share price at expiry will be reduced by the payment of the dividend.

Finally, we look at American options. Given that we have already seen that the market price of options with time to expiry will include a time value, the adage that an option is worth more alive (unexercised)

124   *Share Options*

than dead (exercised) will hold true for American options on non-dividend paying shares. But this is not the case with American options on dividend paying shares. The American call holder might well be better off exercising the call before the expiry date, paying the exercise price (thus acquiring the share) and receiving the dividend. The decision to exercise is worthwhile if the dividend is greater than the market value of the option at the time the dividend is paid. The additional flexibility afforded by the American option relative to the European will justify a higher premium but, given that an option is worth more alive than dead, it follows that this extra premium will be relatively small.

7.6 Pricing Put Options

7.6.1 Applying Our Simple Model Again

The pricing of a European put option in our single period, single jump world draws on exactly the same ideas as we used to price the European call. That is to say, we will have to construct a portfolio of shares and put options in such a way as to generate a risk-free payoff at expiry.

The details of our model with one period and one jump in share price are as follows:

- The share price at $t=0$ is £100, which is equal to the exercise price of the put option.
- The share price at $t=1$ can be either £120 or £90.
- The appropriate risk-free rate of interest over the period $t=0$ to $t=1$ is 4%.

First, we consider the $t=1$ option values associated with holding the put option. If the share price at $t=1$ is £120, the option would expire worthless; the holder would not wish to exercise the put to sell the shares for £100 when the share could be sold in the market for £120. If the $t=1$ share price is £90, the put option would have a value of £10; the holder of the put would be able to buy the share in the market for £90, exercise the put and sell the share for £100.

We can set out the cash flows associated with buying the share as in Figure 7.30. The corresponding cash flows associated with buying the put option at $t=0$ and exercising it as appropriate at $t=1$ are shown in Figure 7.31.

The portfolio which ensures a risk-free payoff at $t=1$ comprises one share and three put options. Note that, unlike the call option, the put option has a higher value the lower the share price. Hence the risk-free portfolio requires positive quantities of each. The gap between the $t=1$ share prices is £30 and between the $t=1$ option prices is £10.

Share Options

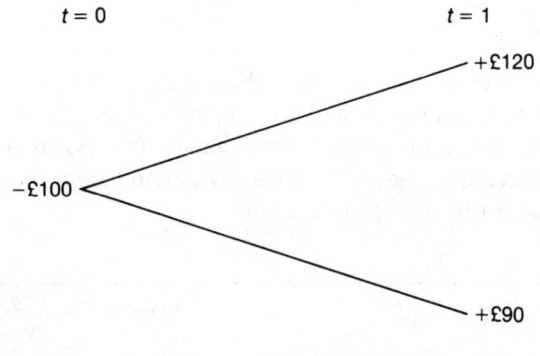

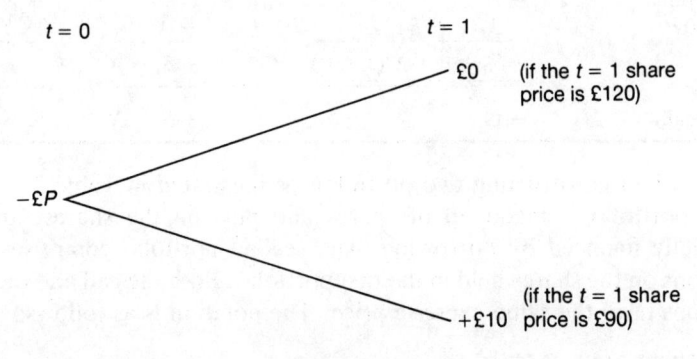

```
t = 0                    t = 1
                         +£120
-£100
                         +£90
```
Figure 7.30

```
t = 0                    t = 1
                         £0     (if the t = 1 share
                                 price is £120)
-£P
                                 (if the t = 1 share
                         +£10    price is £90)
```
Figure 7.31

Hence the hedge ratio is 1/3:1. The combined cash flow profile is shown in Figure 7.32. Given the total $t=0$ cost (of the share and the put options) of £115.3846 (£120/1.04), the $t=0$ price of each put option will be £5.1282.[9]

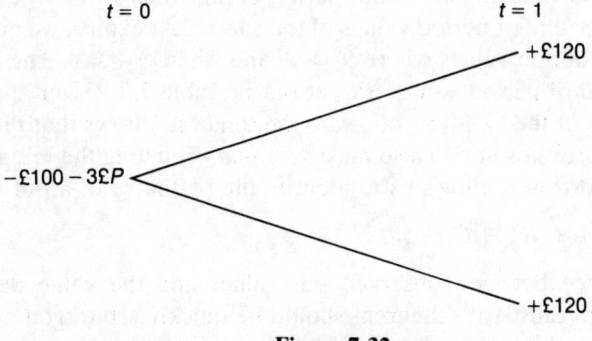

```
t = 0                    t = 1
                         +£120
-£100 - 3£P
                         +£120
```
Figure 7.32

7.6.2 Put-Call Parity

Pricing put options is easy once we know the price of call options. All that we need to do is to appeal to the put–call parity pricing theorem.[10] The basis of this theorem is that instruments (or portfolios of instruments) that have the same value at expiry should have the same initial cost. It's that no free lunch rule again!

Table 7.3

	Cost at t = 0	Value at t = 1 (expiry) $S_1 > X$	$S_1 \leq X$
Buy share	$- S_0$	$+ S_1$	$+ S_1$
Buy put	$- P$	0	$+ X - S_1$
Borrow	$+ X/(1 + R)$	$- X$	$- X$
	$- S_0 - P + X/(1 + R)$	$+ S_1 - X$	0
Buy call	$- C$	$+ S_1 - X$	0

Consider constructing two portfolios as illustrated in Table 7.3. The first portfolio is made up of shares and puts on the shares, and is partially financed by borrowing. The second portfolio comprises call options on the shares held in the first portfolio. Both the call and the put options have the same exercise price. The notation is as follows:

S_0 share price at $t=0$
S_1 share price at $t=1$ (expiry)
C price of the call option
P price of the put option
R risk-free interest rate
X exercise price of the options.

We can now examine the initial costs at $t=0$ and the $t=1$ expiry values for the two portfolios. The end of period option values will, of course, depend on the end of period values of the shares. At expiry, we need to consider the option values where $S_1 > X$ and where $S_1 \leq X$. The initial costs and end of period values are set out in Table 7.3. Given that the expiry values of the two portfolios are the same, it follows that the cost of the two portfolios at $t=0$ also must be equal. Equating the initial cost of the two portfolios allows us to identify the $t=0$ price of a put as[11]

$$P = X/(1 + R) + C - S_0$$

Any difference between observed put values and the value derived under the put–call parity theorem should be quickly arbitraged away.

One further observation is worthwhile here. Where the current price of the share is equal to the discounted value of the exercise price, the prices of the call and the put will be equal. In other words, if the exercise price of the option is set at the current price of the share compounded by the relevant rate of interest, the call and the put options will have the same price.

This can be confirmed by plugging in the following numbers to a Black and Scholes model:

Current share price   £100
Exercise price   £108.3287
Time to expiry   365 days
Risk-free rate of interest 8%
Volatility   15%

Both the call and the put options have the same price of £5.9785. The exercise price has been set as £108.3287 (rather than £108) because of the continuous compounding ($e^{0.08} = 1.083287$), which matches the assumption of continuous price movement.

7.6.3 A Digression

We have seen here the case where the call and the put have the same price; however, this is but one special instance. There will be a whole series of pairings of call exercise prices and put exercise prices where the prices of the calls and the puts will be the same. Starting from our put–call parity value, we can see that raising the exercise price of the call option will lower its premium.[12] Similarly, lowering the exercise price of the put option will reduce its premium. Hence these pairings will be somehow distributed around the put–call parity value. However, for a given call exercise price it is not a trivial matter to find the put exercise price which ensures that the premium of the two options will be the same.

To illustrate this idea we again use the figures of our world with one period and one jump in share price, except for the exercise price which we now set at £104. Given that this exercise price is the same as the current share price (simply) compounded at the 4% risk-free rate of interest, we know that the price of the call option will be identical to the price of the put option. The details of the share and the option values at expiry are as in Figure 7.33. The $t=0$ price of calls and puts is £7.1795.

Now consider the effect of forcing apart the exercise price of the call and the put options around the exercise price of £104. The higher the exercise price of the call option, the lower its price. Similarly the lower the exercise price of the put option, the lower its price. Therefore, increasing the exercise price of the call option by £1 to £105 causes the

Share Options

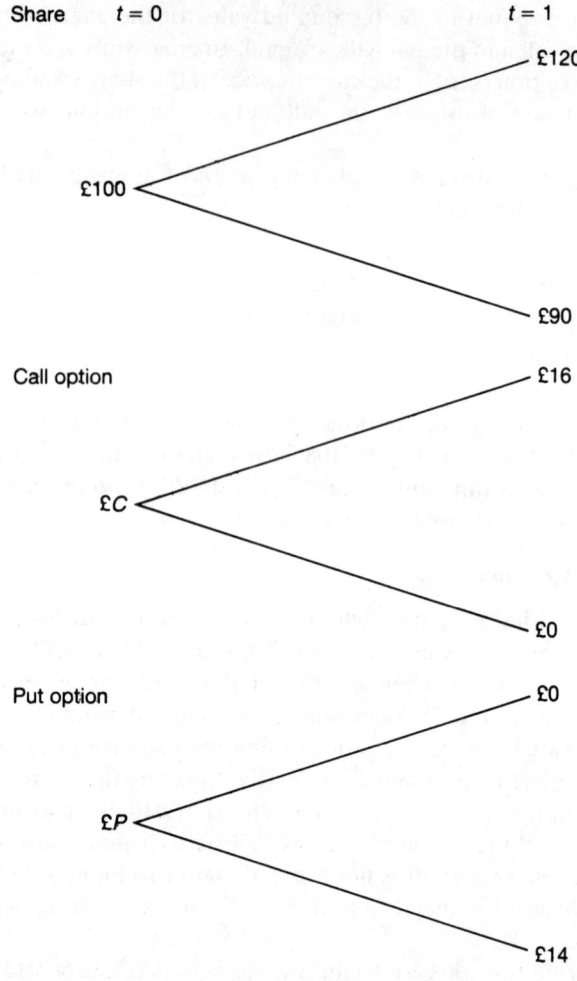

```
Share      t = 0                    t = 1
                                    £120
          £100
                                    £90

Call option                         £16
           £C
                                    £0

Put option                          £0
           £P
                                    £14
```

Figure 7.33

price of the call option to fall to £6.7308. Dropping the exercise price of the put option by the same amount to £103 causes the price of the put option to fall to £6.6667. It is important to note that the changes in the call and put option prices are not the same per unit change in the exercise price around £104.

The reader may wish to confirm that if the exercise price of the call option is set at £112 and if the exercise price of the put option is set at £97 (a movement of +£8 and −£7 around the previous exercise price of £104) the price of both put and call options will be £3.5897.

Matching option premiums is an important idea, and one to which we will come to in Chapter 9.

Share Options

7.7 The Payoff to an Option at Expiration

In Section 7.2 we discussed and illustrated option values at expiration but we did not, at that stage, take account of option premiums.

Let us reconsider the position of a holder of a call option. We assume that the option has an exercise price of £60 and that the holder of the option paid a premium of £5. The payoff profile to the holder of the call at expiry would appear as in Figure 7.34. The corresponding payoff profile to the writer of the call is sketched in Figure 7.35.

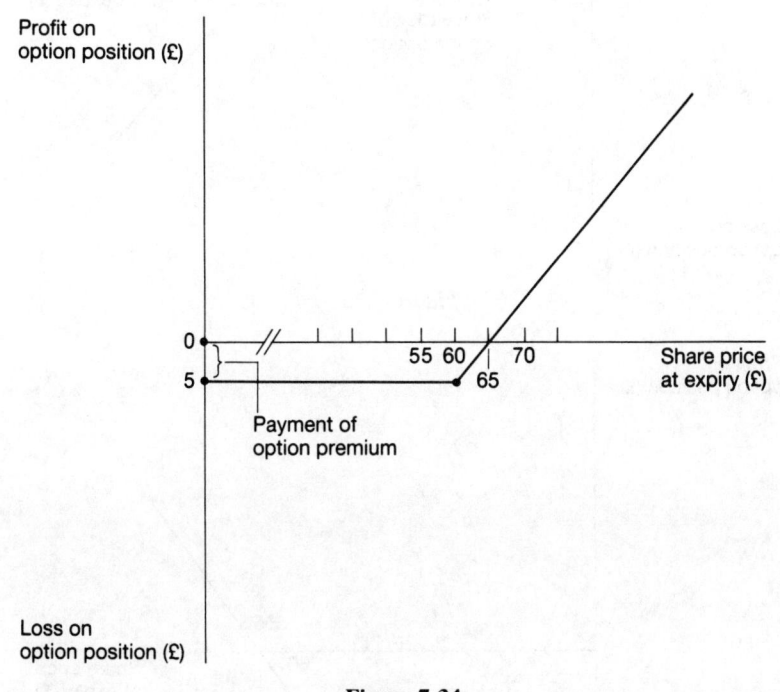

Figure 7.34

However, in drawing Figure 7.34 we have not taken into account the time value of money. The premium would be paid at the time that the option was purchased, but the option value at expiry might be some months later. We can allow for this by compounding up the option premium to the expiry date to calculate a net terminal value of the option premium. Let us assume that, in this case, the net terminal value of the premium is £5.40. Figure 7.36 reflects the new figures. In this instance, the option holder breaks even on the option position if the share price at expiry is £65.40.

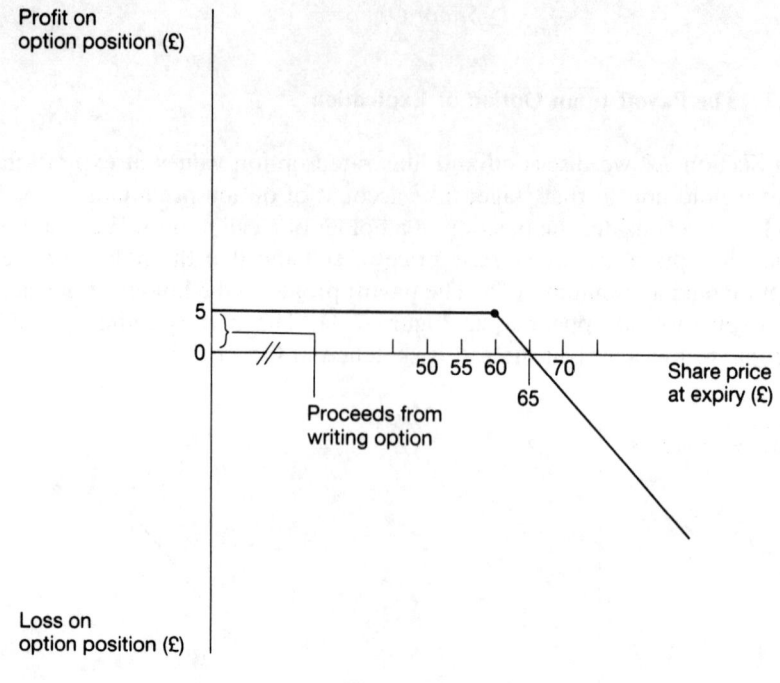

Figure 7.35

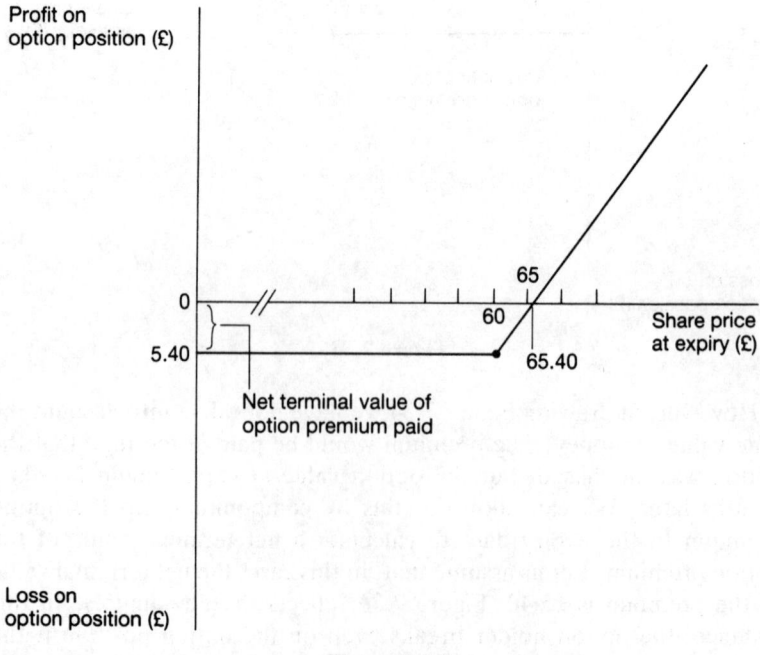

Figure 7.36

Share Options

The payoff profiles at expiry for the holder and the writer of a put option with an exercise price of £60 and an assumed option premium of £5 are shown in Figure 7.37.

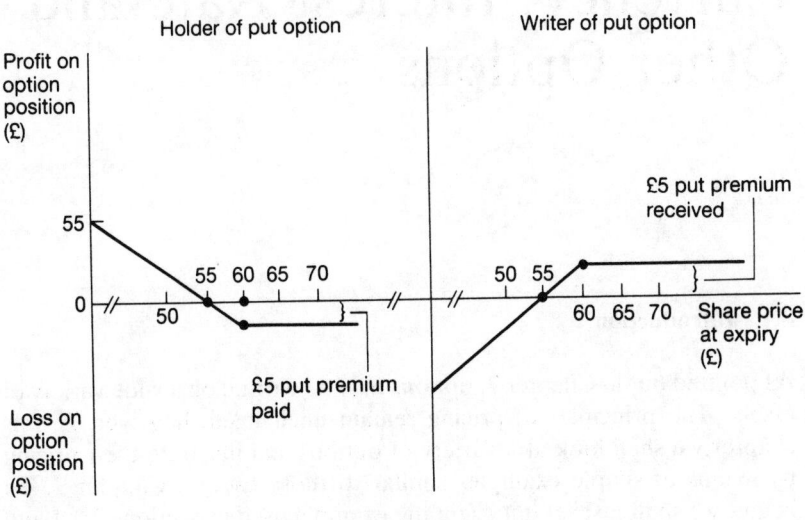

Figure 7.37

7.8 Contract Settlement

If a call option expires in the money and the holder wishes to exercise the option, the option writer is obliged to produce the shares in exchange for an amount of money equivalent to the exercise price.

In the case of puts, if the put holder wishes to exercise, the put writer is obliged to provide the holder with funds equivalent to the exercise price of the put in exchange for the shares.

8
Currency, Interest Rate and Other Options

8.1 Introduction

As pointed out in Chapter 7, options may be written on a wide variety of assets. The principles of pricing remain unchanged, however. In this chapter we shall look at a variety of options and illustrate their pricing by means of simple examples similar to those used in Chapter 7. To begin, we shall just set out again the example used in Sections 7.3.1 and 7.3.2.

To demonstrate the pricing of share options we used a simple binomial example and considered how it would be possible to construct a risk-free portfolio and to replicate an option. We used the example summarized in Figure 8.1 to value a call option with an exercise price of £100. That is, the share has a current price of £100 and will be worth either £120 or £90 in the future. According to the share price, the call option will be worth either £20 or £0 in the future.

8.1.1 Risk-Free Portfolio

The risk-free portfolio described in Chapter 7 consists of buying two shares and writing three calls. The portfolio cash flows are shown in Figure 8.2, where £C is the call option price. As can be seen, the portfolio will be worth £180 in the future whatever the share price outcome.

The net present value of the portfolio is given by

$$-200 + 3C + \frac{180}{1+R} = 0$$

That is, in a competitive market a risk-free project, with its future cash

Currency, Interest Rate and Other Options

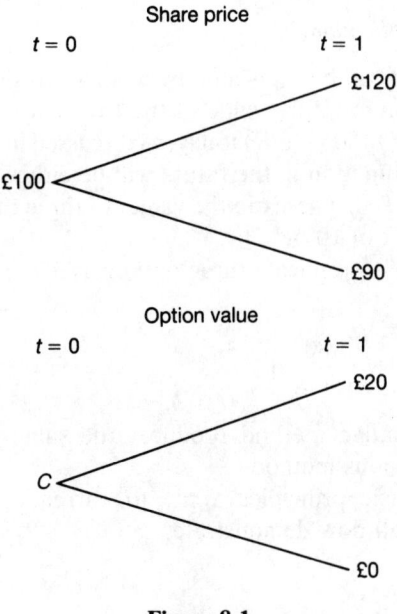

```
                      Share price
         t = 0                        t = 1
                                        £120
          £100
                                        £90

                     Option value
         t = 0                        t = 1
                                        £20
           C
                                        £0
```

Figure 8.1

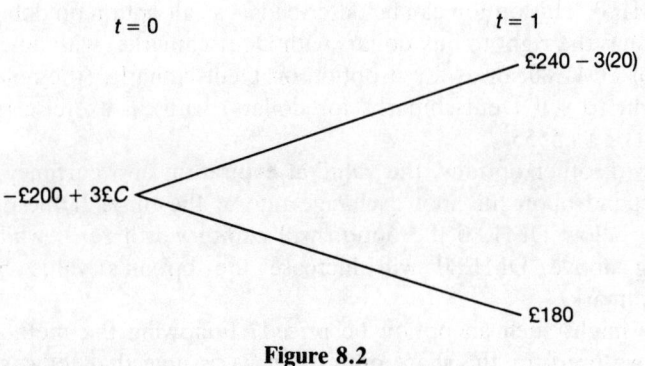

```
         t = 0                        t = 1
                                        £240 − 3(20)

      −£200 + 3£C

                                        £180
```

Figure 8.2

flows discounted by the risk-free rate of return R, will have a net present value of zero. Thus the call option can be priced today as

$$C = £\frac{1}{3}\left(200 - \frac{180}{1+R}\right)$$

As we saw in Section 7.3.1, an interest rate of 4% would give a value of £8.9744 to the option.

8.1.2 Option Replication

The option payoff can be replicated by buying two shares and using the guaranteed minimum future value of the two shares (£180) as security for a borrowing of £180/(1 + R) today, as discussed in Section 7.3.2. The value of this combination in the future will be either £180 − £180 = £0 or £240 − £180 = £60. These are the values of three call options, each of which has a payoff of £0 or £20.

The cash outlay to replicate three options is 3£C = £200 − 180/(1 + R). Therefore

$$C = £\frac{1}{3}\left(200 - \frac{180}{1+R}\right)$$

Hence this alternative method produces the same price for the call option as the previous method.

These same basic principles apply to currency and interest rate options, as we shall now demonstrate.

8.2 Currency Options

Consider the pricing of a currency option allowing its owner to buy $100 for DM180. This option can be described as a call option on dollars (the holder has the right to buy dollars with Deutschmarks) with an exercise price of DM1.80, or as a put option on Deutschmarks (the holder has the right to sell Deutschmarks for dollars) with an exercise price of $1/1.80 or $0.5555.

As with other options, the value at expiration of a currency option will depend upon the spot exchange rate at the time. If the dollar is trading below DM1.80 the option will expire worth zero, while each pfennig above DM1.80 will increase the option's value by one Deutschmark.

How might such an option be priced? Following the methodology which we used for the share option, let us assume that today's dollar spot rate is DM1.80 and that, in the next period (year), only one of two outcomes is possible: either DM2.00 or DM1.60. Thus, in the event of the dollar's exchange rate being DM2.00, the holder of the call has the right to receive $100 (which will be worth DM200) for an outlay of DM180, and the option will be worth DM20. If the rate goes to DM1.60, the holder has the right to receive $100; this will be worth only DM160, and so the holder would not exercise the option. It follows from this that the call option on $100 will expire worth either DM20 or DM0. This is shown in Figure 8.3.

Currency, Interest Rate and Other Options 135

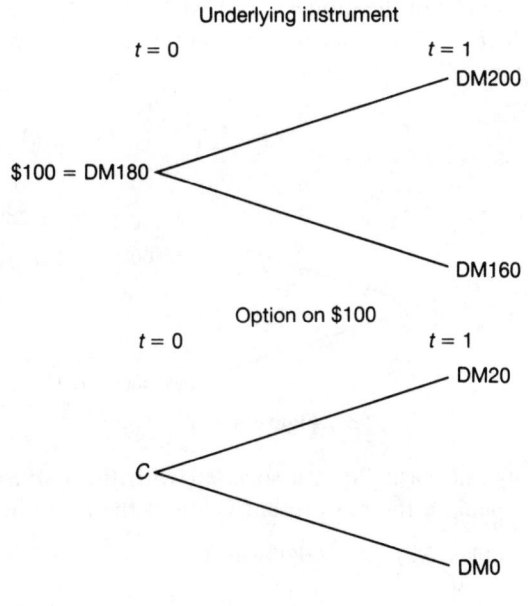

```
                    Underlying instrument
        t = 0                         t = 1
                                    ⟋ DM200
                                  ⟋
    $100 = DM180 ⟨
                                  ⟍
                                    ⟍ DM160

                    Option on $100
        t = 0                         t = 1
                                    ⟋ DM20
                                  ⟋
            C ⟨
                                  ⟍
                                    ⟍ DM0
```

Figure 8.3

8.2.1 Risk-Free Portfolio

Constructing a risk-free portfolio with currency options is analogous to constructing a similar portfolio with share options in a situation where the share pays a dividend. In this case the 'dividend' is the interest on the 'foreign' currency. Just as a call option on a share can be valued by considering a portfolio involving the purchase of the share and the writing of an option, so the call option on the dollar can be valued by considering a portfolio involving the purchase of the dollar, the receipt of interest (dividends) on the dollar and the writing of an option.

The purchase and deposit of $100 today (for DM180) will yield $100(1 + $R_\$$) in the next period.[1] This will be worth either DM200(1 + $R_\$$) or DM160(1 + $R_\$$) depending on the spot exchange rate in the next period. The range of outcomes is therefore DM40(1 + $R_\$$). As we have seen, the corresponding outcomes for the option are DM20 or DM0, a range of DM20. Therefore a risk-free portfolio can be constructed by buying $100 for DM180 and selling 40(1 + $R_\$$)/20 call options on the dollar. Today's cost will be DM180 less DM[40(1 + $R_\$$)/20]C, where C denotes today's price for each call option.

The value of this portfolio in the next period will be either DM160(1 + $R_\$$), should the dollar be worth DM1.60 (and the options therefore expire out of the money), or DM200(1 + $R_\$$) less DM[40(1 + $R_\$$)/20]20, which is also equal to DM160(1 + $R_\$$). The cash flows are shown in Figure 8.4.

$$-DM180 + \frac{40(1 + R_\$)}{20} C \begin{cases} DM200(1 + R_\$) - \frac{40(1 + R_\$)}{20} 20 = DM160(1 + R_\$) \\ \\ DM160(1 + R_\$) \end{cases}$$

Figure 8.4

Constructing the cash flows associated with the risk-free portfolio allows us to calculate the net present value of the portfolio as follows:

$$-180 + \frac{40(1 + R_\$)}{20} C + \frac{160(1 + R_\$)}{1 + R_{DM}} = 0$$

Hence

$$C = DM \frac{20}{40(1 + R_\$)} \left[180 - \frac{160(1 + R_\$)}{1 + R_{DM}} \right]$$

Thus if $R_\$$ = 10% and R_{DM} = 5% the option will have a price of DM5.6277.

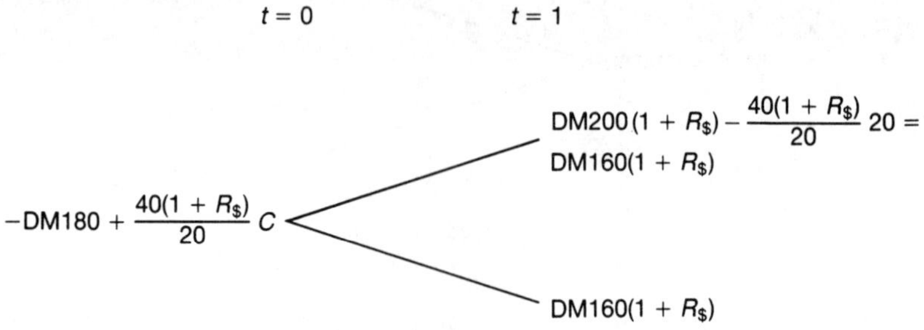

Comparison with the share option formula will show that we have included the dollar interest rate in the equation. Should this rate ever be zero, the equation would reduce to the simple, no-dividend share option equation. The inclusion of the dollar interest rate shows that the higher this rate, the lower the value of the call option on the dollar.

8.2.2 Option Replication

Given the detail in Section 8.2.1, the currency option payoffs can be replicated by buying $100 and borrowing today an amount DM160(1 + $R_\$$)/(1 + R_{DM}), which is the present value of the guaranteed minimum Deutschmark value of the $100 (i.e. DM160(1 + $R_\$$)) at the option's expiration date.

The future value of the combination will be either 200(1 + $R_\$$) − 160(1 + $R_\$$) = DM40(1 + $R_\$$) or 160(1 + $R_\$$) − 160(1 + $R_\$$) = DM0. That is, DM40(1 + $R_\$$) or DM0 is the expiry value of 40(1 + $R_\$$)/20 call options, each of which has a value of DM20 or DM0.

The cash outlay needed to replicate the options is given by

$$180 - \frac{160(1 + R_\$)}{1 + R_{DM}} = \frac{40(1 + R_\$)}{20} C$$

Therefore

$$C = DM \frac{20}{40(1 + R_\$)} \left[180 - \frac{160(1 + R_\$)}{1 + R_{DM}} \right]$$

as before.

In Section 7.3.5 we showed the Black and Scholes model for a European call option on a share. A similar formula for a European currency call option is

$$C = e^{-R^*T} S N(d_1) - e^{-RT} X N(d_2)$$

where

$$d_1 = \frac{\ln(S/X) + [R - R^* + (\sigma^2/2)]T}{\sigma \sqrt{T}}$$

$$d_2 = \frac{\ln(S/X) + [R - R^* - (\sigma^2/2)]T}{\sigma \sqrt{T}}$$

and the notation is as follows:

S exchange rate (domestic currency price of one unit of foreign currency)
X exercise price
T time to expiry
R, R^* domestic and foreign interest rates
σ standard deviation of percentage changes in exchange rate
N cumulative normal distribution function.

A comparison with Merton's formula in Section 7.3.6 shows that the two are identical. In Merton's formula R^* is replaced by δ, which denotes the continuous constant dividend yield.

8.3 Interest Rate Options: Some Preliminaries

In principle, interest rate options are similar to other options. However, there are a few conceptual and computational problems associated with such options.

Suppose that an individual must make an interest payment on a £100 loan at a fixed date in the future. Suppose further that, somewhat unusually, the interest payable on that future date is determined by the spot twelve month interest rate ruling at that time. To protect himself against an adverse movement in rates, he may choose to buy a European call option with a notional principal of £100 on the twelve month rate with an expiration date the same as that on which the interest payment is due.

Suppose, for the sake of argument, that he buys a call option with an exercise price of 10%. If, on expiration day, the twelve month interest rate is 10% or below, the option will expire unexercised. Higher interest rates will trigger the exercise of the option, whereupon the option writer will pay an amount compensating the option holder for the extra interest cost in excess of the 10% interest rate. Hence the option value can be shown as in Figure 8.5.[2]

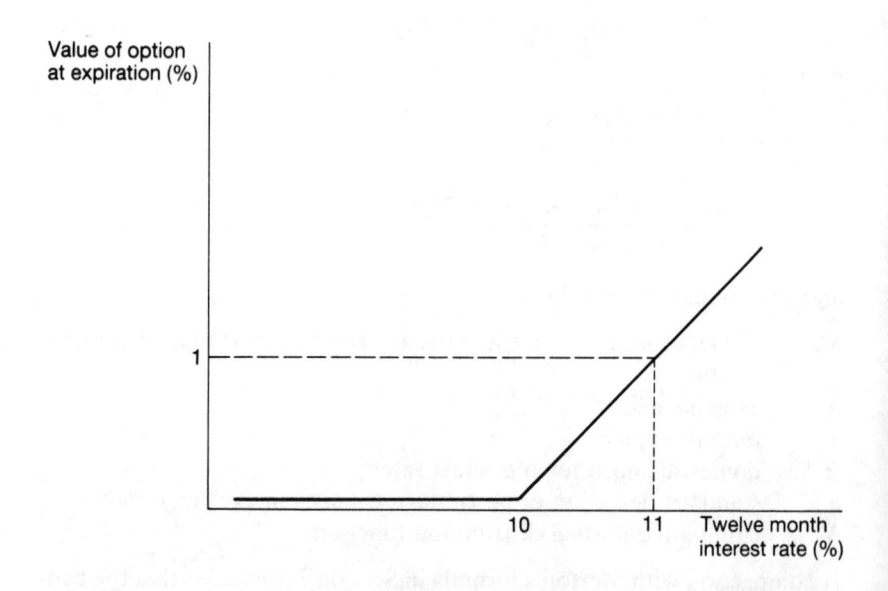

Figure 8.5

As indicated so far, the exercise of an interest rate option does not require the making of a deposit or a loan because the settlement process involves the exchange of a sum of money determined by the difference between the spot rate at expiration and the exercise rate, multiplied by the notional amount on which the option is written.

Let us consider the pricing of the European call option discussed above. As before, let us assume only two interest rate outcomes, 12% and 7%. In this case the interest paid on a £100 loan or deposit will be either £12 or £7, while the call option with an exercise price of 10% will expire with a value of either £2 or £0. This is illustrated in Figure 8.6.

Currency, Interest Rate and Other Options

8.3.1 Risk-Free Portfolio

A risk-free portfolio can be constructed either by taking a loan and buying call options, or by depositing money and selling call options. Using the latter route, which is similar to that used so far, we can see that the risk-free portfolio can be constructed by depositing £200 for one year and selling five call options. If the interest rate is 7% the depositor will receive £214 and the call options will expire with a value of zero, while if the interest rate is 12% the depositor will receive £224 but will

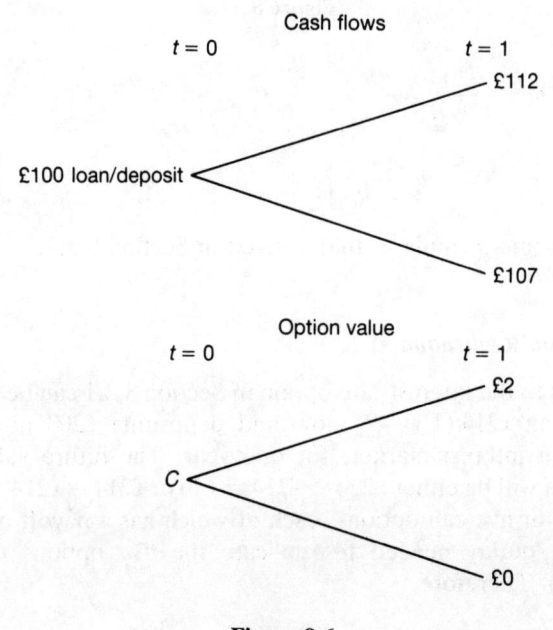

Figure 8.6

have to pay out £2 on each of the five call options. (Note that we are continuing with the somewhat unusual assumption that interest is paid at the spot rate ruling at the end of the period.)

The flows are shown in Figure 8.7. The net present value of the portfolio is given by

$$-200 + 5C + \frac{214}{1+R} = 0$$

Hence

$$C = £\frac{1}{5}\left[200 - \frac{214}{1+R}\right]$$

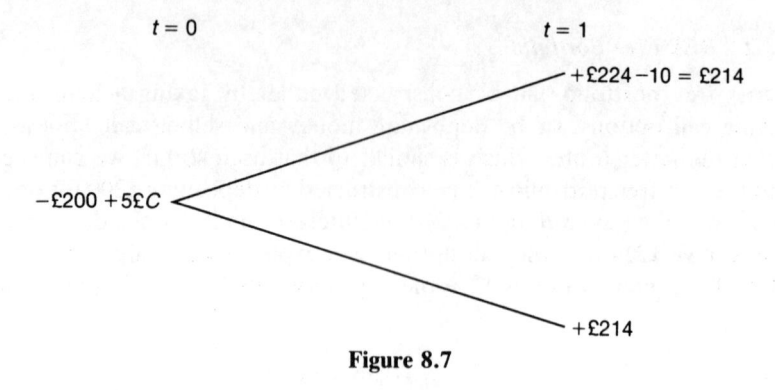

Currency, Interest Rate and Other Options

```
        t = 0                          t = 1
                                  ┌─ +£224 −10 = £214
                                  │
   −£200 +5£C ◄───────────────────┤
                                  │
                                  └─ +£214
```

Figure 8.7

$$5C = 200 - \frac{214}{1 + R}$$

$$C = £\frac{1}{5}\left[200 - \frac{214}{1 + R}\right]$$

This is the same formula as that derived in Section 8.3.1.

8.3.2 Option Replication

The payoffs to the interest rate option in Section 8.3.1 can be replicated by borrowing £214/(1 + R) now and depositing £200 now (in our unusual spot interest market) for one year. The future value of the combination will be either £224 − £214 = £10 or £214 − £214 = £0. This is the value of five call options, each of which has a payoff of £2.

The cash outlay needed to replicate the five options is £200 − 214/(1 + R). Therefore

8.4 Interest Rate Options: Practical Considerations

The system of interest payments which we have discussed above is rather unusual. Far more common is the system under which interest is paid at the end of the period according to the rate prevailing at the *start* of the period. Consider, for example, a three year floating rate loan with interest payable at six monthly intervals. This loan would usually involve the first interest payment after six months, with the amount determined by the six month interest rate ruling at the start of the loan period. The second payment would be determined by the six month rate seen after six months and would be made at the end of the first year, and so on until the end of the loan period. This makes the valuation of

Currency, Interest Rate and Other Options

interest rate options somewhat more complicated than in Section 8.3, although the principles remain unchanged.

To illustrate the issues raised by the payment of interest at the end of each period, consider an individual who has borrowed £100 for two years with floating interest payments to be made at the end of each year. He will know the amount of interest to be paid at the end of year 1 as soon as the loan is agreed, because that amount will be determined by the one year rate pertaining on the agreement date. He will not know, at the start, the amount to be paid at the end of year 2 but he *will* know this amount after just one year of the loan's life.

If this borrower is concerned about the amount to be paid at the end of year 2, he may decide to buy a call option with a notional principal of £100 and an exercise price of 10% in order to protect himself. A common name for such an option would be an interest rate cap at 10%. When valuing this option we face the extra complication that it will expire at the end of year 1 although its value will not be received until the end of year 2. That is, if the twelve month interest rate at the end of year 1 ($t=1$) exceeds 10%, the owner of the option will receive at the end of year 2 ($t=2$) an amount compensating him for the excess.

To complete the setting up of this example, let us assume that the one year rate next year (that is, starting at $t=1$) will be either 12% or 7%, and let us denote today's one year rate and two year rate as $_0R_1$ and $_0R_2$ respectively. We can summarize the position in our usual diagrammatic form as in Figure 8.8.

Loan

$t = 0$ $t = 1$ $t = 2$

                               £100(1+$_0R_1$) (1.12)

£100 ——— £100(1+$_0R_1$) redeposited

                               £100(1+$_0R_1$) (1.07)

Option

$t = 0$ $t = 1$ $t = 2$

                               £2

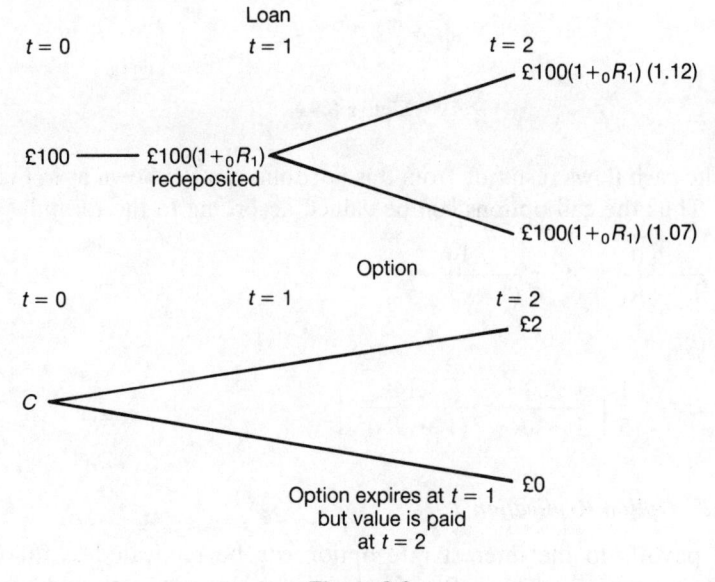

C

                               £0

Option expires at $t = 1$ but value is paid at $t = 2$

Figure 8.8

142 Currency, Interest Rate and Other Options

We can now illustrate the pricing of this option in the usual way, either by constructing a risk-free portfolio or by replicating the option's value.

8.4.1 Risk-Free Portfolio

A risk-free portfolio can be constructed by depositing £200/(1 + $_0R_1$) for one year (at $_0R_1$%), redepositing the proceeds for a further year at the then prevailing interest rate (12% or 7%), and selling five call options. This produces a guaranteed value of £200(1 + 0.07) = £214 at the end of the two year period. If the one year interest rate next year turns out to be 12%, the initial deposit will be repaid as £224 but each of the call options will have a negative value of £2, giving a net value of £214. If the one year rate next year turns out to be 7%, the initial deposit will be repaid as £214 and the options will expire with a value of zero.

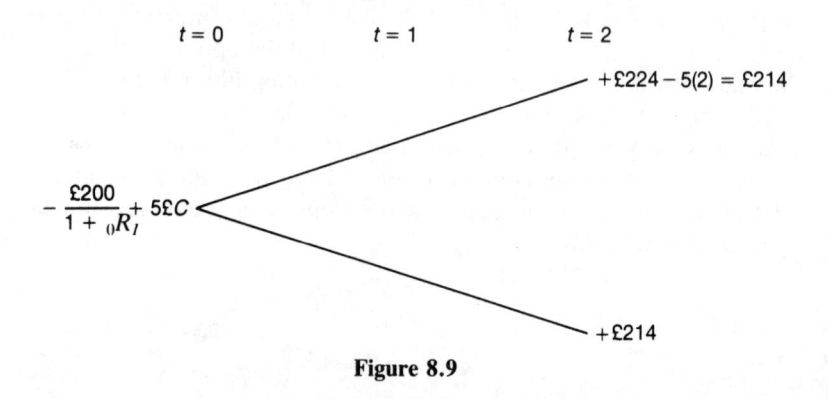

$t = 0$ $t = 1$ $t = 2$

+£224 − 5(2) = £214

$-\dfrac{£200}{1 + {_0R_1}} + 5£C$

+£214

Figure 8.9

The cash flows resulting from this portfolio can be shown as in Figure 8.9. Thus the call options can be valued according to the formula

$$\dfrac{-200}{1 + {_0R_1}} + 5C + \dfrac{214}{(1 + {_0R_2})^2} = 0$$

Hence

$$C = £\dfrac{1}{5}\left[\dfrac{200}{1 + {_0R_1}} - \dfrac{214}{(1 + {_0R_2})^2}\right]$$

8.4.2 Option Replication

The payoffs to the interest rate option can be replicated as follows. First, borrow £214/(1 + $_0R_2$)² for two years, make a cash addition of

£200/(1 + $_0R_1$) − £214/(1 + $_0R_2$)² and deposit the resulting £200/(1 + $_0R_1$) for one year at $_0R_1$%. This will give £200 at $t=1$. Then redeposit this amount for a further year at the then prevailing one year rate. At the end of two years the deposit will have generated cash of either £224 or £214, of which £214 must be used to repay the original borrowing. Hence the value of the deal is either £10 or £0. Thus for a cash outlay of £200/(1 + $_0R_1$) − £214/(1 + $_0R_2$)² the investor has replicated five call options. Each call option therefore costs

$$C = £\frac{1}{5}\left[\frac{200}{1 + {_0R_1}} - \frac{214}{(1 + {_0R_2})^2}\right]$$

which is the same as in Section 8.4.1.

8.5 Interest Rate Options: Pricing Caps and Floors

8.5.1 The Mechanics

As already mentioned in Section 8.4, call options on interest rates of the kind discussed are often known as caps. Put options – useful to those who would lose from a fall in interest rates – are often known as floors. The option pricing process which we have shown allows us to calculate the cash price of a one period cap, that is a single option.

Most caps and floors cover several periods and are therefore made up of a string of options, each with an appropriate expiration date. The cash price of such a string is simply the sum of the cash prices of each of the options involved.[3]

Quite frequently, interest rate options are priced using a standard Black and Scholes share option pricing computer program requiring the following five inputs:

Price of the underlying instrument S
Exercise price of the option X
Time to expiry of the option T
Interest rate R
Volatility σ

In this situation some care has to be exercised when entering the required numbers. We shall illustrate this by reference to our two period example with a 10% cap on the second interest payment and a notional principal of £100.

Price of the underlying instrument

We need to distinguish between option expiry and the date of cash settlement to the option holder. The option gives the holder the right to receive cash settlement at the end of year 2. However, the amount of that cash settlement is known at the end of year 1, so that the option expiry date is at the end of year 1. The price of the underlying instrument therefore depends on today's forward rate $_1R_2$, but is adjusted for the fact that the cash payment determined by the interest rate at the end of year 1 is not actually made until the end of year 2. Hence today's price of the underlying instrument is $S = {_1R_2} \times £100/(1 + {_0R_2})^2$.

Exercise price of the option

Similarly, the cash equivalent of the 10% exercise price must also be discounted before entry into the program because the cash value of the option is not paid until the end of the interest period. Thus the exercise price is $X = 10\% \times £100/(1 + {_1R_2})$.

Time to expiry of the option

The time to maturity of the option is one year.

Interest rate

The interest rate is today's one year spot zero rate $_0R_1$.

Volatility

Volatility can be entered in the usual way.

8.5.2 Case Study: Pricing a Three Year Cap

We now examine the pricing of a three year cap at 8% on six month floating rates.

As we have seen, caps are made up of strings of European call options on interest rates and are usually priced using the Black and Scholes formula. Apart from volatility, all the necessary information is implicit in the yield curves for the relevant period.

For this study we assume the yield curves shown in Table 8.1. The par yield curve (coupon payments semi-annually) has been used to calculate the zero rates and the implied six month forward rates.

Since a cap on interest rates at 8% only has value at maturity of its component options if the relevant interest rate is above 8% the payoff profile is the profile of a call option with an exercise price at 8%. This is shown in Figure 8.10.

Each of the options has this same profile at maturity, which is also the repricing date for the reference interest rate.[4] For the first interest rate

Table 8.1

Time to maturity (months)	Par	Yield curves (%) Zero	Forward
6	5.45	$_0R_6 = 5.45$	—
12	5.65	$_0R_{12} = 5.7338$	$_6R_{12} = 5.8579$
18	5.90	$_0R_{18} = 5.9975$	$_{12}R_{18} = 6.4237$
24	6.24	$_0R_{24} = 6.3625$	$_{18}R_{24} = 7.3307$
30	6.50	$_0R_{30} = 6.6448$	$_{24}R_{30} = 7.6358$
36	6.70	$_0R_{36} = 6.8643$	$_{30}R_{36} = 7.8159$

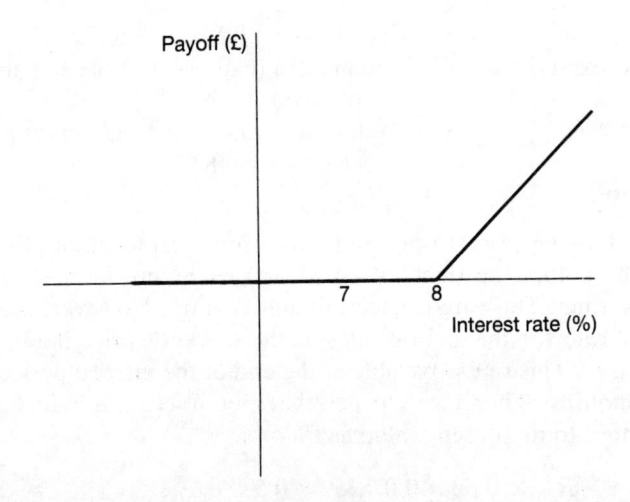

Figure 8.10

period the actual interest rate is already known and thus the payment at the end of the period is known. It is zero if the six month interest rate is below 8%, and it is equal to the difference between 8% and the actual rate if this rate is above 8%. The first period, therefore, is not really an option at all because there is no uncertainty as to the payment.

A three year cap on interest rates which are reset every six months consists of five interest rate options and covers six interest rate periods, as shown in Figure 8.11. For example, the fifth option has a time to expiry of 30 months and covers the interest period between 30 and 36 months. This call option at 8% gives the holder the right to receive the then (in 30 months' time) ruling six month interest against paying 8%.

We start by pricing this fifth option using the Black and Scholes model. This model requires the following inputs:

Underlying price S see below

146   Currency, Interest Rate and Other Options

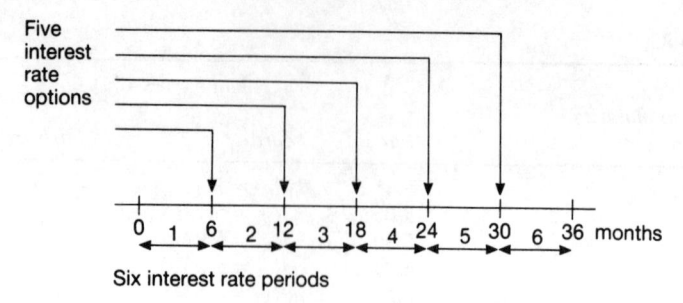

Figure 8.11

Exercise price	X	see below
Time to expiry	T	30 months (expressed as the actual number of days)
Interest rate	R	relevant zero rate for the option period: $_0R_{30} = 6.6448\%$
Volatility[5]	σ	16%

The underlying price to be used needs some explanation. The option gives the holder the right to receive the six month interest rate in 30 months' time. This rate is uncertain until expiry. However, the current forward rate for this period $_{30}R_{36}$ is the market's price implicit in the yield curve. This rate is payable at the end of the interest period, that is in 36 months. Therefore, to get the spot price, this rate has to be discounted to its present value as follows:

$$S = \frac{_{30}R_{36} \times 0.5}{(1 + _0R_{36})^{36/12}} = \frac{0.078159 \times 0.5}{(1.068643)^3} = 3.2022\%$$

The exercise price for this fifth option also has to be discounted, as the end of the option period is the beginning of the sixth and last interest period. This means that the exercise price of 8% has to be discounted back to month 30 from month 36 by the respective forward rate, taking *half* of the rate as we are dealing with six month interest rate options:

$$X = \frac{8\%/2}{1 + (6/12) \,_{30}R_{36}} = \frac{0.04}{1 + (1/2)\,0.078159} = 3.8496\%$$

Thus the inputs to the Black and Scholes model are as follows:

Price   3.2022%
Exercise price 3.8496%
Time   913 days (i.e. 30 months)
Interest rate   6.6448%
Volatility   16%

Currency, Interest Rate and Other Options

The price of this, the fifth, option which expires in 30 months' time is 0.297%.

This procedure is then followed for each of the other four options. Today's price of the cap is the sum of the five individual option premiums. Following this procedure gives a price for the three year cap of 0.698%, which, ignoring transaction costs, would be payable as an up-front premium. If the six month interest rate for the first interest period is above the exercise price, the present value of the differential payment would be added to this premium. We have therefore shown that the premium payable for this three year cap on a notional principal of £1 million would be £6980. Very often the up-front premium is converted into an annual premium to allow its simple addition to any annual interest rate or spread.

The up-front premium is effectively the present value of an annuity (the premium is payable semi-annually in this case). The formula for an annuity is:

$$A = \frac{\text{present value}}{[1 - (1 + i)^{-n}]/i}$$

where i is the par interest rate (or swap rate) for the relevant period and n is the number of periods. In our example this gives

$$A = \frac{0.698\%}{[1 - (1 + 0.0670 \times 0.5)^{-6}]/(0.067 \times 0.5)}$$

$$= 0.130\% \text{ semi-annually}$$

This is equivalent to 26 basis points per annum. Thus, for example, a company which can raise three year floating rate funds by paying six month interest rates plus 60 basis points spread would have to pay six month interest rates plus 86 basis points if the underlying interest rate were to be capped at 8%. In return, the company would have a guarantee that, whatever the level of interest rates seen in the market, it would never pay more than 8.86% during the life of the cap.

8.6 Compound Options

As we have said, options may be written on a wide variety of items – and options themselves are no exception. Options on options, usually known as compound options, are a fast developing product.

The holder of a European call (or put) option on an option has the right, but not the obligation, at expiry to buy (or sell) an option at a prearranged exercise price. Thus, for example, one might hold a three month call option with an exercise price of $3 on a six month call option to buy DM180 for $100. Then, after three months have elapsed, one has the right, but not the obligation, to buy the six month currency option for a price of $3. Clearly if at that time such six month currency options carry a premium in excess of $3, the expiring three month option will be exercised. In other circumstances the option will not be exercised.

To illustrate the pricing of a compound option, we shall refer back to the two period example which we used in Section 7.3.3 to introduce the pricing of share options. We set out the example once again in Figure 8.12. We saw from this example that, if $_0R_1$ is 4% and $_1R_2$ is 6%, a two period call option on the share with an exercise price of £100 would be worth £13.9978 at the start of the first period, and, depending on the share price at the time, would be worth either £25.6604 or £4.8428 at the start of the second period. These values are shown in our diagram in brackets below the share price.

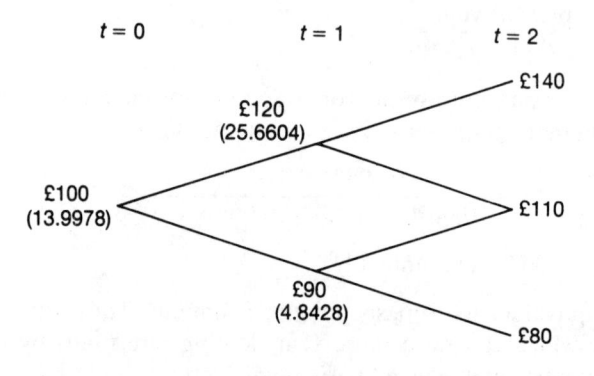

Figure 8.12

We shall now price a compound option which gives its holder the right to buy at $t=1$ a one period call option on the share with an exercise price of £100. Clearly a whole range of exercise prices for such compound options could be quoted. The most frequently quoted exercise price in today's marketplace is the price of the equivalent ordinary option spanning the whole period covered by the compound option. Hence, using our example, we shall consider an exercise price of £13.9978. Thus the buyer of our compound option will have to pay a sum of £C_c (an amount which we are just about to calculate) at $t=0$. Then at $t=1$, when the option expires, he can (if he wishes) pay a further £13.9978 for the second option, which gives him the right, but not the obligation, to buy at $t=2$ one share for £100.

Currency, Interest Rate and Other Options

8.6.1 Risk-Free Portfolio

It is probably already becoming clear to the reader how £C_c can be calculated. Today's price of the underlying asset (the option to pay £100 at $t=2$ for one share) is £13.9978. At the end of the first period, the price of the underlying asset will be either £25.6604 or £4.8428. This being so, our compound option will expire with a value of either £11.6626 (£25.6604 − £13.9978) or £0. Following our usual convention we can show this as in Figure 8.13.

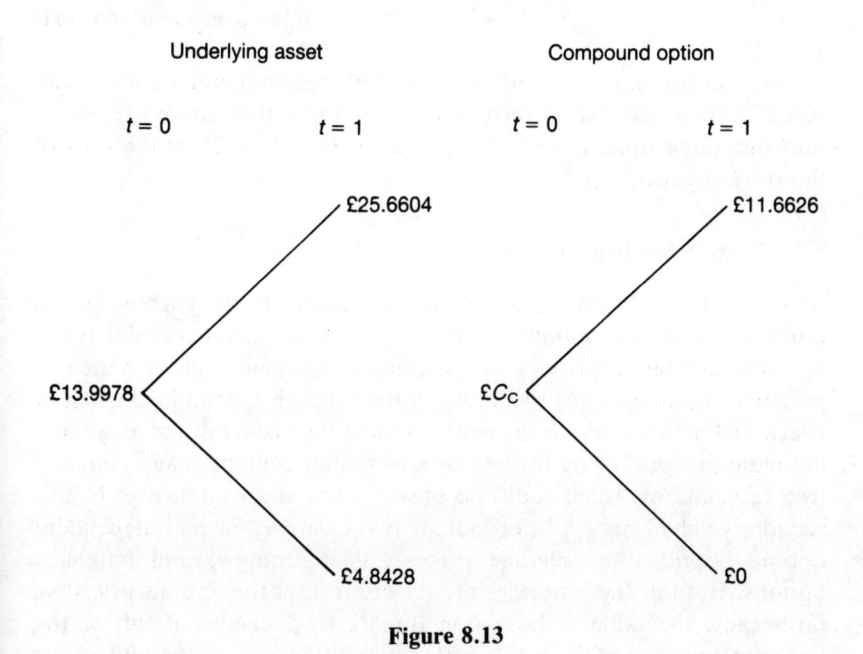

Figure 8.13

A risk-free portfolio can be constructed by buying one unit of the underlying asset and selling 1.7850 units ((25.6604 − 4.8428)/11.6626) of the compound option. The $t=0$ cash needed to construct the portfolio is £13.9978 − 1.7850 £C_c. The $t=1$ value of the portfolio will be either £25.6604 − 1.7850(£11.6626) = £4.8428 or £4.8428 − 1.7850(0) = £4.8428. Hence the net present value equation for the portfolio is

$$-13.9978 + 1.7850\, C_c + \frac{4.8428}{1.04} = 0$$

This gives C_c as £5.2332.

8.6.2 Option Replication

Using the option replication approach, we can see that £4.6565 (£4.8428/1.04) can be borrowed at $t=0$ against the guaranteed minimum value of the underlying asset of £4.8428 at $t=1$. Hence the net cash outlay required at $t=0$ for the purchase of the underlying asset is £9.3413 (£13.9978 − £4.6565). This cash outlay will produce a payoff at $t=1$ of either £20.8176 (£25.6604 − £4.8428) or £0. But recall that £20.8176 or £0 is the payoff to 1.7850 call options. Each call option has therefore a payoff at $t=1$ of either £11.6626 or £0. The net cash outlay at $t=0$ of £9.3413 is the cost of 1.7850 options. The cost of the compound option is £5.2332.

Thus our problem is solved! The buyer of the compound option would pay £5.2332 at the start of the two periods. Then, if he chose to exercise the compound option, he would pay a further £13.9978 at the start of the second period.

8.7 Path-Dependent Options

So far we have shown the pricing of options on shares, currencies and interest rates and of options on options. It can be demonstrated that any option which can be priced through a simple binomial model can then be priced for more complex scenarios, either through a formula like that of Black and Scholes, that is the mathematical approximation of an infinite binomial process, or by the use of a computer running many binomial tree calculations which could be of any form and complexity. In this section we shall have a brief look at two examples of path-dependent options: options on average prices (Asian options) and lookback options. Both of these options are different from the options priced so far because the value of the option at maturity depends not only on the final outcome but also on the path which the prices of the underlying instruments have taken to get to their final outcome.

Options on average prices have their final value determined by an average of the prices of the underlying instruments seen during the period between initiation and expiry of the option. Lookback options have their final value determined by the most favourable underlying price seen during the options' life. These general features can already give an intuitive idea about the values of such options relative to the options discussed so far.

Volatility describes price fluctuations in both directions, up and down, which are favourable and unfavourable for the value of an option. Averaging these price movements means, at least partly, cancelling out movements in opposite directions and thus leads to lower

Currency, Interest Rate and Other Options 151

volatility and lower option prices. Lookback options, on the other hand, 'preserve' volatility movemenls; that is, the best possible price is taken from a series of underlying prices. This means that only favourable volatility counts towards option value. This should, of course, give lookback options a higher value than normal options. Therefore one would expect the values of average and lookback options to be lower and higher respectively than the values of normal options for the same scenario of prices.

Let's look at this in more detail using the same two period example as before.

8.7.1 Options on Average Prices (Asian Options)

The final value of an Asian option is determined by the average underlying price, such as the daily average of closing prices of the underlying instrument during the life of the option. For a call option with an exercise price of £100, based on average prices during the life of the option, the value of expiry is calculated according to the following formula:

$$\frac{\Sigma \text{ prices in each averaging period}}{\text{number of averaging periods}}$$

In our simple example with two periods this can be shown as in Figure 8.14.

Share price			Average share price	Value of call option
t = 0	t = 1	t = 2		
		£140	£130	£30
	£120			
		£110	£115	£15
£100				
		£110	£100	£0
	£90			
		£80	£85	£0

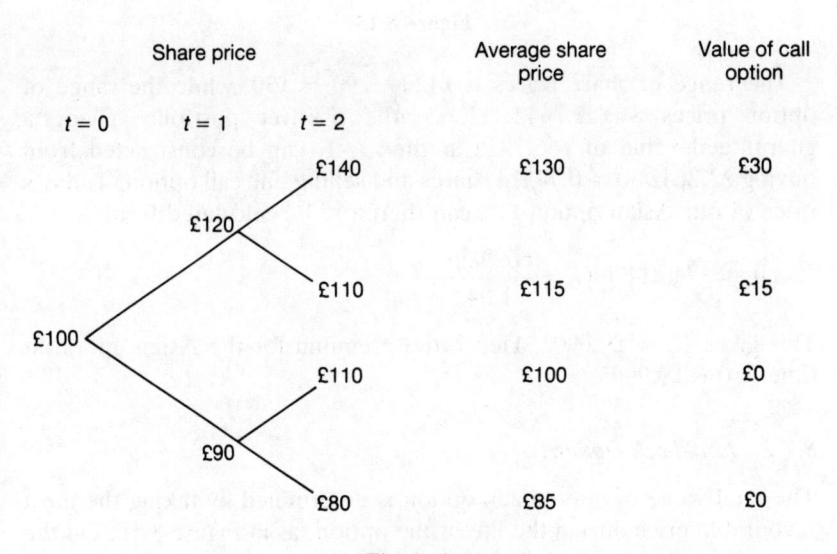

Figure 8.14

As with valuing the two period option in Section 7.3.3, one has to value each branch of the tree separately. On the upper branch the range of the share price is £140 − 110 = £30, while the range of values for the call option is £30 − 15 = £15. Hence a risk-free portfolio, producing a guaranteed value of £80 at time $t=2$, can be constructed by buying one share and selling two calls. Hence on the upper branch the option value £C_u at $t=1$ can be calculated from

$$0 = -120 + 2C_u + \frac{80}{1.06}$$

to give C_u = £22.2642. On the lower branch the option only has values of zero, so that £C_l is zero. Referring back to $t=0$, the option value tree becomes that in Figure 8.15.

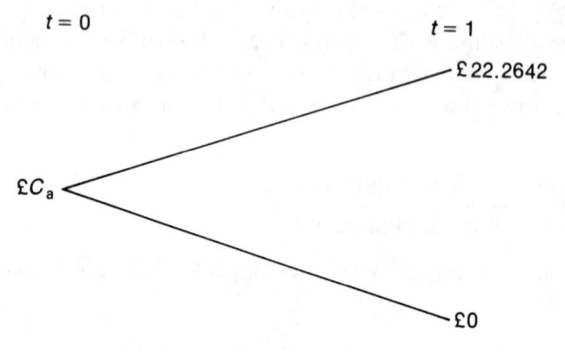

Figure 8.15

The range of share prices is £120 − 90 = £30, while the range of option prices is £22.2642. Hence the risk-free portfolio, giving a guaranteed value of £66.7926 at time $t=1$, can be constructed from buying 22.2642/30 = 0.74214 shares and selling one call option. Today's price of our Asian option £C_a can therefore be calculated from

$$0 = -74.214 + C_a + \frac{66.7926}{1.04}$$

This gives C_a = £9.9903. Hence the premium for the Asian option at time $t=0$ is £9.9903.

8.7.2 Lookback Options

The final value of a lookback option is determined by taking the most favourable price during the life of the option, as in Figure 8.16. On the upper branch the range of share prices is £140 − 110 = £30, while the

Currency, Interest Rate and Other Options

```
         Share price              Value of call option
t = 0      t = 1      t = 2
                      £140              £40
            £120
                      £110              £20
  £100
                      £110              £10
             £90
                      £80               £0
```

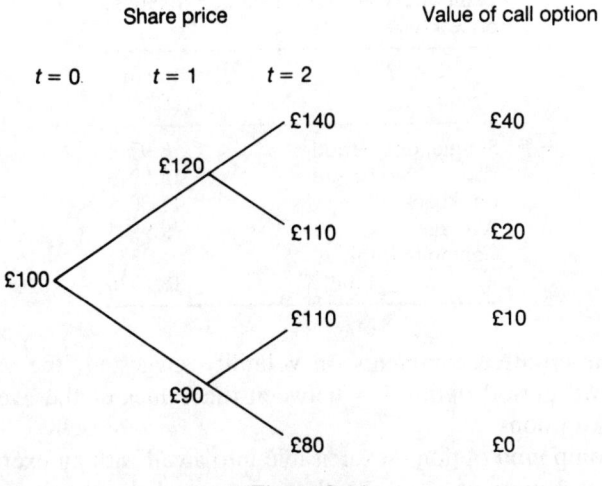

Figure 8.16

range of option values is £40 − 20 = £20. The construction of the risk-free portfolio shows that C_u = £29.6855. On the lower branch, the range of share prices is £110 − 80 = £30 while the range of option values is £10 − 0 = £10. The construction of the risk-free portfolio shows that C_l = £4.8428.

Referring back to $t=0$, the option value tree becomes as in Figure 8.17. Hence the premium C_{lb} for the lookback option at time $t=0$ is £15.8039.

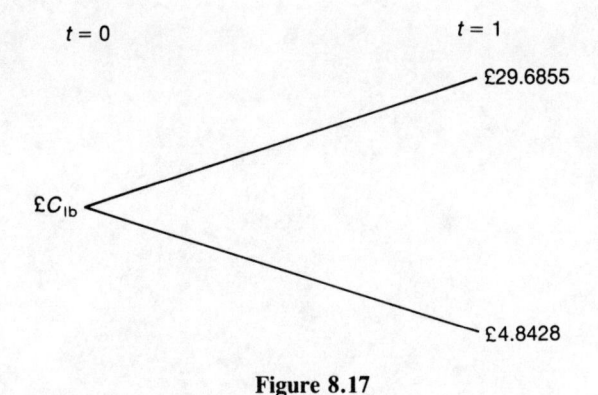

```
      t = 0                        t = 1
                                   £29.6855

      £C_lb

                                   £4.8428
```

Figure 8.17

8.7.3 Summary of Share Option Values

Table 8.2 summarizes the values of the various options described in Sections 7.3.1, 7.3.3, 8.6 and 8.7.

Table 8.2 Call option values (exercise price £100)

Option	Value (£)
Simple: one period	8.9744
two period	13.9978
Lookback	15.8039
Average	9.9903
Compound: initial	5.2332
total	18.6926

As our intuitive comments on volatility suggested, the value of a simple two period option lies between the values of the average and lookback options.

The compound option – exercisable into a call with an exercise price of £100 at a price of £13.9978, the premium of the simple two period option – has initially the lowest cost. However, one has to bear in mind that to obtain the second call option at $t=1$ a further payment of £13.9978 has to be made. Therefore the comparison should be with a price of £5.2332 + present value (£13.9978) = £18.6926. This,[6] the highest price in the table, reflects the fact that this option has two decision points: one at $t=1$, to buy or not to buy the underlying option; and another at $t=2$, to buy or not to buy the underlying share.

9
Using Derivative Products

9.1 Introduction

We have now spent some considerable time examining four of the main instruments of financial innovation: forwards, futures, swaps and options. Before that, in Chapters 2 and 3, we looked at the volatility of financial markets and the impact of this volatility on individuals, firms and nations.

We now turn to ways in which the financial instruments can be used to reduce or otherwise change the impact of volatility. Using instruments to reduce the impact of volatility is often known as hedging. In the process of looking at hedging we see that each of the instruments is really very similar to each of the others, and this will lead us to the building-block approach to financial engineering, first suggested by Smithson (1987).

9.2 The Building-Block Approach

The idea of hedging exposure provides a good vehicle with which to introduce the building-block approach to financial engineering. In Figure 1.5 we introduced the concept of an exposure profile and we developed the concept further in Chapter 2. If it were possible to find a financial instrument whose value at expiration could be shown as a mirror image of the exposure profile, this instrument could be used as a hedge and could completely eliminate its user's exposure. Adding such a financial instrument with a payoff exactly the opposite to the entity's own underlying exposure would remove that exposure, because any change in the environment which worsens the underlying exposure

156 *Using Derivative Products*

would improve the payoff to the instrument and vice versa. This is illustrated in a general way in Figure 9.1.

Three well-known financial instruments with profiles similar to those shown in Figure 9.1 are fowards, futures and swaps. Let us look at each of these again in turn.

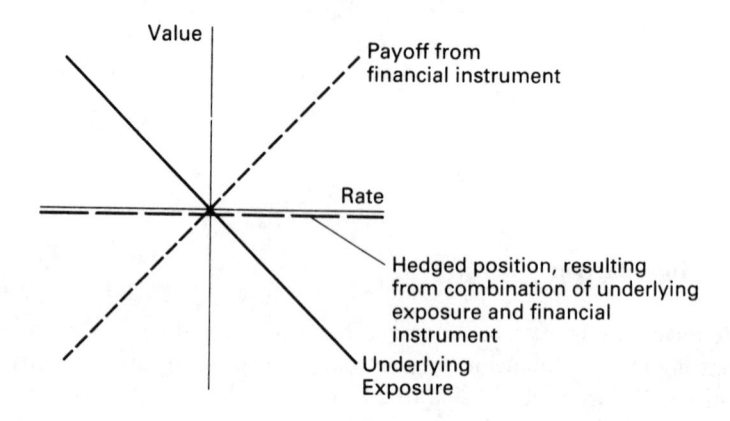

Figure 9.1 Exposure hedged by using a financial instrument with an opposite payoff

9.2.1 Forwards

Currency forwards

A currency forward contract involves an arrangement between two named counterparties and is therefore non-traded. The contract imposes an obligation on each party to exchange currencies as specified. No action is required by either party until the contract reaches its expiration date, whereupon the exchange of currencies takes place.[1]

At expiration, the value of the contract will depend upon the difference between the forward rate written into the contract[2] and the spot rate on the expiration date. Should this spot rate turn out to be equal to the forward rate, the contract will expire with a value of zero, because there is no price difference between taking delivery of the currency at the preagreed rate and buying it on the spot market. However, should the spot rate at expiration turn out to be different from the forward rate, the contract will have a value equal to the difference between the two rates multiplied by the amount of currency involved in the exchange.

Figure 9.2a shows the exposure faced by a German importer who has agreed to pay $1 million. The forward rate for his payment date is

Using Derivative Products 157

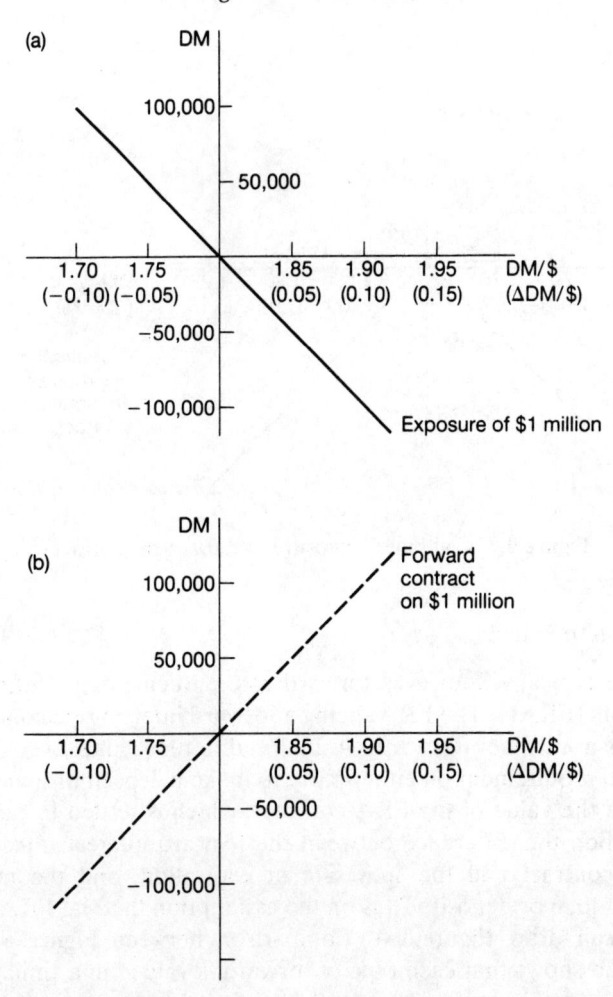

(a)

[Graph showing DM on vertical axis with values 100,000, 50,000, -50,000, -100,000; horizontal axis DM/$ with values 1.70 (-0.10), 1.75 (-0.05), 1.85 (0.05), 1.90 (0.10), 1.95 (0.15) (ΔDM/$); downward sloping line labeled "Exposure of $1 million"]

(b)

[Graph showing DM on vertical axis with values 100,000, 50,000, -50,000, -100,000; horizontal axis DM/$ with values 1.70 (-0.10), 1.75, 1.85 (0.05), 1.90 (0.10), 1.95 (0.15) (ΔDM/$); upward sloping dashed line labeled "Forward contract on $1 million"]

Figure 9.2 (a) Exposure faced by German importer (b) selected forward contract

DM/$ 1.80. Each 5 pfennig deviation from this rate will change the value of his obligation by DM50,000.

Figure 9.2b shows the payoff to a forward contract to buy $1 million for DM1.8 million. Each 5 pfennig deviation from the forward rate will change the value of the forward contract by DM50,000.

Figure 9.3 shows the combination of the German importer's exposure and the currency forward contract. The forward contract removes the exposure. This is a specific example of the general case illustrated in Figure 9.1.

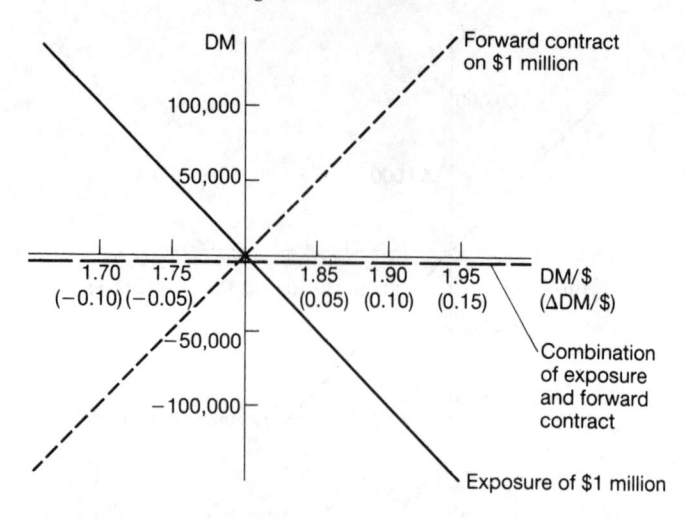

Figure 9.3 Combined exposure and forward contract

Interest rate forwards

These are typically known as forward rate agreements or future rate agreements (FRAs). The FRA, being a forward interest rate contract, is similar to a currency forward. A major difference, however, is that there is no requirement on either party to make a deposit or loan. At its expiration the value of the FRA contract, which is settled in cash, will depend upon the difference between the forward interest rate written into the contract and the spot rate at expiration, and the notional amount of loan or deposit. Thus on the assumption that the FRA rate is 8%, we can draw Figure 9.4. Comparison between Figure 9.4 and Figure 9.2b shows that each type of forward is valued in a similar way. Hence we can summarize the payoff of any forward contract by means of the general picture shown in Figure 9.5.

9.2.2 Futures

For our purposes here, we consider only the value of the futures contract at expiration. If we ignore the daily process of marking-to-market, we can see that a futures contract looks very similar to a forward contract. If the spot rate at expiration turns out to be equal to the rate embedded in the currency futures contract, the futures contract will expire with a value of zero. This is because there would be no difference in cost between taking delivery of the currency as per the contract and buying the currency on the spot market (or, in the case of

Using Derivative Products 159

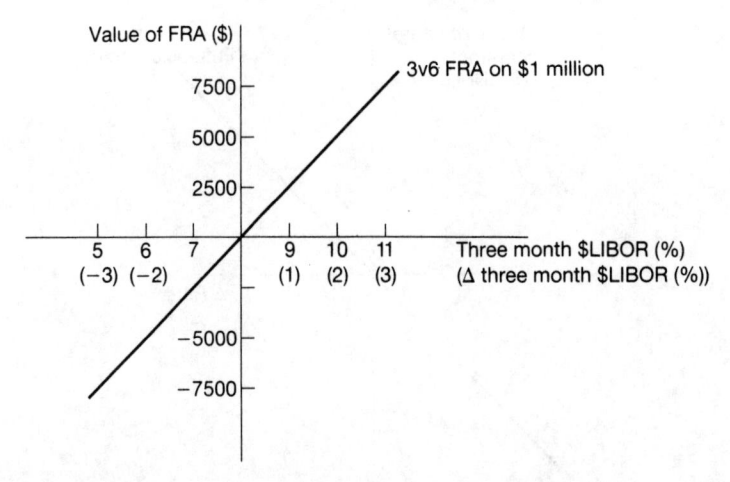

Figure 9.4 Payoff to a three against six FRA on $1 million. Each 1% deviation from the forward (reference) interest rate will change the terminal value of the FRA contract by $2500

an interest rate future, between a loan or deposit made at the interest rate in the contract and one made at the spot rate). However, should the spot rate at expiration turn out not to be equal to the rate embedded in the futures contract, the contract will have a value determined by the extent of the difference between the two rates and the size of the contract. This is illustrated in Figure 9.6. This figure looks the same as Figure 9.5, thus showing the similarity between a forward contract and the corresponding futures contract.

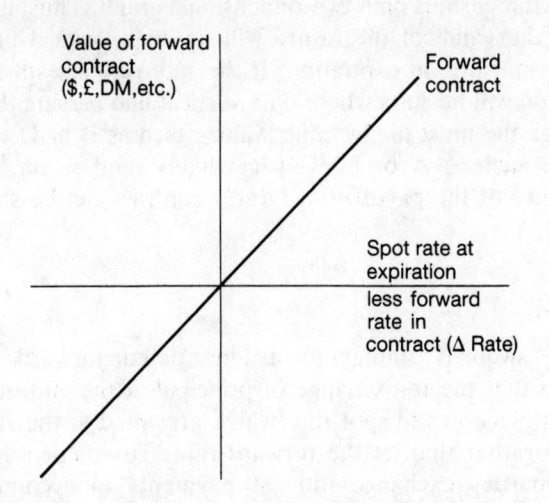

Figure 9.5 General picture of the payoff to a forward contract

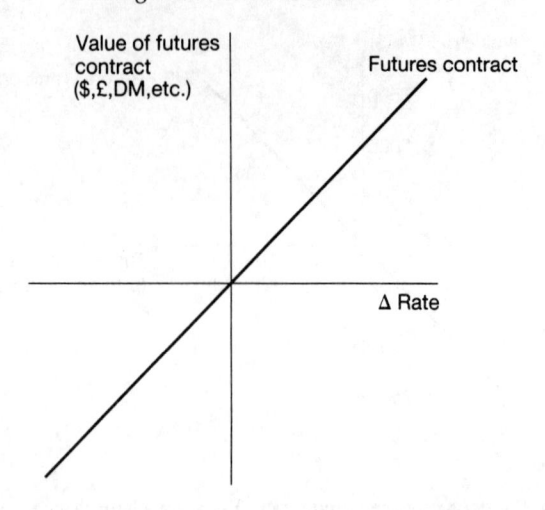

Figure 9.6 Simplified picture of the payoff to a futures contract

However, as explained in Section 5.5 once the process of marking-to-market is taken into account, we cannot determine so simply what will be the value of the futures contract at expiration. This is because the payments into or out of the margin account give rise to interest income or financing costs and, therefore, the exact value of the contract will depend upon the daily movements in the forward rate for its expiration date and hence the futures price.

Showing this pictorially involves the common problem of dealing with several dimensions on a two-dimensional graph. Thus, as shown in Figure 9.7, the value of the future will lie on a vertical line passing through the spot rate at expiration. If the spot rate at expiration is S^* then the value will lie somewhere on a vertical line passing through S^*, and C will be the most likely value; values such as B or D will be less likely, those such as A or E even less likely, and so on.[3] Thus the general picture of the payoff to a futures contract can be shown as in Figure 9.8.

9.2.3 Swaps

A currency swap is similar to a long dated forward, with the complication that the re-exchange of principal at the end of the swap period takes place at the spot rate which prevailed at the start of the swap period rather than at the forward rate. To compensate for this the counterparties exchange interest payments to account for the differential between spot and forward rates, which effectively convert

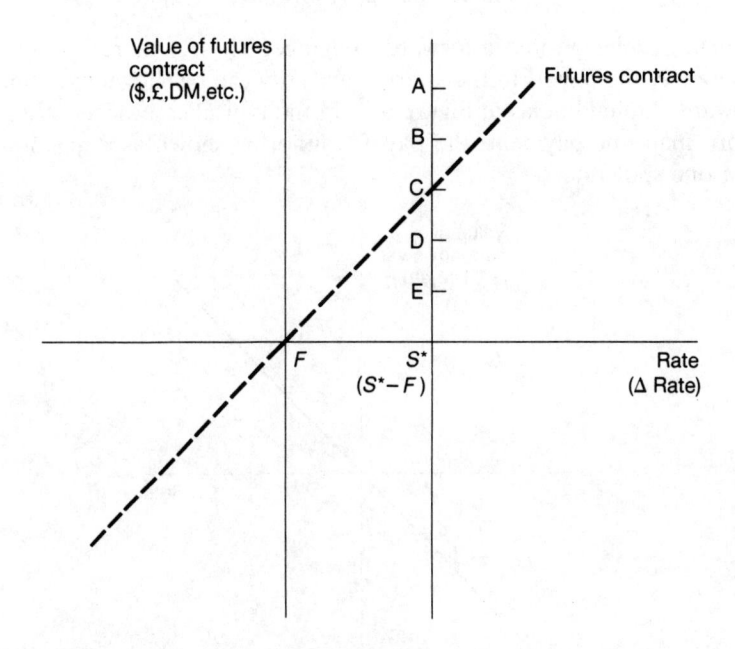

Figure 9.7 Payoff to a futures contract when the spot rate at expiration is S^*

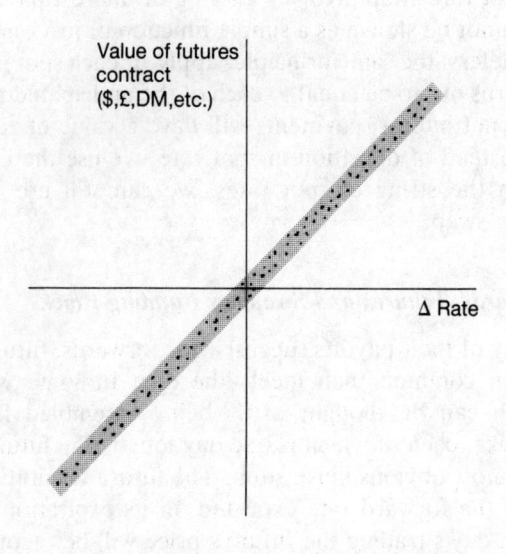

Figure 9.8 General picture of the payoff to a futures contract

the spot exchange into a forward exchange. Thus, if there is only one exchange, the payoff to the swap at maturity can be shown by a simple upward sloping line as in Figure 9.9. In the typical case, where there is more than one payment, the payoff cannot be shown as a function of just one spot rate.

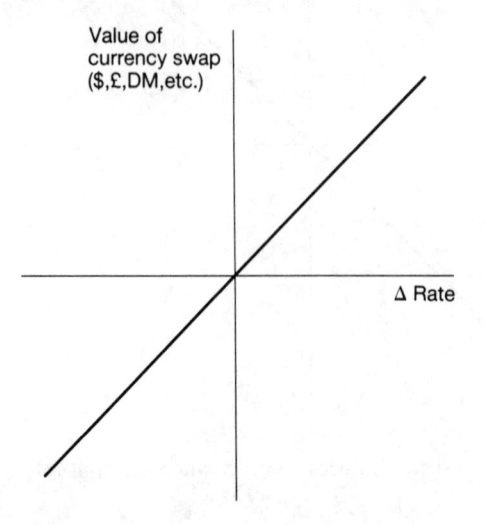

Figure 9.9 Payoff to a currency swap

The interest rate swap involves a string of interest payments. Hence its payoff cannot be shown as a simple function of just one spot interest rate. Nonetheless, the same principles apply. If each spot interest rate in the future turns out to be equal to each of the anticipated forward rates, the string of net interest payments will have a value of zero.[4]

Thus if, instead of deviation in spot rate, we use the concept of net deviations in the string of spot rates, we can still use Figure 9.9 to represent the swap.

9.2.4 Forwards, Futures and Swaps as Building-Blocks

The similarity of their payoffs suggests that forwards, futures and swaps have more in common than meets the eye. In some ways they do, because each can be thought of as being assembled from financial building-blocks, each of which is one day long.[5] The futures contract is perhaps the most obvious illustration. The future will initially be priced according to the forward rate expected on its expiration date. At the close of each day's trading the future's price will be recorded, and any change from the previous day's close will lead to a marking-to-market of the contract with a corresponding cash flow in or out of the margin account. This process explicitly recognizes that the futures contract has one day fewer to run before expiration.

The least obvious illustration is perhaps the forward contract. Neither party is obliged to do anything until the contract matures and, apart from accounting considerations, it is not valued during its life. However, it can still be constructed from one day blocks.

To continue with the analogy, a forward can be thought of as being made up of one day blocks joined together so tightly that the 'cracks' between them cannot be seen. The forward looks and behaves like a solid block spanning the period between its birth and its expiration. A future covering the same period is made up of the same one day blocks but they are loosely joined so that the daily cracks between them are visible. The marking-to-market process effectively pulls the daily blocks off one by one, leaving behind an ever-shortening string of blocks as time passes towards maturity. The swap with its six monthly difference cheque, is less extreme than either the future or the forward. Its one day blocks are joined together so tightly over six month periods that a crack is visible only between each of these six month periods. The difference cheque process effectively pulls the six month blocks off one by one, leaving behind the ever-shortening remainder of the swap.

These ideas, whose power will be seen later, are illustrated in Figure 9.10.

9.2.5 Options

Unlike the three instruments discussed so far, the owner of an option contract is not obliged to exercise it. In practice, the owner will exercise the option only when it will be to his advantage to do so. Consider a call option on the dollar which allows its owner to buy $10,000 for DM18,000 at a prearranged date in the future. If on that date the dollar is worth more than DM1.80, the owner of the option will exercise it. He provides DM18,000 and the writer of the option is obliged to hand over $10,000; this sum is worth more than DM18,000 at the then spot exchange rate. Hence the payoff at expiration depends on the exercise price of the option and the spot price at expiration, as shown in Figure 9.11. If someone came by such an option free of charge and used it to hedge an underlying exposure, the result would be as shown in Figure 9.12.

In practice the owner of the option will have paid a premium for it, so that the net payoff or profit from the option will be its value at expiration less the net terminal value of the premium paid. This profit,

A forward

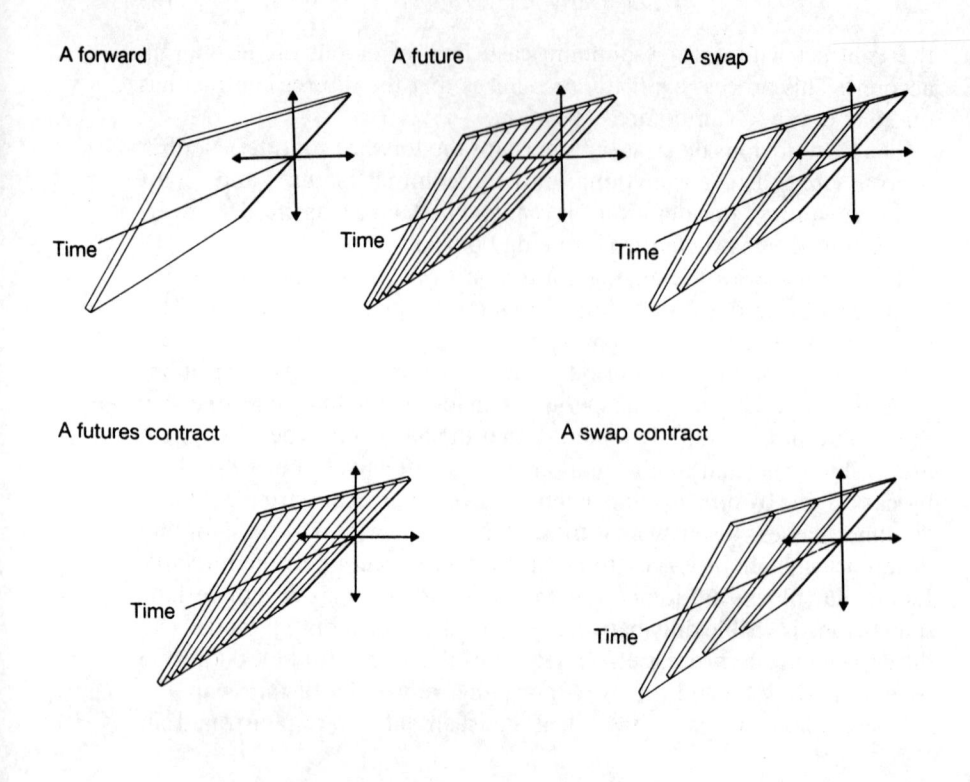

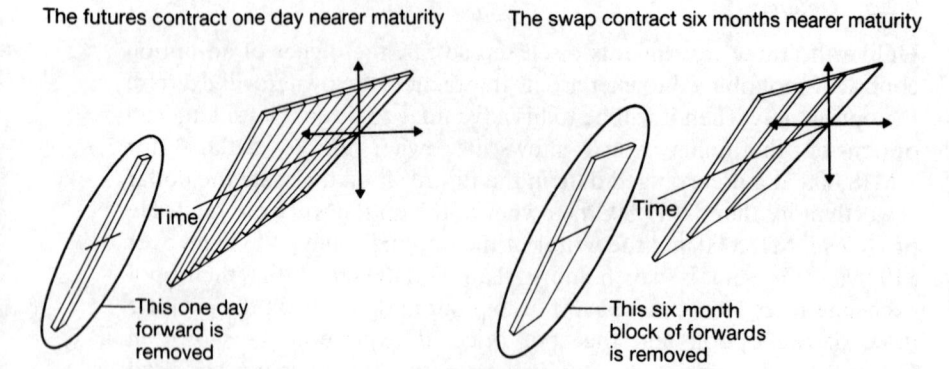

A future

A swap

Time

Time

Time

A futures contract

A swap contract

Time

Time

The futures contract one day nearer maturity

The swap contract six months nearer maturity

Time

Time

This one day forward is removed

This six month block of forwards is removed

Figure 9.10

Using Derivative Products

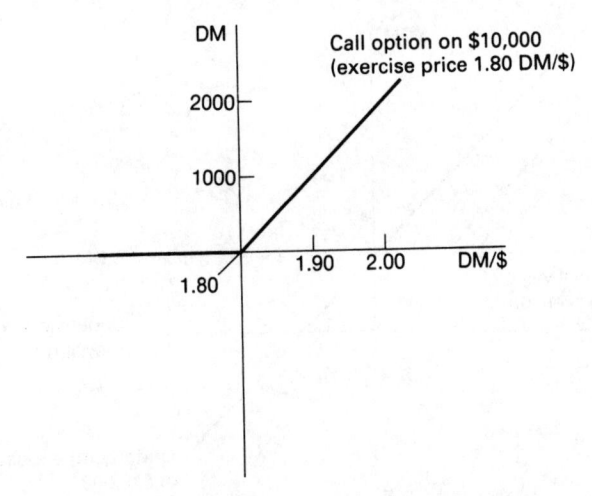

Figure 9.11 Payoff to a call option on $10,000

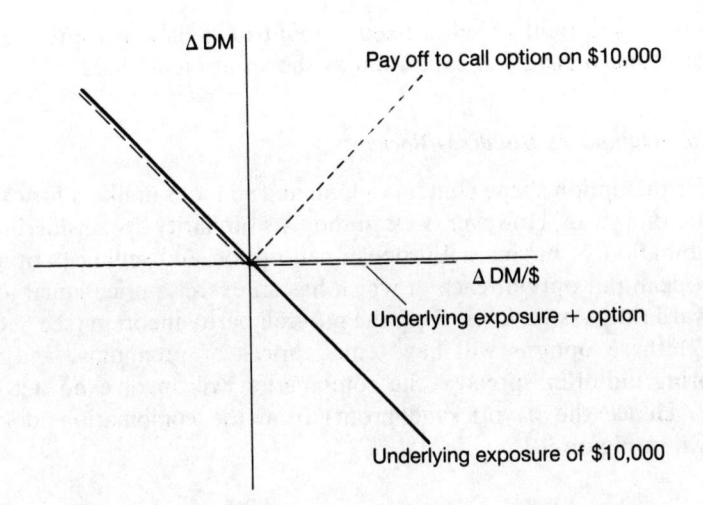

Figure 9.12 Hedging with a free call option

together with the results of using the option to hedge, is shown in Figure 9.13.

It is worth noting that the profit to the writer of the call option is the reverse of the profit to the owner. If the owner pays DM18,000 for $10,000 which are worth more than DM18,000, he makes a profit on the deal; the provider of the $10,000 makes a corresponding loss.

Now consider a put option on the dollar. Because the put option gives

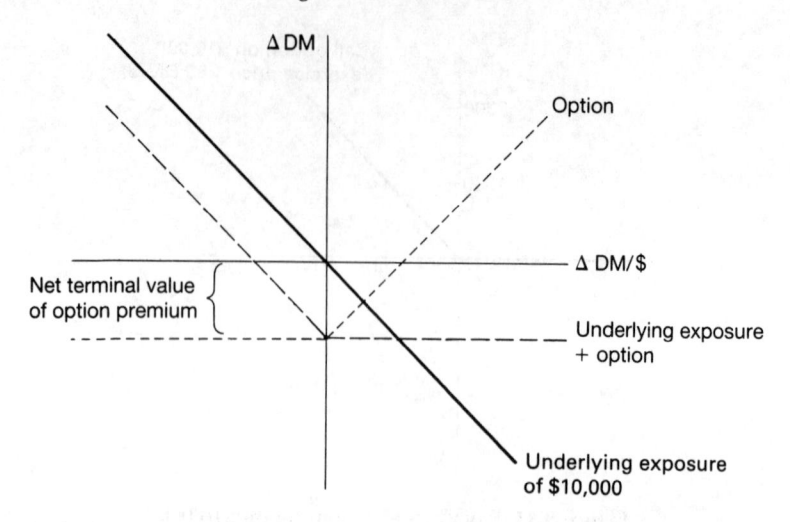

Figure 9.13 Hedging with a call option carrying a premium

its owner the right to sell a fixed amount of dollars at a prearranged price, it has a payoff at expiration as shown in Figure 9.14.

9.2.6 Options as Building-Blocks

So far the option shape contains a kink and so looks unlike a forward, a future or a swap. However, we can show its similarity by considering the combination of buying a European call option and selling (writing) a European put option, each of which has an exercise price equal to the forward rate. As we know from the put–call parity theorem (see Section 7.6.2) these options will have equal prices or premiums, and so – ignoring bid-offer spread – the combination will involve no net cash flow. Hence the payoff (and profit) from the combination looks as shown in Figure 9.15.

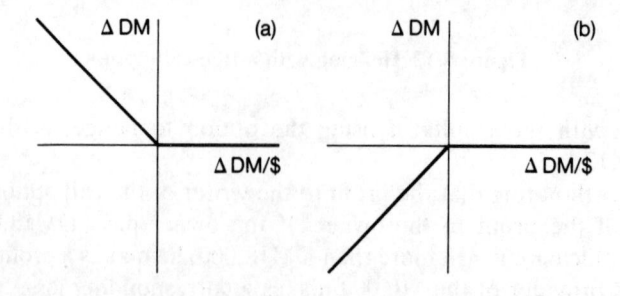

Figure 9.14 Payoffs to a put option (a) to owner (b) to writer

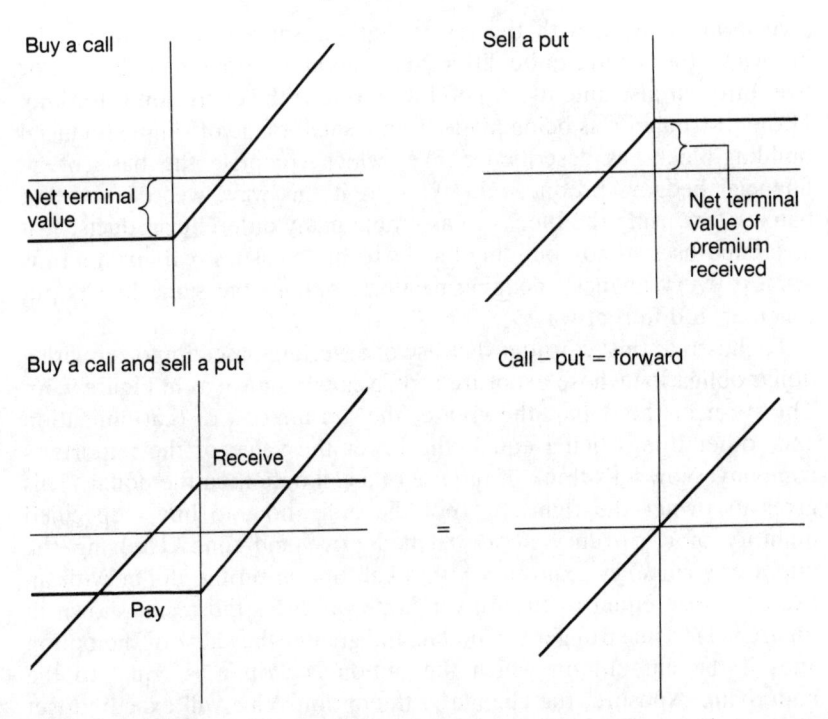

Figure 9.15 Buying a call option and selling a put option produces a forward contract

Thus options, swaps, forwards and futures can be seen to belong to the same family. Perhaps the one day option is the basic building-block. Take a one day call and subtract a one day put, and the combination becomes a one day forward as shown in Figure 9.15. Clip together one day forwards with appropriate cracks and the combination becomes a forward or a future or a swap. In fact, we have already seen that an option can in turn be constructed from an investment in an underlying security and the raising of a loan. Perhaps, then, a cash market instrument plus a one day loan are the basic building-blocks.[6] The search for the basic building-block may be interesting in its own right, but for our purposes it is sufficient to remember that forwards, futures, swaps and options can be thought of as variations on a theme.

9.3 Financial Engineering

These days, the market seems to be full of new-fangled financial hedging instruments. Banks sometimes add to the confusion by giving them their own brand names, with the result that the same instrument may be known by four or five quite different names and so appears to be four or five different instruments. A good way to beat the confusion is to think of the instruments as being made from a small range of simple financial building-blocks as described above, which comprise the basis of all financial hedging products. Looking at it this way, we can see that bankers are using the blocks to assemble many different products, just as a child uses its toy building-blocks to build castles, cars or aircraft. Almost every financial hedging product contains the same blocks put together in different ways.

To illustrate this, consider the case of a sterling-based importer with a dollar obligation whose exposure profile can be shown as in Figure 9.16. The stronger the dollar, the greater the sterling cost of that obligation and, other things being equal, the lower the value of the importer's company. Now let's think of the use of a call option on the dollar. This gives its owner the right, but not the obligation, to buy a specified quantity of a currency at a specified price and time. Hedging the importer's currency exposure with a call option on the dollar with an exercise price equal to the forward rate produces the result shown in Figure 9.17. The stronger the dollar, the greater the value of the option and, if the amount on which the option is written is equal to the underlying exposure, the change in the option value will exactly offset the underlying change in the value of the importer's company. The sensitivity of the company's value resulting from the combination of the option payoff and the underlying exposure is shown as the line labelled 'Result' in Figure 9.17.

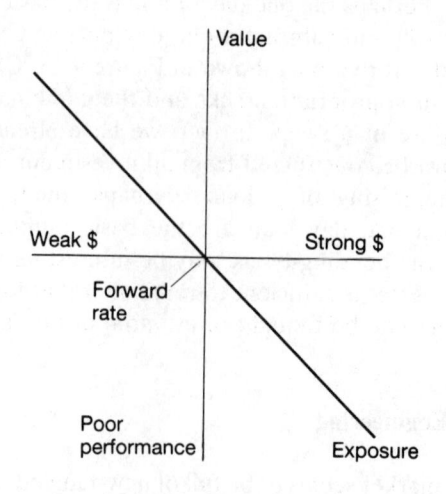

Figure 9.16

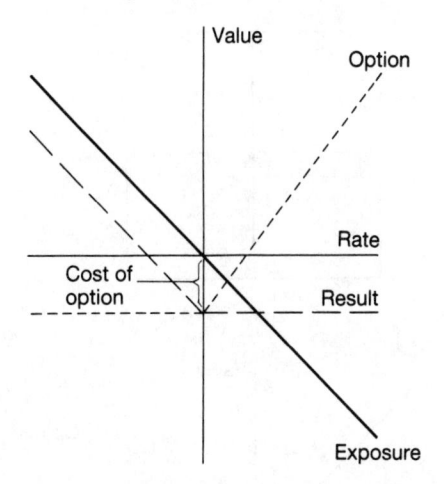

Figure 9.17

So far so good, but the price of such an option is relatively high. To many potential users the price is so high[7] that options don't feature on their shopping list. However, increased familiarity with options and other building-blocks of financial engineering shows how value-for-money solutions can be found. The exercise price of a call option is an important determinant of its price. As indicated in the inset to Figure 9.18, the higher its exercise price the cheaper the call option will be. The option user shown in Figure 9.17 seeks to protect himself from even the smallest adverse movement of the exchange rate from the forward rate prevailing when the option was bought. Hence he buys a call option with an exercise price equal to the forward rate. However, not every potential user will want so powerful, and therefore so expensive, an insurance. Many are well able to live with small movements in rates and want to guard against only the larger adverse movements. To do this, they use an option with an exercise price higher than the forward rate, as shown in the main part of Figure 9.18. It follows then that the cost of such an option will be less and, as a consequence, the result line in Figure 9.18 will lie relatively close to the original exposure.

Now we are beginning to see how to explore value for money. To reduce the cost of protection still more, what about reducing rather than eliminating the company's exposure? This solution can be achieved with an option on a smaller quantity of currency which has a correspondingly lower premium. This is shown in Figure 9.19. The inset compares the payoff to a call option on $1 million with a call option on $0.5 million. If the company's total exposure is $1 million, the option on $1 million will

170   *Using Derivative Products*

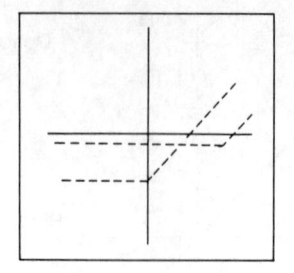

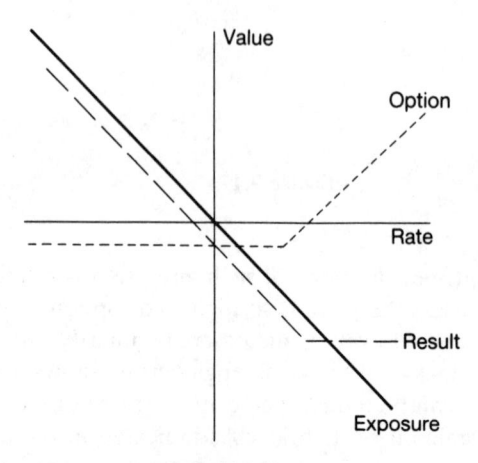

Figure 9.18

produce a result as shown in the main part of Figure 9.18, while the option on $0.5 million will produce a result as shown in the main part of Figure 9.19.

To reduce the up-front cash cost of protection even further, the user can buy a call option and sell a put option, with exercise prices chosen so that the two options have equal premiums. We now have an instrument with several proprietary names: the forward band, the range forward, the tunnel, the zero cost option, the collar, the floor–ceiling swap, the cylinder and so on. This instrument, which often involves no cash outlay, removes all the downside exposure beyond a predetermined point (determined by the exercise price of the call option) and pays for this removal by removing all the upside exposure beyond a different point (determined by the exercise price of the put option). In the middle range the exposure remains. This is illustrated in Figure 9.20.

But this may still not suit the user perfectly. The protection against a stronger dollar shown by the right hand part of Figure 9.20 looks fine. However, the corporation feels that the dollar might well weaken below

Using Derivative Products 171

the rate at which, as shown on the left hand part, no further benefit is enjoyed. The corporation wants to benefit from an even lower dollar than that written into the forward band. This can be done by reducing the exercise price of the put option, while at the same time increasing the amount on which the option is written so that the premiums of the call and the put remain equal. The result is shown in Figure 9.21.

But this, too, may not suit the user. Both Figure 9.20 and Figure 9.21 show a maximum value, that is the result line reaches a maximum level on its left hand extremity. Is it possible to provide protection against the downside risk without an upper limit in the event of a favourable movement in the rate? One way is to take the same call option once again and consider selling a put with the same exercise price and on the same amount as the call. The call is out-of-the-money and the put is in-the-money. Thus, pound for pound or dollar for dollar, the put has a higher premium than the call. To produce equal premiums the put must be written on a smaller amount than the call, and so it will have a smaller

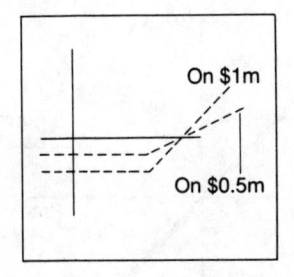

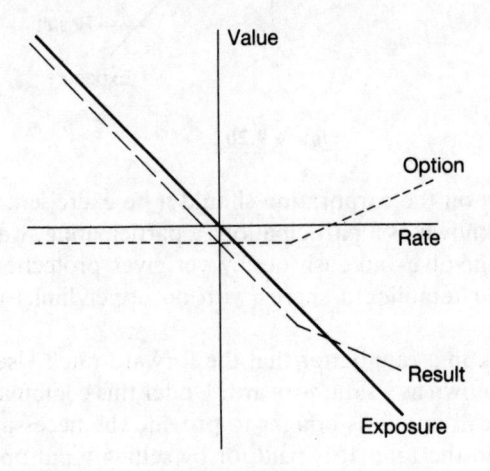

Figure 9.19

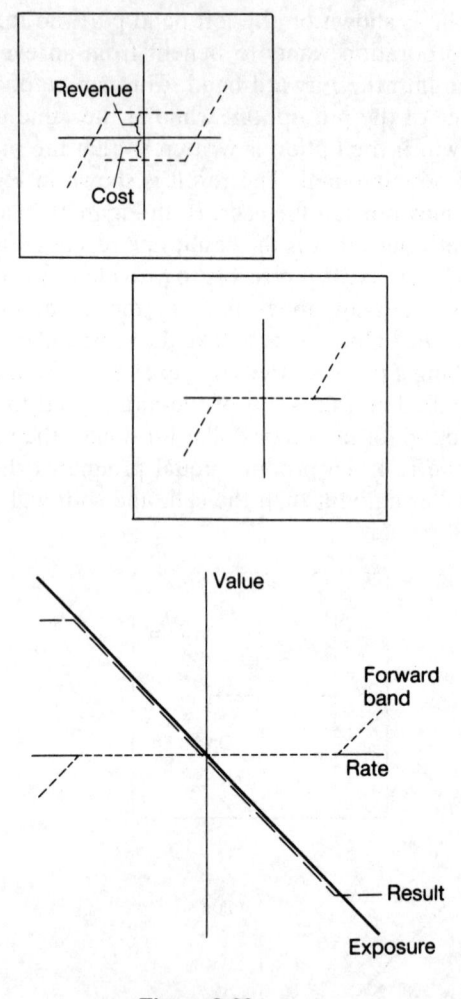

Figure 9.20

adverse impact on the corporation should it be exercised. This put–call combination, known as a participation, a participating swap or a profit-share option, involves no cash outlay yet gives protection against the downside while retaining a share (with no upper limit) in the upside (Figure 9.22).

Want to lock in a rate better that the forward rate? Use the put–call combination known as a ratio forward. Under this combination a deeply in-the-money call option is bought to provide the necessary protection against a rise in the rate. It is paid for by selling a put option with the same exercise price. As this put option is out-of-the-money, it will have

Using Derivative Products

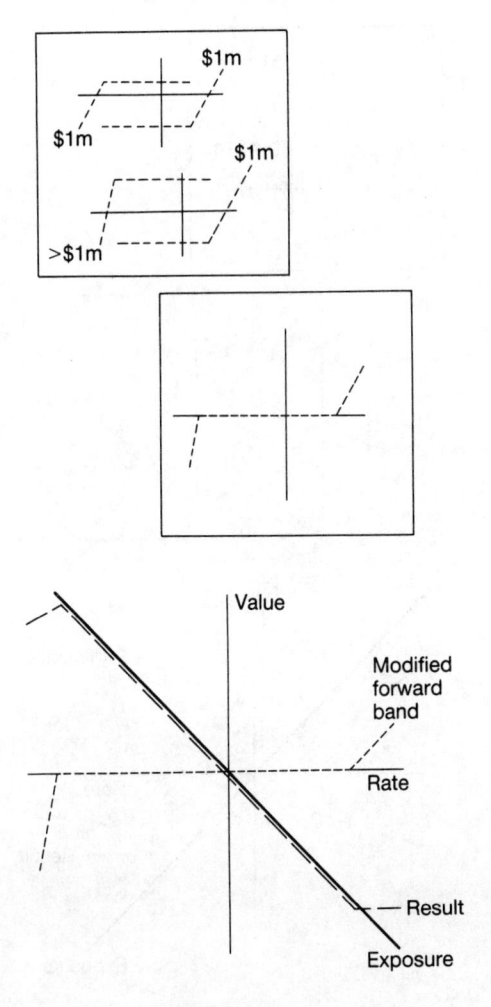

Figure 9.21

a lower premium than the equivalent call option. In order to make the premium of each option equal, the put must be written on a larger sum than the call, thus producing the payoff shown in Figure 9.23.

Want to benefit from exchange rate fluctuations regardless of the direction of the movement? The purchase of two call options (or of course one call option on twice the amount) will produce the steep option payoff in Figure 9.24, which when added to the underlying exposure will produce the desired V-shaped result.

Want to profit from exchange rate stability? Selling two put options (or one put option on twice the amount) will produce the option payoff

174   *Using Derivative Products*

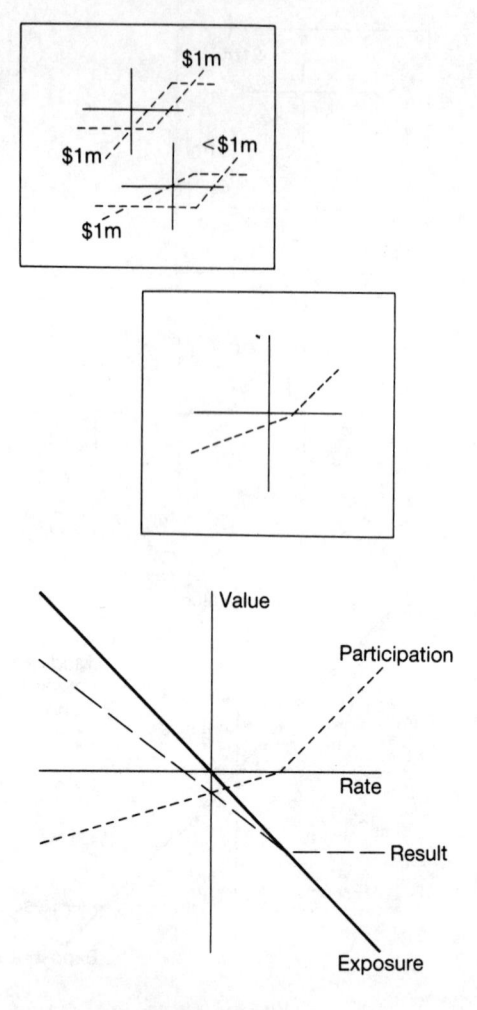

Figure 9.22

shown in Figure 9.25, which when added to the underlying exposure will produce the desired V-shaped result.

The list is endless. If needs and opportunities can be properly specified, then it is usually possible to put together a combination of financial building-blocks which will satisfy those needs and take advantage of those opportunities.[8]

This result is one of the key explanations for the growth of financial engineering. First, it suggests that the instruments can be viewed rather as children's building-blocks, so that many apparently complicated instruments can be constructed from combinations of the simple blocks.

Using Derivative Products

This has encouraged users and suppliers to construct their own instruments. For a fuller discussion of this point see Smithson (1987).

Secondly, it allows banks to manage their own risks associated with the provision of the instruments. For example, a position on an options trading desk – such as long calls and short puts – can be hedged by taking a short position in the forward market.

As is usual in most markets, demand and supply have interacted over time. This historical interaction is shown in a stylized way in Figure 9.26. The starting point of the figure is the upper left hand corner, while the

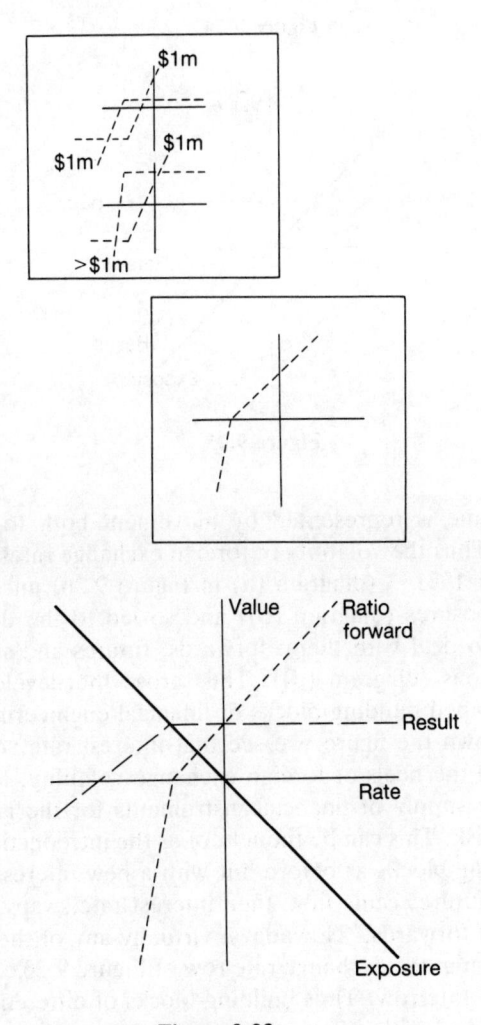

Figure 9.23

176   *Using Derivative Products*

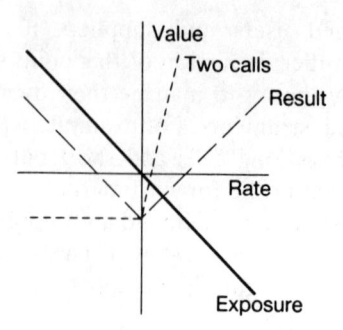

Figure 9.24

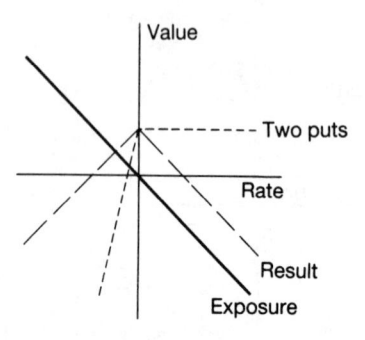

Figure 9.25

passage of time is represented by movement both to the right and downwards. Thus the volatility of foreign exchange rates which became so great after 1971–3 (diagram (a) in Figure 9.26) uncovered foreign exchange exposures (diagram (b)) and so led to the development of instruments to deal with them: forwards, futures and swaps (diagram (c)) and options (diagram (d)). Thus arose the development of the differently shaped building-blocks of financial engineering.

Looking down the figure, we see that interest rate volatility, which came hard on the heels of foreign exchange volatility, led to a similar growth in the supply of financial instruments for the management of interest rate risk. This can be thought of as the introduction of the same shaped building-blocks as before but with a new interest rate 'colour'. Interest rate futures came first, then interest rate swaps, then options, and last of all forwards.[9] Nowadays, virtually any of the shapes which could be shown in the exchange rate row of Figure 9.26 can be repeated in the interest rate row. Thus building-blocks of different colours were developed to deal with different types of exposure.

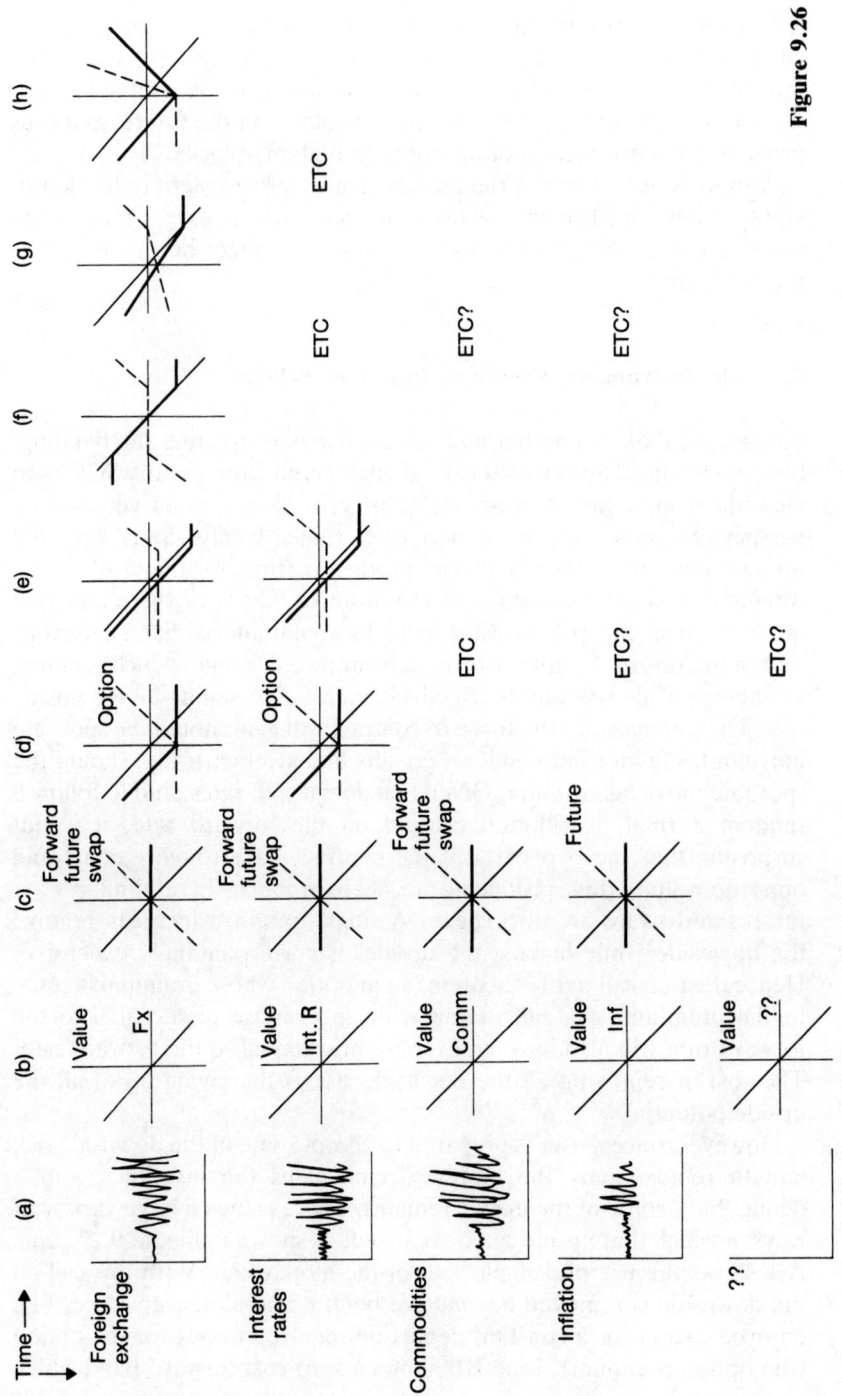

Figure 9.26

Commodity price volatility (third row) has led to the development of commodity-indexed swaps; inflation volatility (fourth row) led to the introduction of futures linked to the consumer price index; and so on. Doubtless some other price will become volatile in the future, and thus provoke the introduction of appropriate building-blocks.

Although not shown in the picture, equity price volatility has led to equity related instruments in the same way. To the extent that equity prices are determined by many variables, they might be thought of as multicoloured!

9.4 The Instruments Viewed as Insurance Policies

Finally, we look at another and powerful way of treating the building-blocks and the shapes which can be engineered from them, which is to view them in terms of insurance. This view shows, from yet another perspective, how they form part of a single family. Start with the forward contract. This is a 'cheap' product costing, for the most creditworthy customers, something of the order of 0.05% of the underlying quantity. It is cheap because it locks in a guaranteed, fixed exchange rate in the future. In other words an insurance is bought which removes all the downside risk and is effectively paid for by selling all the upside risk. The purchaser of the forward contract will gain should the spot rate move in his favour but will lose, equally and symmetrically, should the spot rate move against him. Given that actual spot rates tend to follow a random normal distribution centred on the forward rate, it is not surprising that the two parts of the contract have roughly equal and opposite value, thus producing a cheap product. In a similar way, futures and swaps are also cheap. A single option, which can remove the downside while leaving the upside, is correspondingly expensive. Hence the put–call parity theorem: a put option whose premium is equal to the premium of a call option with an exercise price equal to the forward rate will also have an exercise price equal to the forward rate. The cost of removing all the downside risk is the giving up of all the upside potential.

However, once a user is prepared to accept some of the downside risk and to remove only the more extreme cases (an insurance with a deductible), some of the upside remains. There is then a large variety of ways in which that upside can be enjoyed, as shown in Figure 9.27. Line AA shows the use of a single, out-of-the-money call. With this call all the downside is removed beyond the point a and all the upside can be enjoyed except for a constant deduction required to pay for the option (the option premium). Line BB shows a zero cost forward band which

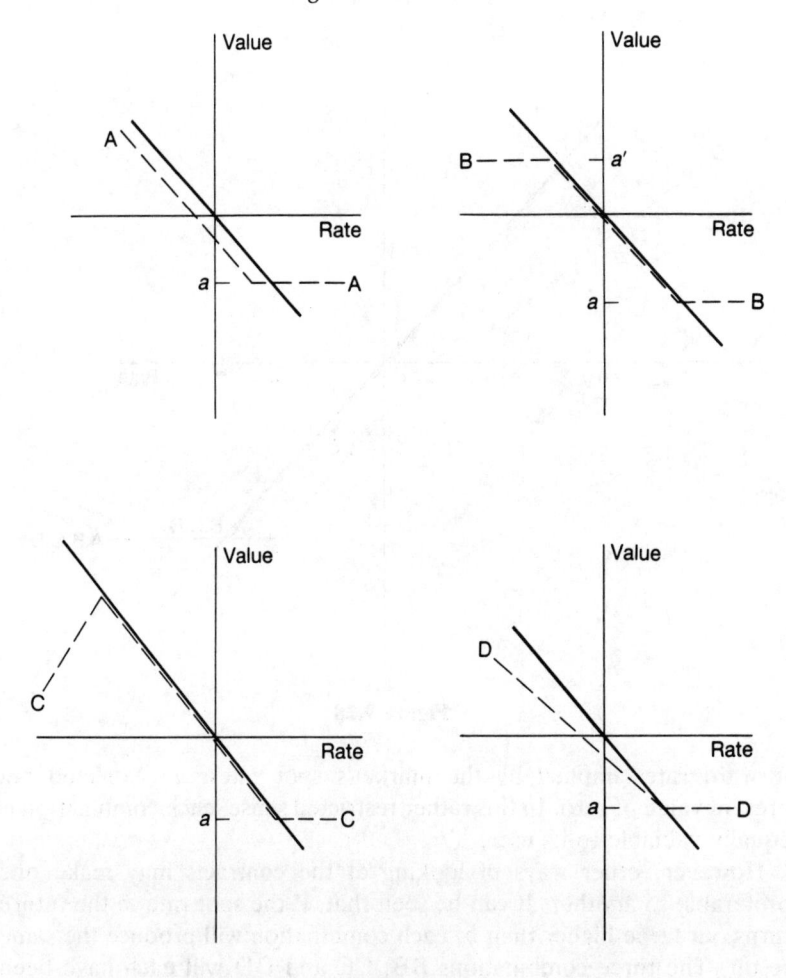

Figure 9.27

removes all the downside beyond point *a* but which pays for this insurance in a different way. Instead of a fixed premium, the forward band allows the user to enjoy all the upside up to point *a'* but none thereafter. Line CC shows the provision of a higher maximum but at the cost of a decline in the upside at more extreme values. Line DD shows the downside protection paid for by giving up a proportion of any upside gain. Further examples can be generated.

Clearly, the relative merits of these possibilities depend upon the objectives of their users and on their users' view of likely future movements. Figure 9.28 superimposes the parts of Figure 9.27. At the moment that each option combination is entered into it has, using the

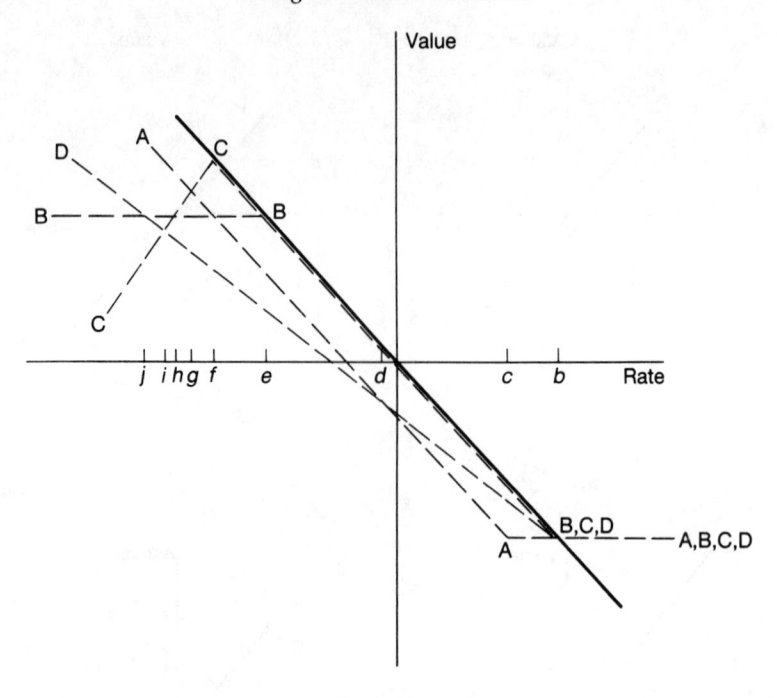

Figure 9.28

forward rates implied by the market's spot rates, an expected net present value of zero. In this rather restricted sense, each combination is equally valuable to its user.

However, other ways of looking at the contracts may make one preferable to another. It can be seen that, if the spot rate in the future turns out to be higher than b, each combination will produce the same result. The three combinations BB, CC and DD will each have been provided at 'zero cost', and each begins to provide protection at rates above b. AA will have been bought for cash (to buy the call option) but it begins to provide protection at the lower rate c. The protection it provides between b and c exactly offsets its cash cost.

We can see that, at very low spot rates, combination CC turns out to be the most expensive of all. Combination AA turns out to be the cheapest because its fixed cost is small relative to the overall gains from the rate movement. At somewhat higher rates CC looks more attractive – and so on. Table 9.1 summarizes the relative values of the payoffs at the different rates.

Hence the choice between the combinations will depend upon the user's attitude to risk, his view compared with the forward implied by the spot markets, his ability and willingness to pay cash for any

Table 9.1

Rate	Payoff
< j	CC < BB < DD < AA
j	CC < DD = BB < AA
> j, < i	CC < DD < BB < AA
i	CC = DD < BB < AA
> i, < h	DD < CC < BB < AA
h	DD < CC = BB < AA
> h, < g	DD < BB < CC < AA
g	DD < BB < CC = AA
> g, < f	DD < BB < AA < CC
f	DD < BB = AA < CC
> f, < e	DD < AA < BB < CC
e	DD < AA < BB = CC
> e, < d	DD < AA < BB = CC
d	DD = AA < BB = CC
> d, < b	AA < DD < BB < CC
b	AA = BB = CC = DD
> b	AA = BB = CC = DD

combination he may want, and the tax and accounting implications. Thus a user who wishes to minimize the worst possible outcome will tend to favour CC less than AA or perhaps (given the implication of rates turning out to lie between d and b) DD. By contrast, a user who feels that a rate in the range g to e is reasonably likely will tend to favour CC above other combinations.

9.5 Some Comments on the Use of Derivative Products

We have looked at forwards, futures, swaps and options at some length, and we have now seen how combinations of these financial instruments can be used to transform exposure profiles. At this point, we pause a little and classify the various uses of these instruments.

9.5.1 Dealing or Trading

Buying and selling can be a profitable activity. However, before profits can be made, something must be available for the trader or dealer to buy or sell!

Many institutions make a good living, albeit in a very competitive market, by trading the instruments which we have discussed in this book. The instruments can also be used as building-blocks to make other instruments. Thus, while banks can deal in forward contracts and, if they wish, can match purchases and sales, they can also make the forward contracts they need by using the spot market and the credit market (that is by borrowing or lending). These activities were illustrated in Chapters 3 and 4.

9.5.2 Arbitrage

Arbitraging can also be a profitable activity. If the prices of the equivalent futures contracts and forward contracts diverge sufficiently, profits can be made by selling the more expensive and buying the cheaper. Of course, by changing the balance of supply and demand, this process will tend to bring the prices closer together again, but someone who can see and exploit the opportunity before most other people can earn some profit in the meantime. This arbitrage activity plays a key role in maintaining the efficiency and competitiveness of different markets. As we shall see in Chapter 11, some arbitrage opportunities may be longer lasting.

9.5.3 Hedging

As we saw in Section 9.4, many financial instruments can be used to change an exposure, either by removing it completely, or by reducing it, or by otherwise tailoring it to make it more favourable.

9.5.4 Speculation

As we indicated at the end of Section 9.4, many users of these financial instruments will have no initial exposure and will use the instruments to create exposures which they hope will prove profitable in the future. This activity is usually described as speculation.

9.5.5 Beating the Market

In terms of the use of financial instruments, hedging and speculation look very similar. However, there is a greater difference than meets the eye: successful speculation involves outperforming the market, while hedging does not.

Consider the ordinary forward contract. A hedger may buy a forward contract in order to remove his foreign exchange exposure, and so match any positive payoff from the contract at expiration with a negative payoff from his underlying exposure and vice versa, as illustrated in Figure 9.1. His expected net payoff will be zero. Strictly speaking, the pure hedger expects the payoff (positive or negative) from his hedge to equal the loss or gain on his underlying position, and so expects no net profit from hedging *per se*.

The speculator, on the other hand, expects to gain from the use of the financial instruments. This means that he expects the future value of the underlying variable (currency, interest rate and so on) to differ from the forward rate embodied in the instruments, and so positions himself accordingly. This, in turn, means that he considers his own forecasts of the future spot to be more accurate than the forward rate seen in the market. Believers in efficient markets will find this a rather dubious claim – certainly if made by more than a tiny minority of speculators.

Turning back now to hedging we can see that, in practice, the difference between hedging and speculation is not as clear-cut as it might seem. This is because few hedgers always hedge 100% of their exposure. Most will change the proportion which they hedge and many will change their chosen method of hedging depending on their view of the current state of the market. To this extent, the hedgers are speculators. We return to these ideas in Chapter 10.

9.6 Case Study: Financial Engineering with Currency Options

The following data are given for 25 May 1988:

Spot DM/$ rate	1.7000
Six month Euro-DM interest rate	3.625% (3⅝%)
Six month Eurodollar interest rate	7.8125% (7¹³⁄₁₆%)
Market estimate of six month volatility	12% per annum

Suppose that an individual, whose performance is measured in Deutschmarks, has contracted to pay $100 on 25 November 1988. He is therefore exposed to the DM/$ exchange rate: the stronger the dollar in November, the worse his performance will be.

The individual may decide to hedge his exposure. On 25 May 1988 he finds the prices for six month European currency options, shown in Table 9.2.

Table 9.2

Exercise price (DM/$)	Call options on $100: premium ($)	Put options on $100: premium ($)
1.6143	—	1.96
1.70	2.37	4.41
1.7043	2.28	4.56
1.72	1.96	—

9.6.1 Constructing a Forward Band

Suppose that our individual wants to construct a zero cost forward band contract on the DM/$ exchange rate. The maximum value (upper limit) on the dollar price against the Deutschmark is to be 1.72. The individual needs to know the corresponding minimum value, and consults Table 9.2 to find the premium for a call option $100 with an exercise price of 1.72. This is $1.96. He then looks for the exercise price of a put option which has the same premium. This is 1.6143. Hence by buying the call option and selling the put he has (ignoring bid–offer spreads) constructed a zero cost forward band, placing a maximum price of DM172 and a minimum price of DM161.43 for his $100. An underlying exposure, a forward band and the combination of the two are illustrated in Figure 9.20.

9.6.2 Constructing a Participation

Suppose that our individual now wishes to construct a participation with an upper limit of 1.70. Table 9.2 shows that a call option with an exercise price of 1.70 will cost him $2.37. A put option with the same exercise price has a premium of $4.41. Hence buying one call on $100 and selling one put on $54 (i.e. 2.37/4.41) will match cash inflows and outflows and produce a zero cost participation. An underlying exposure, a participation and the combination of the two are illustrated in Figure 9.22.

9.6.3 Changing the Participation Rate

In the above example the individual has sold a put option on $54 against his exposure on $100 and therefore enjoys only 46% of any favourable movement in the exchange rate. Suppose that he would prefer to enjoy 50%. As we discussed in Section 9.4, he can obtain a greater upside potential if he gives up some protection on the downside. Table 9.2 shows that a call option on $100 with an exercise price of 1.7043 has a premium of $2.28, while a put option with the same exercise price has a premium of $4.56. Thus a zero cost participation can be constructed by buying a call on $100 and selling a put on $50.

Comparing the two participations shows that, of the individual wants a guaranteed maximum price for $100 of DM170, he enjoys only 46% of the benefit should the dollar turn out to be weaker than DM1.70. If, however, he wants the higher guaranteed maximum price of DM170.43, he enjoys 50% of the benefit should the dollar turn out to be weaker than DM1.7043.

10
The Corporate Hedging Decision

10.1 Introduction

In Chapters 1 and 2 we discussed the increased volatility facing firms and outlined the ways in which firms would be exposed to such volatility. Based on the various price exposures detailed in Chapter 2, we might expect that all firms would wish to undertake hedging activities. Our intuition is, as we shall see, only partially correct.

It is appropriate at this stage to pick up again some of the main points of Chapter 2 that will help us here in reviewing the corporate decision to hedge. We set out the firm's exposure profiles for the various price volatilities but we did not, at that stage, measure the slope of the curve that described the sensitivity of corporate value to those factors. We also noted (Section 2.3) that the market value of an all-equity financed company could be written as

$$V_e = \sum_{j=1}^{\infty} \frac{NCF_j}{(1 + {}_0R_j)^j}$$

We have discussed the calculation of the expected future net cash flow figure, but we have not yet considered the determinants of the required rate of return (the discount rate in the equation).

Consider now the possible effects of corporate hedging activity on the value of the firm. First, it is possible that hedging could affect expectations of the firm's expected future net cash flows. Secondly, hedging activity could affect the rate of return that the shareholders require on their investment. If the required rate of return reflects the riskiness of the investment, hedging might reduce the perceived future riskiness, which would reduce the required rate of return and hence increase the market value of the firm.

The Corporate Hedging Decision

It is this issue of the relationship between risk and return which we address first. In order to do that we have to concern ourselves with the ideas underlying portfolio theory. The bad news is that before tackling portfolio theory itself, we have to have some statistical underpinning.

10.2 Some Statistics

We will be looking here at three principal statistical measures: the mean, the standard deviation and the covariance.

Initially, we will be using historic data describing the monthly returns from holding shares. We will explain how these data are computed later in the chapter.

The hypothetical historic returns for two shares arbitrarily, and not very creatively, labelled share A and share B over a twelve month period are as shown in Table 10.1. In the calculations that follow, we have worked through the statistics for share A. Exactly the same procedures apply for share B!

Table 10.1

Month	Share A (%)	Share B (%)
1	5.5	−0.5
2	3.0	1.5
3	−0.5	4.0
4	4.0	2.5
5	1.5	−1.0
6	2.5	1.0
7	−2.5	3.5
8	−3.5	1.5
9	5.0	0.5
10	3.0	−1.5
11	5.0	3.5
12	1.0	3.0

10.2.1 Mean

The mean (or average) monthly return from share A, written as $\bar{R}_A$, is computed by simply summing the returns and dividing by the number of observations n. For the data in Table 10.1,

$$\bar{R}_A = \frac{5.5\% + 3.0\% + \ldots + 5\% + 1\%}{12} = 2.0\%$$

Formally, this is written as

$$\bar{R}_A = \frac{\sum_{i=1}^{n} R_i}{n}$$

10.2.2 Variance and Standard Deviation

We now need to get a measure of the variability or riskiness of share A's returns. This is usually done by calculating the dispersion of returns around the mean value. We do this by calculating either the variance or the standard deviation of share A's returns (written as σ_A^2 and σ_A respectively).

We first demonstrate the computation of the variance. This is done by calculating the average of the squared individual deviations from the mean. Using the data in Table 10.1, the variance of share A's returns is as follows:[1]

$$\sigma_A^2 = \frac{\sum_{i=1}^{n} (R_i - \bar{R}_A)^2}{n}$$

$$= \frac{(5.5 - 2.0)^2 + (3.0 - 2.0)^2 + \ldots + (1.0 - 2.0)^2}{12} = 7.8750\%^2$$

The problem with the variance figure in this context is that, as you will have noted, its unit is percentage squared. The standard deviation, which is the square root of the variance, allows us to work in the more user-friendly unit of simple percentage. In our example, the standard deviation of share A's return is 2.8062%. Standard deviations are the usually quoted formal measures of risk.

It is left to the reader to confirm that the average monthly return for share B ($\bar{R}_B$) is 1.5%, with a standard deviation of returns of 1.7795%.

10.2.3 Covariance

We need to arm ourselves with one last statistic, and that is the measure of covariance. As its name suggests, this statistic measures how returns across different securities (in this case, shares A and B) are interrelated.

We can get an impression of how the returns covary simply by inspecting the figures. In month 1, the return on share A is above its mean value whereas the return on share B is way below its mean value. Looking at each month in turn should suggest that the returns are not very closely related and, if anything, are negatively related.

The formal measure of covariance is calculated by taking the average of the products of the individual deviations from their respective means! It is somewhat easier to explain using our data for shares A and B in Table 10.1. Remember that we take each month in turn. Thus the covariance between A and B is given by

$$\text{cov}_{A,B} = \frac{(R_{A,1} - \bar{R}_A)(R_{B,1} - \bar{R}_B) + \ldots + (R_{A,12} - \bar{R}_A)(R_{B,12} - \bar{R}_B)}{12}$$

where $R_{A,1}$ denotes the return on share A in month 1, $R_{B,1}$ denotes the return on share B in month 1, and so on. More formally, this can be written as

$$\text{cov}_{A,B} = \frac{\sum_{i=1}^{n} (R_{A,i} - \bar{R}_A)(R_{B,i} - \bar{R}_B)}{n}$$

Thus, in our example,

$$\text{cov}_{A,B} = \frac{(5.5 - 2.0)(-0.5 - 1.5) + (3.0 - 2.0)(1.5 - 1.5) + \ldots + (1.0 - 2.0)(3.0 - 1.5)}{12}$$

$$= \frac{-20.75}{12} = -1.7292$$

10.2.4 Correlation Coefficient

The covariance figure that we have calculated is, of itself, rather meaningless because of the problems of scale. Let us explain. Suppose that in each month the returns on shares A and B were multiplied up by a factor of 10, the return for share A in month 1 now being 55% rather than 5.5%. The mean return for share A and share B would now be 20% and 15%, with standard deviations of 28.062% and 17.795% respectively. The covariance now works out to be −172.92. But remember that the relationship between the shares in each month (share A's return in month 1 is still above its mean, while share B's return is still way below its mean) remains unchanged. In other words the value of the covariance is a function of the scale of numbers used.

The correlation coefficient (which is given the symbol ρ (rho) and which can take a value from −1 to +1) gets over this problem of scale. Dividing our first covariance value of the returns on shares A and B by the product of the standard deviations for shares A and B gives us a value for the correlation coefficient as follows:

$$\rho_{A,B} = \frac{\text{cov}_{A,B}}{\sigma_A \, \sigma_B} = \frac{-1.7292}{2.8062 \times 1.7795} = -0.3463$$

In our scaled-up example, the correlation coefficient remains the same:

$$\rho_{A,B} = \frac{-172.92}{28.062 \times 17.795} = -0.3463$$

We can see that if the covariance term is positive then so is the correlation coefficient, and vice versa.

10.3 Portfolio Theory

Having covered these preliminaries, we can at last turn to the ideas underlying portfolio theory.

10.3.1 *Portfolio Risk and Return*

We start by considering the return/risk characteristics of a portfolio made up solely of the shares A and B whose returns were detailed in Table 10.1. The portfolio that we are going to construct comprises 50% in share A and 50% in share B. These weightings will be designated W_A and W_B. Given these weightings, we can see that the return R_P on such a portfolio in month 1 would be

$$R_P = 0.5 \,(\text{return on share A}) + 0.5 \,(\text{return on share B})$$
$$= 0.5 \,(5.5\%) + 0.5 \,(-0.5\%) = 2.5\%$$

We could obviously repeat this for the other eleven months and then find the mean return on the portfolio (written as $\bar{R}_P$):

$$\bar{R}_P = \frac{2.5\% + 2.25\% + \ldots + 4.25\% + 2.0\%}{12} = 1.75\%$$

Alternatively we could compute the mean return on the portfolio by weighting the mean return on the individual shares:

$$\bar{R}_P = W_A \bar{R}_A + W_B \bar{R}_B = 1.75\%$$

We now turn to the calculation of the variance of the portfolio returns. Recalling that the variance is the average of the squared deviations from the mean, the variance would be calculated thus:

$$\sigma_P^2 = [\tfrac{1}{12}(2.5 - 1.75)^2 + \tfrac{1}{12}(2.25 - 1.75)^2 + \ldots$$
$$+ \tfrac{1}{12}(4.25 - 1.75)^2 + \tfrac{1}{12}(2.0 - 1.75)^2]$$
$$= 1.8958\%^2$$

More formally, this expression can be written as

$$\sigma_P^2 = \frac{\sum_{i=1}^{n} (R_{P,i} - \bar{R}_P)^2}{n}$$

In our example, we can expand the expression by breaking up the R_P terms into the returns on the component shares:

$$\sigma_P^2 = \frac{\sum_{i=1}^{12} [(W_A R_{A,i} + W_B R_{B,i}) - (W_A \bar{R}_A + W_B \bar{R}_B)]^2}{12}$$

Rearranging terms we get

$$\sigma_P^2 = \frac{\sum_{i=1}^{12} [(W_A R_{A,i} - W_A \bar{R}_A) + (W_B R_{B,i} - W_B \bar{R}_B)]^2}{12}$$

The weightings W_A and W_B are fixed, so this can be further rearranged:[2]

$$\sigma_P^2 = \frac{\sum_{i=1}^{12} [W_A (R_{A,i} - \bar{R}_A) + W_B (R_{B,i} - \bar{R}_B)]^2}{12}$$

This can now be expanded in a generalized form to

$$\sigma_P^2 = \frac{\sum_{i=1}^{n} W_A^2 (R_{A,i} - \bar{R}_A)^2}{n} + \frac{\sum_{i=1}^{n} W_B^2 (R_{B,i} - \bar{R}_B)^2}{n} + \frac{\sum_{i=1}^{n} 2 W_A W_B (R_{A,i} - \bar{R}_A)(R_{B,i} - \bar{R}_B)}{n}$$

Despite the algebra, some of this should be familiar! The first and second terms are the weighted variances of the returns on shares A and B, while the third term is the weighted covariance of the returns on the two shares. Thus we can rewrite the expression as

$$\sigma_P^2 = W_A^2 \sigma_A^2 + W_B^2 \sigma_B^2 + 2 W_A W_B \text{cov}_{A,B}$$
$$= W_A^2 \sigma_A^2 + W_B^2 \sigma_B^2 + 2 W_A W_B \sigma_A \sigma_B \rho_{AB}$$

Thus, plugging in the data for shares A and B with weightings of 0.5 and 0.5, the portfolio variance will be

$$\sigma_P{}^2 = (0.5)^2(2.8062)^2 + (0.5)^2(1.7795)^2 + 2(0.5)(0.5)(2.8062)$$
$$(1.7795)(-0.3463)$$
$$= 1.8958\%^2$$
$$\sigma_P = 1.3769\%$$

Before we move on to discuss portfolio selection decisions, we need to say a few words about the calculation of returns from holding a share. There are a number of ways of working out the return, and obviously a range of periods over which the historic return can be measured. One of the most common ways of calculating the return over the period from time 0 to time 1 is of the form

$$R = \frac{P_1 + D}{P_0}$$

where P_1 denotes the price of the share at the end of the period, P_0 denotes the price at the start of the period, and D denotes the dividends paid during the period. That is to say, the return is the share price change over the period plus any dividends paid during the period.

10.3.2 Portfolio Selection Decisions

We can now turn to portfolio selection decisions involving, as they do, decisions about the future allocation of resources on the basis of expected risk and return. This sort of data is very hard to come by. Fortunately, most of the evidence suggests that statistics taken from past periods are likely to provide us with reasonable estimates of future risk and return relationships.

As a real-life example, in Table 10.2 we have set out extracts from a series of actual returns calculated over a period of five years for two

Table 10.2

Month	Share X (%)	Share Y (%)
1	1.72	1.73
2	5.93	8.55
⋮	⋮	⋮
59	0.97	7.60
60	−4.35	0.44
Mean	$\bar{R}_X = 2.45$	$\bar{R}_Y = 3.48$
Standard deviation	$\sigma_X = 7.45$	$\sigma_Y = 10.34$
Covariance	$\text{cov}_{X,Y} = +20.34$	
Correlation coefficient	$\rho_{X,Y} = +0.264$	

actively traded shares quoted on the London Stock Exchange. We will call them share X and share Y. Their returns are measured on a monthly basis. The table also shows summary statistics for the shares.

We have plotted the risk/return data for these two shares in Figure 10.1.

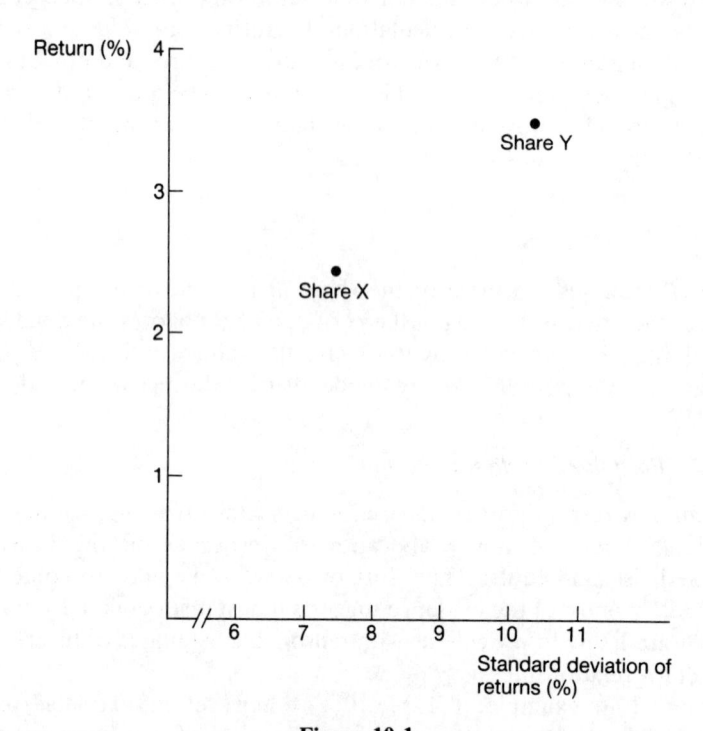

Figure 10.1

Using the data in Table 10.2, and creating an equally weighted portfolio of shares X and Y, that is setting $W_X = W_Y = 1/2 = 50\%$, the return on the portfolio is equal to

$$\bar{R}_P = (1/2)(2.45\%) + (1/2)(3.48\%) = 2.965\%$$

The portfolio variance will be

$$\sigma_P^2 = (1/2)^2(7.45)^2 + (1/2)^2(10.34)^2 + 2(1/2)(1/2)(7.45)(10.34)(+0.264)$$
$$= 50.7729\%^2$$

The combination of return and risk coordinates for this particular weighting of 50% in share X and 50% in share Y (return of 2.965% and standard deviation of 7.126%) has been plotted on Figure 10.2. In the

The Corporate Hedging Decision

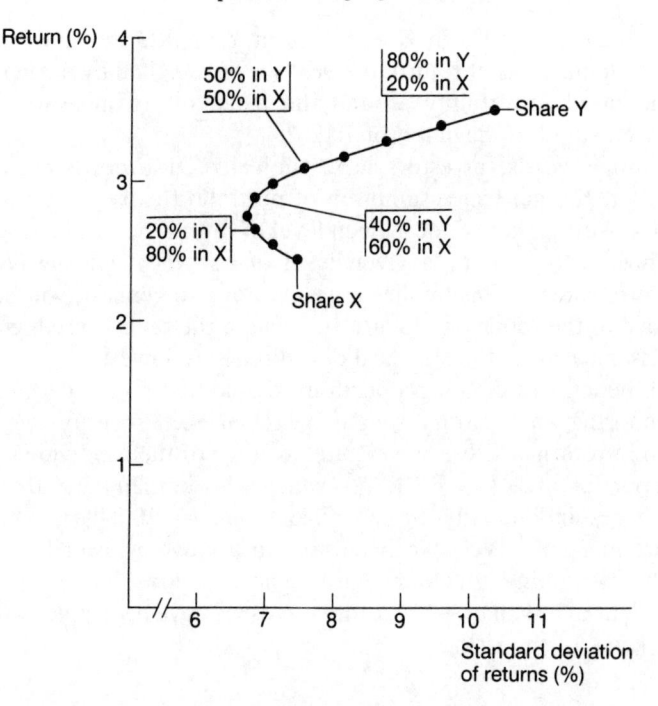

Figure 10.2

same figure we have also plotted the risk/return points for ten other weightings of share X and share Y. Some of the coordinates are given in Table 10.3. Of course, any point on the solid line joining the eleven dots is also achievable by changing the weighting between the two shares.

However, this analysis does not actually tell us what proportion of share X and share Y to hold. The answer is that it would depend upon the individual investor's risk preference. For instance, suppose the investor held a portfolio of 60% in share X and 40% in share Y. The average return from such a mix is, as shown in Table 10.3, 2.862% with a standard deviation of 6.845%. The decision to hold such a portfolio

Table 10.3

Share X weighting (%)	Share Y weighting (%)	Return (%)	Standard deviation (%)
20	80	3.275	8.784
50	50	2.965	7.126
60	40	2.862	6.845
80	20	2.656	6.805

194   *The Corporate Hedging Decision*

rather than, say, 50% in X and 50% in Y implies that the benefit of moving up in terms of return to 2.965% is outweighed by having to take on increased uncertainty around the mean return measured by the increased standard deviaton of 7.126%.

In other words, investors have subjective risk/return preferences. However, the general assumption of portfolio theory is that investors are risk averse: that is, for a given level of return they will always try to minimize risk, and for a given level of risk they will always try to maximize return. This implies that investors, in general, will be trying to move to the top left of Figure 10.2 where the returns are highest and the risk measures (the standard deviations) are lowest.

The benefits of creating a portfolio should be becoming self-evident. By choosing an arbitrary weight of 1/2 in each security, we have a portfolio return which is a weighted average of their individual returns but a portfolio risk ($\sigma_P = 7.126\%$) which is lower than the risk of *each* of the shares individually ($\sigma_X = 7.45\%$, $\sigma_Y = 10.34\%$). This is an important result. We have been able to achieve a lower level of risk simply by joining together shares whose returns had a correlation coefficient of less than +1. In other words we have been able to diversify away some of the risk.

10.3.3 *Covariances Simplified: Sharpe's Market Model*

Suppose now that we extend the two share case discussed above to, say, ten shares. Our portfolio return would now be

$$W_1\bar{R}_1 + W_2\bar{R}_2 + \ldots + W_{10}\bar{R}_{10}$$

Our portfolio variance would be

$$\sigma_P^2 = W_1^2\sigma_1^2 + W_2^2\sigma_2^2 + \ldots + W_{10}^2\sigma_{10}^2 + 2W_1W_2 \text{ cov}_{1,2} + 2W_1W_3 \text{ cov}_{1,3} + \ldots + 2W_1W_{10} \text{ cov}_{1,10} + 2W_2W_3 \text{ cov}_{2,3} + 2W_2W_4 \text{ cov}_{2,4} + \ldots + 2W_2W_{10} \text{ cov}_{2,10} + \ldots$$

where $\text{cov}_{1,2}$ denotes the covariance of the returns between share 1 and 2, and so on. We haven't set out all the covariance terms simply because, in total, there are 45 of them! It should be clear to you that, in terms of portfolio risk, the individual riskiness of a share (measured by its own variance of returns) is effectively swamped by the covariance terms. Thus, in our example, there are ten variance terms and 45 covariance terms.

Let's now consider adding an eleventh share to our ten share portfolio. The expression for the portfolio return would now include $W_{11}\bar{R}_{11}$. However, there would be eleven additional terms in the expression for the portfolio variance, namely

The Corporate Hedging Decision

$$W_{11}{}^2\sigma_{11}{}^2, 2W_1W_{11}\text{ cov}_{1,11}, 2W_2W_{11}\text{ cov}_{2,11}, \ldots, 2W_{10}W_{11}\text{ cov}_{10,11}$$

That is, the expression would include the variance of the eleventh security's returns, and ten other terms measuring how the eleventh security's returns covary with the returns of each of the other ten shares. This is significant in the sense that if return is a function of risk, the most important ingredient in the risk expression is how the return on an individual share covaries with the returns on all the other shares, rather than its own individual variability or riskiness. Remember too that these covariances can be positive or negative.

Extending the idea to encompass say 50 securities makes the calculation of the portfolio variance rather unmanageable, given that we would be dealing with a total of 2450 covariances.

At this point we can introduce a simplification suggested by William Sharpe in 1963. The simplification was the replacement of the covariances across all the individual securities with a single figure that would capture the covariance between the returns on an individual share and the return on a market-wide index.

Consider the inclusion of a marginal 51st share in a 50 share portfolio. Given our previous discussion, we would have needed to consider the additional 50 covariance terms individually. The Sharpe simplification reduces to the single problem of measuring how the returns on the 51st share covary with the market. Given that the 50 shares are a reasonably representative sample of the shares that make up the whole market, the results from such a simplification are unlikely to be much different from the result that would be obtained from considering each of the individual covariance terms.

If we plot the returns on share X against the corresponding returns on the market-wide index, we get a graph similar to that in Figure 10.3. In order to simplify matters we have, in Figure 10.3, plotted only a sample of the 60 observations in Table 10.2.

We can get a measure of how the returns on share X covary with the market returns by running an ordinary least squares regression on the data. The regression provides a numerical relationship between the variables, and is of the form

$$R_X = \alpha_X + \beta_X R_M + \epsilon_X$$

where the notation is as follows:

R_X return on share X
α_X intercept term (alpha)
β_X regression coefficient (beta)
R_M return on the market

196   *The Corporate Hedging Decision*

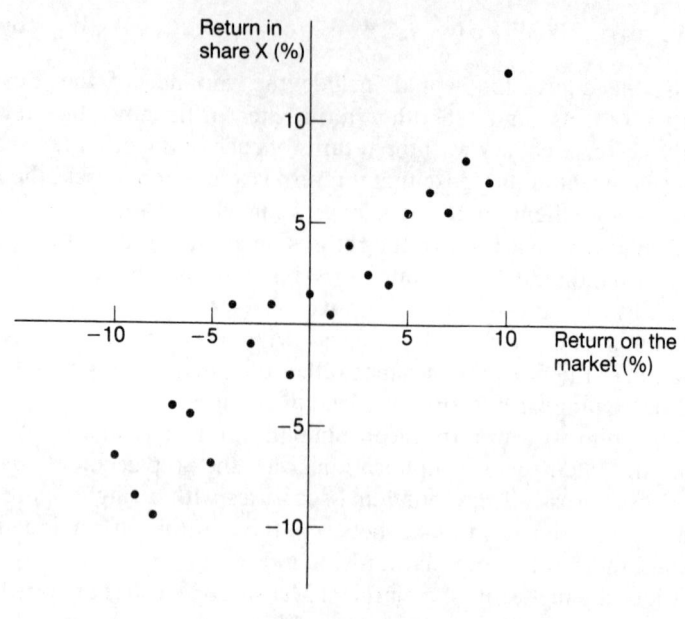

Figure 10.3

ϵ_X error term: a random variable with an expected value of zero and a constant variance.

The regression line is fitted to the data in Figure 10.4. Without going into the details of regression, suffice it here to note that the α value of 0.6 is not statistically different from zero. In Figure 10.4 the β value is the slope of the regression line, and its value of 0.94 relates the return on share X to a per unit return on the market index.

The returns for share Y plotted against the returns on the market are set out in Figure 10.5, together with the least squares regression line.

The coefficient β_i on share i is formally defined as

$$\beta_i = \frac{\text{covariance } R_i, R_M}{\text{variance } R_M}$$

In other words, β measures the standardized covariance of the returns on share i with the returns on the market. This is exactly the statistic that we suggested above would be the appropriate measure of risk in a portfolio context.

In Figure 10.6, we have repeated Figure 10.4 and have also drawn in the average return for share X as a dashed horizontal line running through the vertical axis at 2.45.

Consider again the ideas underlying the calculation of the variance of

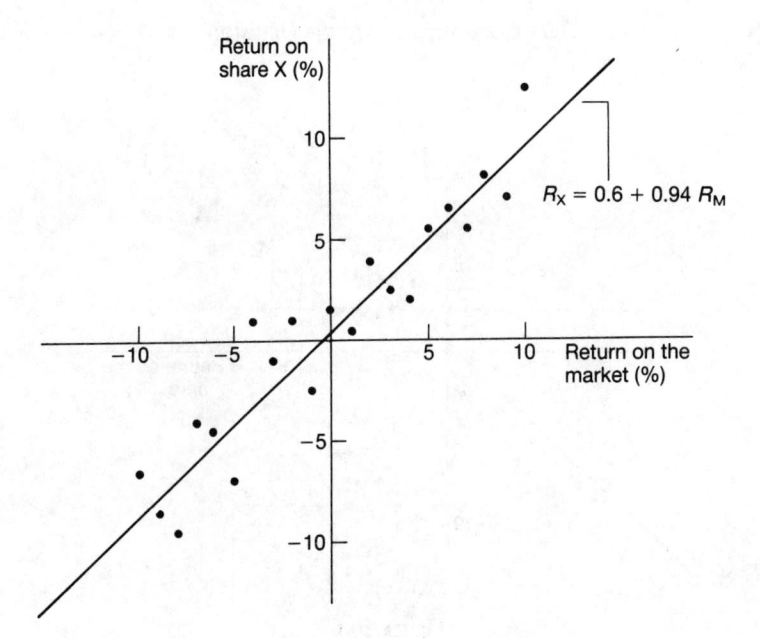

Figure 10.4

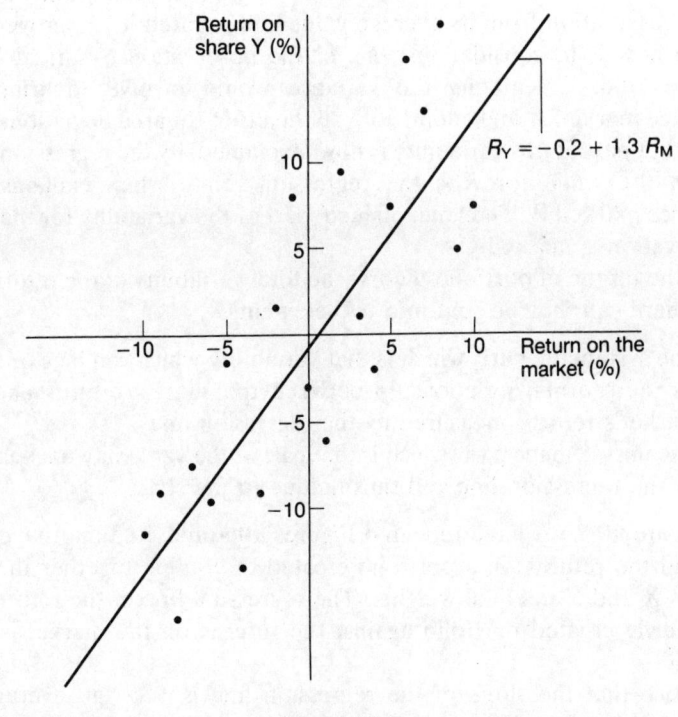

$R_X = 0.6 + 0.94 R_M$

Figure 10.5

$R_Y = -0.2 + 1.3 R_M$

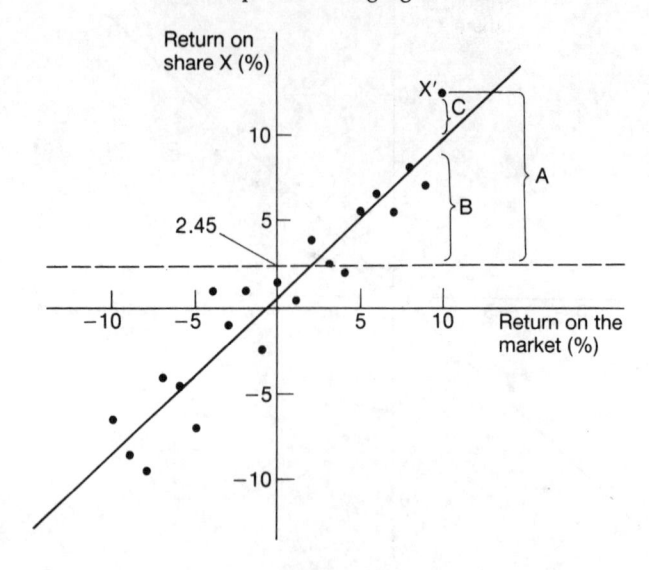

Figure 10.6

returns. In the calculation of the variance, you will recall that we took each observation from its average value and squared it. What we want to do now is to consider just one of the observations, marked X' in Figure 10.6. Calculating the variance would involve squaring the distance marked A and adding it to all the other squared deviations. But note that part of this variability is now 'explained' by the regression line. Given the value for R_M, the regression relationship 'explains' the distance marked B. The 'unexplained' part of the variability for that one observation is marked C.

In the jargon of portfolio theory, the total variability of the returns on any share can thus be split into two elements:

- The systematic part, which is that variability which can be explained by the 'normal' relationship between the share's returns and the market's returns measured by the regression line
- The unsystematic part, which is that part of the variability unexplained by the regression line and thus unique to the share.

In Figure 10.7 we have repeated Figures 10.4 and 10.5 and have also plotted the returns on a portfolio created by joining together the two shares X and Y in equal weights. The regression line of the returns on this newly created portfolio against the returns on the market is also plotted.

Notice that the slope of the regression line is 1.12, an average of individual β values. It should be evident that the variability around the

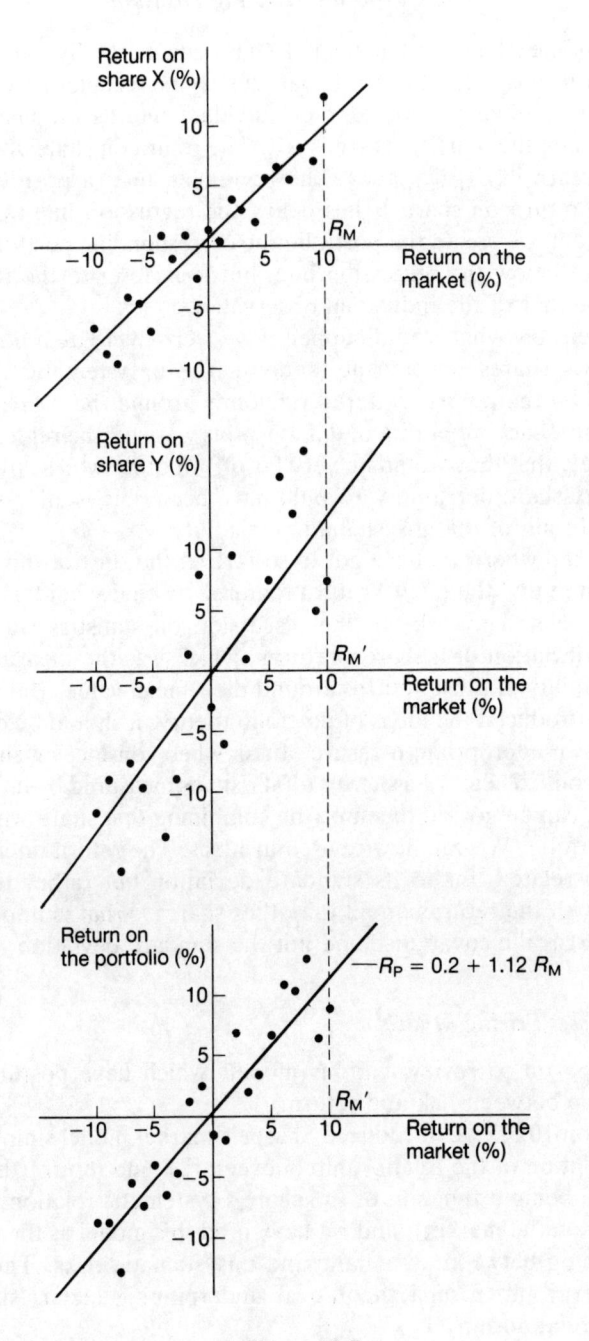

Figure 10.7

regression line (the unsystematic risk) has been markedly reduced. This reduction in unsystematic risk is particularly noticeable if we consider just one pair of observations, the individual returns on share X and share Y when the market return is R'_M. The return on share X when the market return is R'_M lies above the regression line (a positive error), while the return on share Y lies below the regression line (a negative error). When we create the portfolio the corresponding portfolio return for R'_M lies below the regression line, but it is closer to the regression line than either of the individual observations.

Consider now what would happen if we were to create a portfolio of say, twenty shares selected at random. The unsystematic variability measured by the points scattered randomly around the regression line would cancel each other out, and if any plots were off the regression line it is unlikely that they would be very far off! In other words, by creating this twenty share portfolio we would have been able to diversify away most, if not all, of the unsystematic variability.

Let's recap where we have got to so far! At the start of this chapter, we suggested that the rate of return required by equity holders in a firm might be related to risk. In the discussion on statistics we met the standard deviation of a share's returns, which was the measure of the total variability of those returns around their mean value. But now that we have introduced the ideas of portfolio theory, it should be clear that this is not an appropriate measure of risk when considering shares in a portfolio context. Part of a share's total risk, as measured by its standard deviation, can be got rid of simply by combining that share with others into a portfolio. We can now revise our ideas. The return on any share should be related not to its standard deviation but rather to how it covaries with the returns on all the other shares. What is important in this context is the covariance and not the standard deviation.

10.3.4 Asset Pricing Models

We now go on to review various models which have postulated the relationship between risk and return.

In Section 10.3.2 we introduced Sharpe's market model simplification as a description of the relationship between risk and return (the return on a share being a function of the share's systematic relationship with the return on the market), and we have used this model as the basis for distinguishing between systematic and unsystematic risks. This model has, however, no formal theoretical underpinning and is simply an empirical relationship.

Sharpe's model is not the only return generating model that has been suggested. The capital asset pricing model (CAPM), derived originally

The Corporate Hedging Decision

as an equilibrium pricing model, also postulates a linear relationship between return and risk but relies upon theory and several assumptions to underpin the relationship. The form of the CAPM is

$$R_i = R_f + (R_M - R_f) \beta_i$$

where R_i denotes the return on the ith asset, R_f denotes the return on a risk-free asset and β_i denotes the systematic risk of the ith asset.

A newer model, based on the ideas of arbitrage pricing theory (APT), explains the risk/return relationship in terms of a firm's sensitivity to several distinct economic factors rather than just to the market in general. An important implication of APT is that companies may differ in their sensitivity to these factors so that changes in some economic variables will have a greater impact on certain companies than on others. What is more, the relationship on a company's return to the return on the factor can be either positive or negative. While the theory itself specifies neither the number nor the identity of the factors necessary to explain company returns, four factors have been suggested: unexpected changes in industrial production growth; unexpected changes in the term structure of interest rates; spreads on bond portfolio returns; and unexpected inflation.

In general, studies using Sharpe's market model, CAPM or APT have used regression/factor models to quantify risk. Although these models entail different theoretical frameworks and assumptions, any β is a measure of covariability rather than total variability.

10.3.5 Hedging and Unsystematic Risk

We now go on to consider what causes these variations in share price returns, and the implications for corporate hedging strategy.

Recall that at any point in time, a company's market value will be determined by the present value of its expected future net cash flows. It is important to note that the expected future net cash flows in the numerator are 'fixed' across individuals given the information set at any one point in time. Changes in a company's market value will then result from changes in a company's cash flow expectations that occur because of company-specific events, as well as those changes that happen to affect companies on a market-wide basis.

If we could measure changes in the expected future net cash flows and attribute the changes to newly available information relating to the changes in interest rates, foreign exchange rates and so on, we could quantify the impact of such information on a company's market value. Given no perceived change in the rate of return (the denominator in the equation in Section 10.1), movements in the share prices reflect the change in the present value of a company's revised expected future net cash flows.

We now examine the implications of the risk/return tradeoff in the context of the corporate hedging decision. At first glance, it may appear that managers should hedge against all the unexpected changes in the price of economic variables which cause the total variability in corporate market value measured by the variance of the share price returns. However, we have noted above that some part of the total risk can be got rid of by the shareholders themselves simply by joining securities together in a portfolio. We have seen above that the expected return on a security should be based only a measure of how the security's riskiness covaries with that of the market. That is to say, the expected return is a function of that security's market β, the measure of its systematic risk.

Now if fluctuations in corporate market value brought about by changes in the price of economic variables constitute unsystematic risk (that is, they are specific to the firm), then portfolio theory advises that they should not be hedged. Such volatility could be diversified away by the shareholders by holding the security in a randomly selected portfolio of shares.

And if shareholders are costlessly able to diversify away the unsystematic element of total risk simply by creating a portfolio of a number of securities, it follows that they would not wish managers, working on their behalf, to expend corporate resources on hedging risks which they have already been able to hedge for themselves. Shareholders, in this scenario, would only be interested in systematic risk and would express their preference for risk by selecting a diversified portfolio with a particular expected β value reflecting their own, individual risk preference.

Nevertheless, there are instances where the shareholders would wish the managers to undertake hedging activities on their behalf. For example, shareholders would wish the managers to hedge unsystematic variability in corporate value in those instances where hedging activity at a company level would secure real economic benefits (and thus add to corporate value) which were not accessible to the shareholders at a personal level.

10.4 The Corporate Hedging Decision

We now go on to discuss the instances where corporate managers are likely to undertake hedging activities. Much of this material draws on the seminal work of Dufey and Srinivasulu (1983).

It is common practice, which we have implicitly adopted, to assume

The Corporate Hedging Decision

that firms aim to maximize their shareholders' wealth V_e (see the equation in Section 10.1). It is a clear that setting out to maximize V_e is an extremely difficult task involving assessment of the expected future environment in which the corporation will operate and decisions on the corporation's reactions to those assessments. To the extent that fluctuations in net cash flows affect V_e, either via the denominator or via the numerator of the valuation equation (see Sections 2.3 and 2.4), the assessments of the future environment involve scenarios or probabilities rather than simple point forecasts, thus making the whole process even more difficult. One reason, perhaps, why successful entrepreneurs are hard to find!

It would be helpful for analytical purposes if the average levels of the expected future net cash flows were independent of the degree of fluctuations around those levels. To a limited extent, such independence might exist. That is, the better the firm's investment decision, the stronger its product lines, the more effective its marketing and so on, the greater the expected future net cash flows will tend to be, regardless of whether or not those flows fluctuate over time. However, there may be some circumstances in which this independence is not seen. For example, lenders such as banks may price their loans according to the perceived risk of default, and their perception may be influenced by the volatility in the firm's cash flows. In this case, a reduction in volatility can reduce the cost of funds and so raise the levels of net cash flows during a period of borrowing. Similarly a progressive tax system will lead to greater tax payments on a volatile cash flow than on a stable one. Hiring and firing costs and, in the extreme, bankruptcy costs will also lead to lower cash flows under volatility than under stability. One further factor may be customer confidence. A would-be buyer of a durable may want to be sure that its seller will be in business during the whole life of the durable, and the volatility of the seller's cash flow may influence the degree of confidence in the seller's long term ability to service the durable.

At first sight, it might be thought that the discount rate used in the denominator of the valuation equation would depend upon the expected levels of the net cash flows and on the degree of certainty with which the cash flows can be estimated. The rate would depend on the levels of the flows because, to the extent that the net cash flows represent income to their recipients, low incomes will produce a high marginal utility and hence a high discount rate. It would depend on the degree of uncertainty because of the general principle that uncertain flows are discounted more heavily than certain flows.

While this may be so in certain cases, the situation with respect to a publicly traded firm is less clear-cut. If the value of the firm is captured in freely tradeable securities, and those securities form part of more general portfolios, we have seen from portfolio theory (and there is considerable empirical evidence to support the argument) that the appropriate discount rate depends only upon the securities' systematic risk.

It is sometimes argued that, because a firm with volatile cash flows is 'riskier' than one with stable cash flows, the owners of such a firm will be interested in hedging to reduce volatility. However, it can be seen from the above that this argument is not usually correct. To the extent that the owners of a firm are free to buy shares in other firms and hence own (parts of) other firms they will be able to diversify away unsystematic risk, with the result that the riskiness of any one individual firm becomes unimportant. By choosing an appropriate combination of (parts of) firms, owners can choose a combination of risk and return which best suits them.

The main users of hedging are therefore likely to be owner managed firms, which represent a large proportion of their owners' total wealth, together with firms which can raise the level of their expected future net cash flows by reducing future cash flow volatility.

So far we have ignored any conflicts of interest; we have implicitly assumed that owners, shareholders and managers have identical interests. It is possible that, in large corporations, interests differ – and different individuals may follow different interests even if, in the aggregate, their actions lower the value of the firms. Thus managers may feel reluctant to announce large changes in earnings, purchasing managers may have in their job description an instruction to stabilize input costs, and so on. These types of situation can also lead to a demand for hedging, even if hedging for such reasons might not be in the best interests of the shareholders.

However, how can we square this with the large amount of hedging activity which appears to be going on in the market? Let us look again at some of the principles of hedging. In general, the price to a purchaser of hedging instruments will be made up of three parts: the underlying central price, the bid–offer spread and other transactions costs, and the charge to reflect the credit risk. Consider a one year currency forward contract under which the buyer is obliged to provide, for example, DM1.8 million in return for $1.0 million. The figure of DM1.8 million is arrived at by calculating the central forward rate for DM/$ (which is in turn a function of the spot exchange rate and the spot interest rates for a one year maturity in each of the currencies), adding the seller's spread and then adding a further amount to take account of the risk to the seller that the buyer will be unable to provide the DM1.8 million when the contract matures. In what follows we shall ignore credit risk (thus

The Corporate Hedging Decision

implicitly assuming that the buyer falls into the best possible credit rating category). For the time being we shall also ignore bid–offer spreads, and we shall assume that transactions costs are zero. Given these simplifications, the exchange rate written into the forward contract will be the forward rate for the currencies concerned.

The payoff to the buyer of the forward contract at expiration will depend upon the difference between the rate in the contract and the spot rate at expiration multiplied by the amount on which the contract is written. Applying this to our example gives a payoff as DM1 $(S - 1.80)$ million, where S denotes the spot rate at expiration.

There has been a considerable amount of research which suggests that, in liquid markets with no institutional constraints, the forward exchange rate is an unbiased predictor of future spot rates. If this is so, the expected value of the payoff to a forward contract will be zero. To put matters in another way, the process of repeatedly hedging over a fixed period could be expected to generate zero profits and, given enough repetitions, would actually produce zero profits.

It follows from this that, if hedging with forward contracts is to produce a profit, the hedger must be able to outperform the forward rate. That is, the buyer must at least either identify a period in which the spot rate will turn out to be lower than the forward rate and leave the position unhedged, or identify a period in which the spot rate will turn out to be higher than the forward rate and hedge for a sum greater than his underlying exposure. As we have already pointed out in Section 9.5.5, believers in the efficiency of markets would argue that such an ability is very rare indeed.

So far we have set the discussion of these issues in terms of currency forward contracts. However, the same issues apply in other markets and to other products. As we have seen, interest rate forward contracts (FRAs) also have forward rates written into them. Research in this area also suggests that forward interest rates are unbiased predictors of future spot rates. Thus, profitably hedging interest rate exposure with interest rate forwards also involves outperforming the forward rate.

Futures and swaps, whether on currencies or on interest rates, also embody forward rates in their prices. Options, too, involve the same issues. The payoff at expiration to the holder of an option can never be negative, but the premium which must be paid for the option is meant to reflect this. The expected value of buying a fairly priced option and holding it to expiration is zero. Repeated hedging with options will produce no greater profits than repeated hedging with the other three instruments.

Let us briefly sum up the argument so far. What we are claiming is that using hedging of the kind we have just outlined is unlikely to yield profits. That is, the hedging activity in itself will not be profitable. That is not the same thing at all as claiming that hedging is useless. In the circumstances outlined above, hedging will improve the overall value of the firm and will therefore be well worth while. The hedger should use instruments which are simple to administer and should hedge his exposure for as long as it will be seen or for as long as it can be predicted with any accuracy. If instruments of long enough maturity are unavailable (either in the market or through synthetics) the more distant exposure must be left unhedged.

Somehow, though, this approach seems at odds with casual empiricism, which suggests that a great deal of very active and successful hedging and speculation is going on. There are several possible reasons for this. First, forward rates are far from accurate predictors, even if unbiased. Over limited periods, many other forecasting methods will perform better than the forward, and the search for and application of these methods may drive many of the users of hedging instruments. There may be occasions where even though the brain accepts the 'efficient markets' view of the world, the heart does not. For example in February 1985 both spot and forward rates showed the dollar close to parity against the pound sterling. To many people the gross relative overvaluation of the dollar seemed unsustainable, and some large positions were taken as a result. Conversely, in late 1980 and early 1981, when the dollar traded in spot and forward markets close to $2.40 against the pound, its relative undervaluation was seen as unsustainable. Many participants in the market acted upon these feelings and used financial instruments such as currency forwards to lock in a rate close to $2.40, often with some success. In these situations, some lessons can be drawn for the use of different hedging instruments. For a company highly exposed to the $/£ exchange rate due to large exports from the UK, locking in the 1985 dollar rate with forward contracts would have guaranteed a high profit margin. In 1988, with a strong pound, the use of forwards would have meant locking in a smaller profit or possibly a loss; at this end of the cycle the use of options was more advisable.

Although reports of successful hedging abound, we should retain a reasonable degree of scepticism. The fallibility of human nature and memory may play a part here. Asked about their past performance, hedgers may well tend to remember their successes rather than their failures!

Furthermore, sampling techniques may be defective. Successful hedgers may retain their jobs while unsuccessful hedgers are quickly moved on. A sample of current hedgers whose records can be examined may therefore contain a disproportionate number of successful hedgers and so be unrepresentative of the hedging population.

The Corporate Hedging Decision

Also the criteria of success may be flawed; correct or good prediction may be confused with outperforming the market. Thus, after a period in which interest rates have fluctuated greatly, a hedger may point to his success in anticipating the movements up and down and in changing the interest sensitivity of his loans or deposits accordingly. However, to the extent that the actual spot rates corresponded to the forward rates implied in the yield curve at the start of the period, this active hedging policy may not really have reduced borrowing rates or raised deposit rates. Indeed, it may have been expensive in terms of transactions costs. Similar (but cheaper) results would have been obtained from fixed rate loans or deposits arranged at the start of the period and left untouched until the end.

Finally, hedging instruments have non-hedging uses. Thus some of the activity which may look like hedging could owe its origins to other factors. We look at this issue in Chapter 11.

10.5 Quantifying Corporate Exposure

In this section we discuss one of the possible methods of identifying and quantifying a company's exposure profiles. It should be stressed at the outset that the approach adopted here is somewhat rough and ready, but it does provide a starting point for a more detailed analysis.

In Section 10.3.5 we suggested that hedging carried out by corporate management would be redundant in the case where shareholders hold well-diversified portfolios. The shareholders would have eliminated the unsystematic risk themselves and would clearly not wish corporate management to use their resources to hedge such (unsystematic) volatility as well! However, we have also outlined the instances in which the shareholders would wish corporate managers to undertake hedging activity. In general, these would be occasions where hedging at the corporate level adds value to the company.

We start by accepting Sharpe's model as a description of the process generating expected returns, which implicitly assumes that shareholders hold diversified portfolios and are therefore only interested in systematic risk. If there was no price volatility (no interest rate changes, foreign exchange rate changes and so on) over a period, the return on any share would be equal to its β multiplied by the return on the market.

If there is price volatility over a period, it is likely that it would impact on the market (causing the return on the market to change) and that it would also impact on the return on the individual share. What we are interested in measuring is the share price return over and above the

208   *The Corporate Hedging Decision*

systematic movement. Once we have identified that element in the share price return, it is possible to relate it to the external price volatility.
Our model is of the form:

$$R_{i,0-1} - \beta_{i,M}R_{M,0-1} = \alpha_i + \beta_{i,1}R_{P1} + \ldots + \beta_{i,j}R_{Pj} + \epsilon_i$$

where the notation is as follows:

$R_{i,0-1}$ realized return on company i's shares over the period $t=0$ to $t=1$
α_i intercept term
$\beta_{i,M}$ company i's market beta coefficient based on historic data over a period ending at $t=0$
$R_{M,0-1}$ realized return on a market index over the period $t=0$ to $t=1$
$\beta_{i,j}$ company i's sensitivity to unanticipated changes in R_{Pj}
R_{Pj} realized return to any economic variable calculated as the percentage change in the price of the economic variable over the period $t=0$ to $t=1$
ϵ_i error term, which is a random variable with an expected value of zero.

10.5.1 Case Study: World Travel Group

The model is most easily explained by outlining the hypothetical historical data that we would need to carry out such a risk exposure analysis for the World Travel Group PLC that we met in Section 2.8. The data are:

* WTG's share price returns from say, month 1 to month 100
* The monthly returns on a market-wide index, say the FT-SE index, for the same 100 months.
* The monthly return on holding a barrel of oil over the period from month 61 to month 100.
* The monthly return on holding one dollar, one peseta and one Turkish lira over the period from month 61 to month 100.

We start by calculating WTG's market β by regression WTG's share price returns against the returns on the FT-SE index using the first 60 months' data.

Now consider month 61. We know the historic return on WTG's share in month 61 and we also know the return on the market for month 61. WTG's expected return for month 61 would be the return on the FT-SE index in month 61 times WTG's β calculated over the period from month 1 to month 60. The difference between WTG's actual share price return in month 61 and the expected return for month 61 is what we are

The Corporate Hedging Decision

interested in, and this is the first value of our dependent variable. We can now relate this 'unexpected' return (or abnormal return) to the unexpected changes in interest rates, foreign exchange rates, commodity prices and so on that are observed in month 61.

This exercise is now replicated using data for each of the months 62 to 100. It is now possible to regress the 40 dependent observations (months 61 to 100) against the corresponding independent variables measuring unexpected changes in interest rates and so on.

10.5.2 Case Study: Sears PLC

To give perhaps a more concrete example, the same model was applied to a British quoted company, Sears PLC, one of the UK's leading retailing groups with some 6000 outlets in the US, the UK and mainland Europe.

The following independent variables were defined:

R_M realized monthly return on the *Financial Times* All-Share Index
$R_{£/Y}$ realized monthly return on holding one yen
$R_{£/\$}$ realized monthly return on holding one dollar
$R_{£/DM}$ realized monthly return on holding one Deutschmark
R_{oil} realized monthly return on holding one barrel of oil
R_{int} realized monthly change (return) in three month LIBOR.

In all cases the returns have been computed by calculating the price change in each month as a percentage of each opening monthly value. They are positively signed when, respectively, interest rates rise, each currency rises against sterling, and oil prices rise.

The result of regressing Sear's monthly unexpected returns against the five independent variables indicates:

$$\text{unexpected return} = \alpha_i + \beta_{int}R_{int} + \beta_{£/Y}R_{£/Y} - \beta_{£/\$}R_{£/\$} -$$
$$(-0.37) \quad (+1.04) \quad (+2.46) \quad (-2.62)$$

$$\beta_{£/DM}R_{£/DM} + \beta_{oil}R_{oil}$$
$$(-1.72) \quad\quad (+1.62)$$

T-statistics are in parentheses, and the R^2 statistic is 34%. We consider the coefficients that are significant at the 95% level.

The positive coefficient on the £/yen return series suggests that firm cash flow expectations may be revised upwards in response to a weakening of the pound *vis-à-vis* the yen. The negative coefficients on the other exchange rate variables indicate that cash flow expectations are revised downwards in response to a weakening of the pound *vis-à-vis* either the US dollar or the Deutschmark. The yen exposure is intriguing because the firm has no operations in Japan; nor does it seem that Japan is an important supplier of the footwear and fashion goods that Sears sells. However, the coefficient could be a sign of a hidden interrelationship between Sears's firm value and the value of the yen. This could result from, say, the firm targeting the purchase of goods that are priced in a third currency, are in limited supply and are also the buying target of Japanese retailers.

There is, though, always an alternative interpretation for the coefficients of economic variables. For example, the positive coefficient on the £/yen return series might indicate the firm's relative insensitivity to unanticipated changes in this exchange rate that negatively impact the overall UK market. Sears's annual report cites tourist spending at its department store Selfridges as an important determinant of its performance, so the increased spending by yen earning tourists that could result from a higher £/yen rate might dampen the market-wide negative impact of a weaker pound.

Risk exposure to the dollar and the Deutschmark could occur because the firm has outlets in the UK and in West Germany and countries whose currencies are linked to the Deutschmark. A weaker pound would increase operating costs denominated in dollars and Deutschmarks and could lower the pound denominated mark-up on purchased goods not priced in sterling, though it would also increase dollar and Deutschmark profits translated into pounds. The negative coefficients could be a sign that the latter effect is being denominated by the two former detrimental ones.

Taking the Sears regression coefficients at face value suggests that a 1% increase in the £/$ rate would have reduced Sears's market capitalization by an amount in the region of £21 million.

It is important to stress here that we are not suggesting that the coefficients on the economic variables (such as on interest rates and oil) are elements of systematic (reward bearing) risk. It may well be the case that replicating the regression on a well-diversified portfolio, made up of a large number of securities, would not record significant coefficients on any variable apart from the market return. Nonetheless, as we have explained earlier, it is still important for corporate management to know and to be able to quantify the firm's susceptibility to (unexpected) changes in the price of economic variables relative to the market. In running the regression, we are effectively measuring such a susceptibility. In other words, the unexpected price movements might impact on the market return and on the firm, but the coefficients noted above measure the effect of such movements on firm value over and above their market impact.

One caveat needs to be mentioned regarding our results. We do not know what level of hedging had been undertaken over the period. It may be that Sears, for instance, did undertake hedging activity. If that was the case, our coefficients measure the firm's exposure to changes in the price of economic variables over and above the systematic market-wide effect and the level of hedging undertaken.

11
Further Uses of Derivative Products

11.1 Introduction

So far we have tended to consider the use of the building-blocks in the context of simple exposure management. However, as financial institutions have gained experience in handling them, so an increasing range of uses has emerged. We now turn to some of these uses, illustrating each with examples.

11.2 Exploiting Opportunities for Arbitrage

Government action may lead to opportunities for regulatory arbitrage. For example, the authorities in country X may decide to make a limited amount of long term funds available at a specially low rate of interest, perhaps to stimulate long term investment. If the rate is lower than normal market rates, there will be plenty of would-be borrowers, particularly if there are few strings attached to the loan. The funds may well have to be rationed by some sort of queueing system under which borrowers have to wait their turn for funds. At first glance it may seem as if, because the funds are paid out only in country X's currency, cheap funds are not available in another currency. However, this is not so. By borrowing in country X's currency and entering into a currency swap between country X's currency and country Y's, a borrower can make for himself a loan denominated in country Y's currency which still contains the interest rate subsidy.

An illustration may be helpful here. Suppose that interest rates are as follows:

Further Uses of Derivative Products

	Country X (%)		Country Y (%)	
	Zero	Par	Zero	Par
Six months	8.0		4.5	
Twelve months	10.0	9.72	5.0	4.93

Suppose also that the spot exchange rate is 1.00X/1.80Y. (These are the same figures as we used in our currency swap example in Section 6.1.) Finally, suppose that country X now offers special access to one year funds at 2% below market rates.

A borrower based in country Y now borrows 100X for twelve months at 7.72% (that is, 9.72% − 2%). This means that the borrower will have to pay 3.86X in six months' time and 103.86X at the end of one year. He now enters into a currency swap on the same terms as we discussed in Section 6.1. As a result, he pays out 100X today, 4.44Y in six months' time and 184.44Y at the end of the year. In return he receives 180Y today, 4.86X in six months' time and 104.86X at the end of one year. Let us now summarize the borrower's cash flows:

	Loan in X	+	Swap	
Today	+100X	−100X	+180Y
Six months' time	−3.86X	−4.44Y	+ 4.86X
One year's time	−103.86X	−184.44Y	+104.86X

	= Loan in Y + subsidy
Today	= +180Y
Six months' time	= −4.44Y + 1.00X
One year's time	= −184.44Y + 1.00X

The final column shows figures which are the same as those associated with an ordinary borrowing of 180Y made in country Y (+180Y − 4.44Y − 184.44Y) with an additional two inflows of 1.00X. At today's spot exchange rate each of these inflows is valued as 1.80Y, thus providing what could be loosely described as a 2% subsidy on the 180Y loan.

To give another example of arbitrage, consider a situation known as credit arbitrage. Suppose that company AAA can borrow fixed at 10.8% and floating at LIBOR + 0.25%, while company BBB can borrow fixed at 12.0% and floating at LIBOR + 0.75%. As would be expected, either type of borrowing is cheaper for AAA than for BBB. However, the credit spread between the companies is different for the two types of borrowing.

In this case the two companies can use a swap to reduce their borrowing costs. AAA borrows fixed at 10.8% while BBB borrows floating at LIBOR + 0.75%. AAA and BBB then do a fixed–floating swap, with the fixed rate (x%) determined by the proportion in which they wish to share the savings. That is, AAA receives $x\%$ and pays LIBOR, while BBB receives LIBOR and pays $x\%$. Therefore, net, AAA borrows at LIBOR + 10.8% − $x\%$, while BBB borrows at $x\%$ + 0.75%.

Suppose they wish to share the saving equally. Then they will set x at 10.9%. Hence AAA borrows at LIBOR − 0.1%, and BBB borrows at 11.65%. Thus each company borrows at a rate 0.35% below that available to it in the market.

11.3 Matching Borrowing Costs to Ability to Pay

Many institutions – for example sellers of consumer durables or real estate developers – find that, because of their customers' sensitivity to interest rates, their sales revenues are reduced when interest rates rise. Hence if they finance their operations by means of an ordinary floating rate loan they are doubly exposed, with their debt servicing costs rising just as the income available for debt servicing falls.

At first this may seem an unfortunate but insoluble problem. However, many banks now offer reverse floating loans whose charges are inversely related to market interest rates. A loan agreement under which, for example, a borrower pays 18% minus LIBOR rather than LIBOR, provides the required matching of costs and ability to pay and so removes interest rate exposure. This is illustrated in Figure 11.1, which shows exposure plus an ordinary floating rate loan in the top part and exposure plus a reverse floating loan in the bottom part. Innovative as a reverse floating loan may seem, it is no more than an ordinary floating loan coupled with a fixed–floating interest rate swap whose notional principal is twice that of the loan amount.

To give another example, a while ago the price of oil fell below $10 per barrel, thus forcing a well-known oil company to increase its borrowings. However, because the lower oil price lowered the company's credit rating, it found itself being asked to pay higher interest charges just at the time it needed the money! This problem was solved by issuing a bond which (in essence) paid the greater of either 11% per annum (where 11% was considerably below the rate which the company would normally have to pay) or the value of half a barrel of oil per $100 borrowed.

Under this arrangement, the purchasers of the bond also held call options on the price of oil which took their value in the form of a 'subsidized' interest rate. While the oil price remained below $22 per barrel and the company was relatively badly off, the company paid an exceptionally low rate of interest. When the oil price rose above $22, the

Further Uses of Derivative Products 215

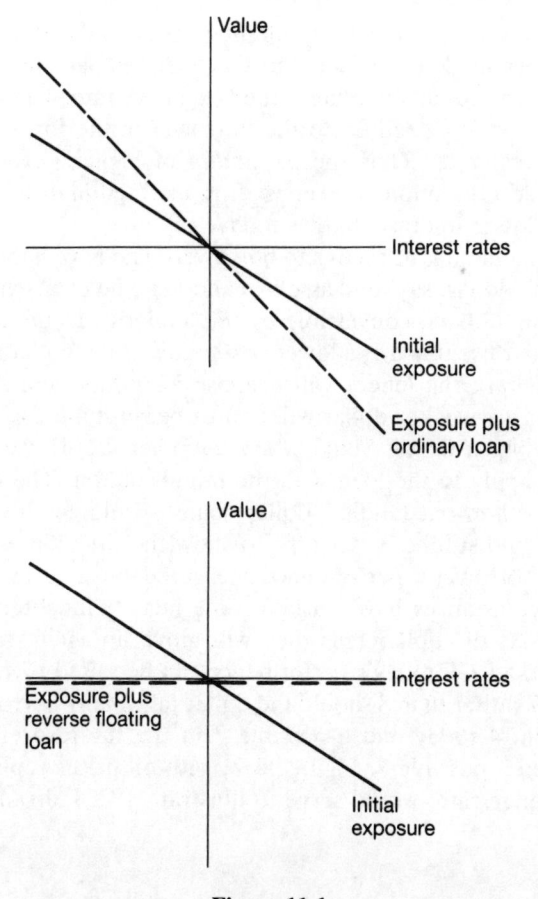

Figure 11.1

company paid the higher interest rates, but at a time when the company was cash rich and well able to pay these rates. Figure 11.2 serves to illustrate this arrangement.

Wouldn't it be helpful to a gold mining firm, which is exposed to fluctuations both in gold prices and also in interest rates, to be able to finance its operation in gold; that is, to make interest and principal payments in the form of gold and thus protect itself from fluctuations both in interest rates and in gold? What a novel approach – yet banks have already made loans with both principal and interest payments fully denominated in gold!

In the exchange rate context, a further example of this kind of management is a currency conversion facility (CCF), sometimes called – a little misleadingly – a dual currency loan. Under this facility a borrower takes out a loan and simultaneously gives the lender the right, at a predetermined future date, to convert the loan into a specified alternative currency at a predetermined exchange rate. The value of this currency option is passed on to the borrower in the form of a below-market interest rate. Thus the *possibility* of higher payments in the future, should the option be exercised, is accepted in order to gain the *certainty* of lower interest charges today.[1]

This arrangement is attractive to borrowers who have liabilities in one currency (the dollar, say) and assets in another (the Deutschmark, say). By borrowing dollars, convertible by the lender to Deutschmarks, the borrower can raise funds at a lower cost today. If the dollar falls against the Deutschmark the lender will exercise his option and some of the benefit from the weaker dollar will be lost because the cost of the loan will then be higher than it would have been otherwise. However, the loss would only apply to the loan with the inbuilt option. The costs of the borrower's other outstanding dollar loans would be lower, so the borrower would still be better off. To show the situation another way, think of a borrower's performance measured on a scale of 0 to 10. Today's circumstances have pushed some heavily indebted borrowers down to 3. As the dollar falls they will move up again, say to 8. By entering into a CCF today's performance can be raised to 4, at the cost of rising to 7 rather than 8 should the dollar fall. Many borrowers would find a certain 4 today and a possible 7 in the future preferable to a certain 3 and a possible 8. Figure 11.2, with oil prices replaced by the $/DM exchange rate, would serve to illustrate a CCF arrangement.

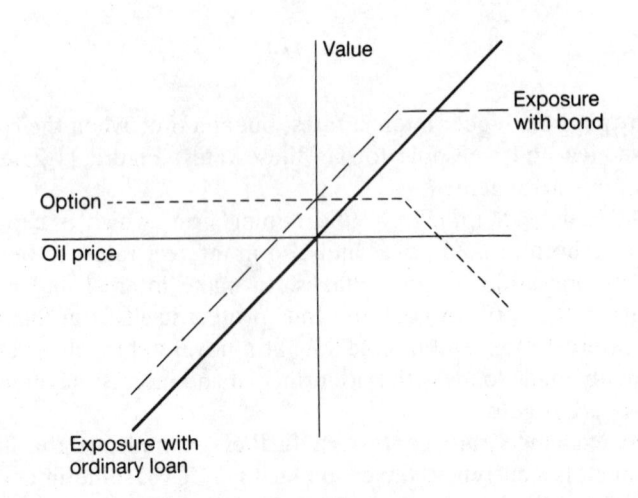

Figure 11.2

Of course, each of these uses can be reversed to make similar changes to rates earned by depositors, rather than to rates paid by borrowers.

11.4 Time and Tax Transformation

In some cases, it is possible to use the building-blocks of financial engineering to transform cash flows over time. An example would be an off-market swap.

Consider an ordinary swap of the kind discussed in Chapter 6. Normally the swap is arranged so that, at inception, the present value of the expected payments on one side of the swap is equal to the present value of those on the other side. Apart from transaction costs, no money changes hands at the time when the swap is set up. However, if one side is set above (or below the current market rate), the expected future cash flows will have different present values so that one counterparty will receive (or pay) cash at the time the swap is set up. This way, provided the tax regulations permit it, a company which currently faces a low rate of tax but which expects a higher tax rate in the future may enter into an off-market swap, which gives it a cash inflow today (taxed at the lower rate) while increasing its cash outflows in the future and thus taking advantage of higher tax relief on its interest payments. By transforming the time profile of its flows, the company has reduced its tax liability. Similar results can be obtained by selling (buying) in-the-money call options and buying (selling) out-of-the-money put options.

Even the simple forward contract can be used to transform cash flows and tax liabilities. For example, country A's interest rates may lie 10% below country B's. This may encourage borrowers in country B to borrow country A's currency and so enjoy lower interest rates. However, this would leave them exposed to exchange rate movements which might more than offset the interest rate gain. This risk can be removed by buying country A's currency forward but, as we have shown, the forward rates will reflect the interest rate differential and so raise the cost of borrowing A's currency until it is equal to that of borrowing B's. However, the pattern of the cash flows will be different. For example a fixed rate loan in B's currency will involve constant high interest payments followed by the repayment of principal. A fixed rate loan for the same amount denominated in A's currency and covered on the forward market will involve initially low, but rising, interest payments followed by a repayment larger than the initial principal. The difference in the two cash flows may make one type of loan preferable to the other,[2] while tax allowances or different tax treatments of interest and principal may again make one loan preferable to another for the borrower and/or the lender.

11.5 Reducing Posted Borrowing Rates

A kind of competition between corporate treasurers seems to be emerging under which participants seek to announce ever-lower borrowing rates. The usual way in which these rates are expressed is with reference to LIBOR. Hence, a treasurer announcing LIBOR plus 20 basis points appears less competent than one announcing LIBOR minus 10 points, and so on.

On the surface such a competition seems laudable. Part of the treasurer's responsibility is to obtain the best possible terms for his or her company. However, the pressure on the treasurer to present borrowing costs in this format may now be leading him away from straightforward cost reduction techniques towards those which contain an element of illusion and even potential danger.

To illustrate some of the possibilities, let us consider a company which is normally able to raise a LIBOR-based floating rate loan at a rate exactly equal to LIBOR. In what ways can this company arrange some other type of loan so that its borrowing charges can be expressed as LIBOR minus x basis points?

One way is to take advantage of regulatory arbitrage (see Section 11.2). A government might provide specially cheap lending to support a particular objective. A company might remain in a queue long enough to qualify for some cheap, but rationed, funds which it doesn't really need. It can then 'sell' these funds to another company which needs them but which hasn't been in the queue long enough to qualify. The first company can take the proceeds in the form not of up-front cash but of an interest rate subsidy, which it can add to its LIBOR borrowing to produce the magic LIBOR minus x quotation.

Another way is to take advantage of competition. A particular bank may wish to enter into or even to create a new market, such as the Eurocommercial paper market. It may be willing to offer special below-market rates to the first few customers which it can introduce to this market. In such a case a quotation of LIBOR minus x can represent a genuine below-market rate of interest.

A further way in which rates can be changed is to accept increased risk and to us the reward to 'subsidize' borrowing costs. To give an example, the oil company which we discussed in Section 11.3 raised funds and contracted to make regular minimum interest payments

Further Uses of Derivative Products

together with additional payments should the price of oil rise above a specified price. The regular minimum interest payment was substantially below the normal market rate and was expressed in terms of LIBOR minus x. However, the reason for the apparently low rate was that this arrangement involved the sale by the borrowing company of call options on oil. Instead of selling the options for outright cash, the company chose to take the revenue in the form of an interest rate subsidy.

A deal of this kind can be presented to the unwary as 'cheap money' and hence as something for nothing, but such a presentation is at best misleading and at worst dishonest. The buyer runs the risk that, should oil prices rise sufficiently, it will pay above-market interest rates. Below-market rates at the outset are no more than the reward for the risk taking. Of course, the decision to take the risk and so enjoy the rewards may be perfectly sensible. If oil prices rise the company will have to pay more but it will also be enjoying higher sales revenues and so can afford to pay more. In the meantime it enjoys low borrowing costs just when its sales are weak. However sensible the decision may be, though, an honest presentation requires that the risk issue be addressed. This type of deal involves more than simply cheap money and should be presented as such. Bonds with warrants provide another, quite common, vehicle for risk taking by selling options and taking the revenue in the form of subsidized interest.

Finally, we turn to arrangements which are sometimes used purely for window dressing. These involve some kind of sleight of hand which appears to reduce the cost of borrowing without actually making any real change at all. Perhaps the most dramatic of these is the reset swap. When the current yield curve is strongly upward sloping, the reset swap can be presented in terms such as 'pay LIBOR minus 52 basis points, receive fixed', while the ordinary or 'plain vanilla' swap might be presented as 'pay LIBOR, receive fixed'. This looks as if the company is saving 52 basis points, but in fact there is no real saving at all. The trick is to redefine LIBOR by altering the relation between the interest rate used to determine the amount to be paid and the date on which the payment is made. Under the plain vanilla swap with floating payments made at six monthly intervals, interest is paid in arrears; the amount paid today is determined by reference to the six month interest rate seen in the market six months ago. Under the reset swap, the amount paid today is determined by the six month interest rate seen today. Hence the expected net present value of the interest payments under the reset swap will exceed those under the ordinary swap. In order to give the two flows equal present value, the reset swap must be quoted as 'LIBOR minus' if the plain vanilla swap is quoted as LIBOR.

220 Further Uses of Derivative Products

The details of the calculations are as follows. Suppose today's LIBOR yield curve shows the following interest rate pattern:

Six month rate   9.0%
Twelve month rate   9.5%
Eighteen month rate 10.0%

A one year plain vanilla swap with a difference cheque exchanged every six months would involve one party contracting to pay LIBOR in arrears and the other party contracting to pay a fixed rate of interest. The party paying the variable rate would view the swap as follows:

- Today: swap agreement signed.
- Six months hence: pays 9% interest and receives prearranged x% interest.
- Twelve months hence: pay interest according to six month LIBOR six months hence and receive prearranged x% interest.

Like all such financial instruments the interest rate x% will be set such that (excluding fees and spread) the expected net present value of the swap will be zero. This involves calculating x% such that the net present value of two payments of x% is equal to the net present value of one payment of 9% followed by another at today's six month forward rate.

Today's forward rate for six months hence can be calculated from today's (spot) yield curve by using the arbitrage equation (see Section 4.2.1):

$$(1 + 0.09/2)(1 + {_6R_{12}}/2) = 1 + 0.095$$

This gives ${_6R_{12}} = 0.0957$ or 9.57%. This six month forward rate is higher than either of the spot rates – something which is a normal feature of a strongly upward sloping yield curve.

To find the fixed rate x% we have to equate the net present value of the two cash flows in the swap:

$$\frac{4.5}{1 + 0.09/2} + \frac{4.785}{1 + 0.095} = \frac{x/2}{1 + 0.09/2} + \frac{x/2}{1 + 0.095}$$

This gives $x = 9.28$. Thus the fixed rate in the swap is 9.28%

Let us now sum up the argument so far. The swap party agrees today to pay LIBOR and to receive fixed interest payments of 9.28%. He knows that in six months' time he will pay £4.50 on each £100 notional principal (as indicated by today's six month interest rate of 9%) and he will receive £4.64 as indicated by the 9.28% swap rate. He will not know the amount of his second payment until six months have elapsed, but today's yield curve indicates a forward rate of 9.57%. If this is what the six month interest rate actually turns out to be he will pay £4.785 as his second payment and will receive £4.64. Today's net present value of these flows is zero.

Under the reset swap the relevant interest rates are those prevailing in the market when the payment is made. The amount of the first payment will be determined by the six month rate in six months' time and the second by the six month rate in twelve months' time. Using the figures shown above, the plain vanilla swap will involve a 9% rate for the first payment while today's forward rate shows a 9.57% rate for the second payment. By contrast, the expected payments to be made under the floating side of the reset swap will reflect today's forward rate of 9.57% for the first payment and 10.04% for the second payment (calculated by applying the arbitrage equation of Section 4.2.1 to today's twelve month and today's eighteen month rates). The fixed side of each swap will be 9.28%. The plain vanilla swap has an expected net present value of zero. The reset swap, with its higher expected floating interest payments, has a negative net present value. In order to give the reset swap a zero net present value, each of the two floating interest payments must be reduced by 52 basis points. Thus the ordinary swap quotation would be given as received fixed and pay LIBOR, while the reset swap quotation – however misleading it may be – would be LIBOR minus 52 basis points!

The message of all this is simple: there simply is no free lunch. If LIBOR is the market rate, lower rates cannot be obtained for nothing. Either the borrower must extract a subsidy from someone else, or the borrower must sell something to provide income which can be used to provide a subsidy. Anything else, such as quoting a reset swap in the same way as a plain vanilla swap, is pure window dressing!

Note that the issue here is one of presentation. Properly presented, reset swaps are a useful innovation to many users. An obvious user would be someone prepared to take a view which differed from the market. The steeper the yield curve, the higher the forward rates contained in it, and hence the greater the amount subtracted from LIBOR in the reset swap quotation. Someone who thought that interest rates would actually fall well below those forward rates would find a reset swap much more attractive than an ordinary swap and, if he were proved correct, the interest costs would indeed be much lower.

11.6 Conclusion

Financial engineering is a rapidly growing area of activity. This reflects the demand for protection in today's volatile world and the ability of the financial system to provide instruments which give such protection.

Increased familiarity with the instruments reveals a growing range of possible uses for them. It is a rare problem which cannot be solved, or at least greatly reduced, by applying the building-block approach of financial engineering.

12
A Brief Look at the Future

In this final short chapter we offer a hostage to fortune and make some suggestions as to the future development of financial engineering.

As we have seen, a major force for the growth of financial engineering has been the increased volatility of financial prices. A forecast of greater stability in these prices would almost certainly lead to a forecast of declining demand for financial engineering.

There are some pointers towards greater stability. There is increased cooperation among the central banks of the Group of Seven (G7) countries on exchange rate stabilization policies. In addition, there is a long term movement towards a tighter exchange rate mechanism within the European Monetary System, with the possibility of eventual currency union.

On the other hand, there are still many signs pointing towards continued volatility. Many countries of the world pursue economic policies which relate to their domestic economies rather than to the international situation, and this often produces divergences in growth rates, inflation rates and balance of payments flows. These divergences in turn tend to lead to large swings in interest rates and exchange rates. The declining economic power of the United States relative to many other countries in the world is a factor which has encouraged this process. A further factor suggesting continued volatility is the tension between the use of the US dollar as a reserve currency and the persistent current account deficit of the US, which forces the country to attract capital inflows from abroad.

The process of globalization is also likely to continue. An increasing number of instruments (and synthetic instruments) will be available in many different locations and in many different time zones. This will reduce arbitrage opportunities and lead to an increasing interdependence among the world's financial markets.

Geographical trends will also lead to important changes. To some extent banking systems depend on the economic strength of their host country. Thus, at the height of the economic power of the British Empire, the British banks dominated the world financial system. Although still important, the influence of British banks has declined along with Britain's economic importance. American banks played a key role in the 1960s and early 1970s but are now declining relative to Japan. As Japan's economic importance grows, so will the power and influence of the Japanese banks.

The whole Pacific basin is growing in importance in terms of both gross national products and also increasingly complex trade and investment flows. The demand for financial engineering is likely to grow faster in this region than anywhere else in the world. However, it must not be forgotten that, despite its fast growth, the region will not overtake the older industrialized areas of the world for some considerable time.

On balance, we expect volatility of financial prices to persist, and therefore we expect continued growth of demand for financial engineering. Within the total growth we expect the use of options and combinations of options such as participations and collars, which allow some individual tailoring of exposures, to grow relative to the use of the simpler instruments such as forwards and swaps, which simply remove exposure. Commodity indexation will spread, with instruments linked to a greater variety of commodities.

We also expect to see a wider range of uses made of existing instruments along the lines discussed in Chapter 11. These are likely to range over the whole field of corporate finance and fund management rather than being concentrated in the narrower risk management sector.

Notes

Chapter 1

1 The name 'derivative products' is used to indicate that the products may be derived from other products and, hence, that the prices of the products depend on the prices of other products. Thus, as we show in Chapter 4, a forward contract can be derived from the spot currency market and the spot markets for borrowing and lending. Some years ago the name 'derivative products' tended to be restricted only to those products which could be derived from spot markets. But, nowadays, the name seems to be used for any product which may be derived from any other.

Chapter 2

1 We have assumed here that the firm continues its operations into the indefinite future and is therefore valued on a going concern basis. This is not, of course, the only approach to corporate valuation but it provides us with a useful starting point to our analysis. Further details on corporate valuation can be found in Copeland and Weston (1988).
2 One of the very important issues which we shall see later is that discount rates reflect the degree of risk associated with the cash flows being discounted.
3 Interested readers are referred to Tiner and Conneely (1987).
4 This case study, which is loosely based on the situation of a British company, was prepared by Dylan Thomas using only publicly available information. It has been simplified and is designed for illustrative teaching purposes only.
5 Figure 2.5 measures the effect of lease interest rate changes on the cash flow attributable to the equity holders in the company. In general the cash flows attached to floating rate obligations are adjusted to take account of interest rate changes so as to leave the present value of the obligation unchanged.
6 We assume here that the securities are held to maturity. An early sale would involve a capital loss, with the result that the cash flows would have been affected by a change in market interest rates.

Chapter 3

1. We should point out that spot rates are usually for delivery after a period of two working days. Thus deals made today refer to a value day two working days ahead. This allows time for documentation and payment to be completed. Thus in a way there is a lag of two working days, and today's spot rate is really a two day forward rate. In what follows, we shall ignore this consideration and use 'spot' and 'today' interchangeably.
2. The market shown in Table 3.1 has a consistent spread of 1/16. Generally world money markets show a spread of 1/8.
3. We have added 'at least' because the bank will usually make a further charge depending upon the borrower's credit-worthiness.
4. Note that, in most markets dealing with maturities longer than one year, compounding and hence the use of exponents is the norm. However, beware of a maturity of less than one year which forms part of a longer series. Some practitioners will continue to use fractions for all periods of less than one year.
5. The spot zero curve assumes only one cash flow at the beginning and one at the end with nothing happening in between, and there are no additional assumptions. In the case of the par rate there are cash flows every six months. *Ex ante* the two cash flow streams have equal present values. *Ex post* they may turn out not to have the same terminal value and therefore not, with hindsight, to have had the same present value. To arrive at the same present or same future value for zero and par rates implies that the reinvestment rates (or discount rates for present value calculations) are indeed those implicit in today's yield curve (for the calculation of implied forward rates see Chapter 4). If these reinvestment rates are not locked in at the beginning of the period (that is, today), then the two transactions ('zero' investment versus 'par' investment) are no longer the same because the latter transaction is subject to interest rate risk. In a very simple way this can be shown by looking at the duration (not maturity) of these two transactions. The zero coupon investment has a duration of exactly two years, while the par rate instrument has a duration of only 1.83 years. However, by locking in all the reinvestment rates for all the intermediate cash flows, the duration would increase to 2.

Chapter 4

1. It is quite common for spot currency and spot interest rates to change frequently. In this case the forward rate for the date in question may also change, thus preventing complete cancellation by means of a reverse contract.
2. Note that yield curves based on different conventions can be unravelled to produce forward rates in analogous ways. Hence in a market where interest is compounded the formula would become $(1 + {_0}R_t)^{t/12} (1 + {_t}R_T)^{(T-t)/12} = (1 + {_0}R_T)^{T/12}$. Markets in which the actual number of days in the month are taken into account would not produce a simple formula but the same

principles would apply. In this case we would replace the general fraction of 1/12 by 28/365, 29/365, 30/365, 31/365 depending on the year and month concerned.
3 Interested readers may like to note one feature of these calculations. If forwards are calculated according to the formula shown in note 2 of this chapter, then a flat yield curve (one whose rates are all equal) will produce forward rates each equal to the single rate shown in the spot yield curve. An upward sloping spot yield curve will produce forward rates progressively higher than those shown in the spot yield curve the further into the future the forwards are calculated. A downward sloping yield curve will produce progressively lower forward rates. Use of the formula shown in the main body of the text will produce slightly less clear-cut results. The production of a whole set of identical forward rates will require a slightly upward sloping spot yield curve. A flatter yield curve will produce progressively declining rates while a steeper yield curve will produce progressively increasing rates.
4 For simplicity, we are ignoring the normal two day delivery process.
5 Note that one (or both) of the parties to the forward contract may fail to honour his obligation, that is may default. Thus the supplier of a forward contract must take into account the central rate, the market's bid–offer spread and the credit risk of the counterparty. As elsewhere in this book, we do not address the issue of measuring credit risk. In general, the longer the time to settlement and the higher the amount of money involved, the greater the credit risk.

Chapter 5

1 Arbitrage activity usually involves selling the overpriced instrument and buying the underpriced substitute. Here we are selling the higher interest rate and buying the lower interest rate. Thus we buy forward contracts, and because the futures contract price is quoted as (100 − interest rate) we need to buy futures contracts.
2 Usually referred to as the cash bond. It is usual in futures markets to refer to the cash market rather than the spot market.
3 Apart from the usual transaction costs and risks, the particular delivery procedure for bond futures leaves some uncertainties which have been discussed above.
4 At the time of writing a forward market in the FT-SE index is emerging.

Chapter 6

1 Note that we are talking only of market valuations. The subjective value of the two payment streams need not be equal, of course. Party B may well feel that the forward exchange rate for the dollar will be far above 1.7182 and may

expect to gain from the swap. Party A may feel that the dollar will be far below 1.7182 and may also expect to gain from the swap. In the event, if one party to the swap turns out to have gained from the swap the other will turn out to have lost. The expectation of a gain is not the only explanation for a party's willingness to enter into a swap. Although some participants in the swap market may be taking positions or 'speculating', many will be interested only in hedging to remove currency risk by locking in guaranteed rates for the future and will not be interested in making any special gain on their swap position. Still others may be using a swap to take advantage of some arbitrage opportunity offered between the two markets involved. We discuss this at greater length in Chapters 9 and 10.

2 As in the case of the currency swap we are talking about market value rather than individual subjective value.

3 Efficient market theory suggests that today's forward rate is the best of all possible estimates of the future spot. We should also note that the use of an FRA would lock in the effective rate in six months' time and so give the swap a certain present value of zero.

4 It can be seen that a similar process could be used to value a swap at any time during its life.

5 To give a numerical example, suppose that, instead of the series of six monthly interest rates (12.1944%, 12.4934%, 12.8130%, 13.5033%) which were implied when the swap was signed, rates actually turned out to be 12.1944%, 12.4934%, 13% and 14%, so that B made to A the series of payments £5.9218, £6.0629, £6.30145 and £6.77078. In this case the terminal value of A's payments to B turns out to be

$$£6.1689(1.124934)^{1/2}(1.13)^{1/2}(1.14)^{1/2} + 6.1689(1.13)^{1/2}(1.14)^{1/2}$$
$$+ 6.1689(1.14)^{1/2} + 6.1689 = £27.1832$$

The terminal value of B's payments to A turns out to be

$$£5.9218(1.124934)^{1/2}(1.13)^{1/2}(1.14)^{1/2} + 6.0629(1.13)^{1/2}(1.14)^{1/2}$$
$$+ 6.30145(1.14)^{1/2} + 6.77078 = £27.5089$$

Thus the $100 swap turns out, at expiration, to have a terminal value of £0.3257 to A matched by a value of −£0.3257 to B.

6 In the early days of swaps a bank used to bring the counterparties together; each counterparty would make its payments to the bank, which would then pass them on to the other counterparty. Sometimes each counterparty was known to the other, sometimes identities were kept secret. Nowadays banks enter into swaps in their own right and a bank may be one of the two counterparties to the swap.

7 With an upward sloping yield curve at the outset of the swap, this is the expected payment pattern. In the case of downward sloping yield curves, the counterparty making the floating rate based payments is expected to pay first and receive in the later periods. This may sometimes create the illusion that a swap in a downward sloping yield curve environment looks 'cheap', since the swap rate is below the current short term interest rates.

Chapter 7

1. In most markets one option contract is usually based on 1000 shares. Thus the holder of one of our call option contracts with an exercise price of £1.50 will have the right, but not the obligation, to purchase 1000 shares for £1500.
2. As usual we are ignoring the bid–offer spreads.
3. The process of holding an asset and writing a call option on the same asset reduces the risk to the writer, and is known as covered call option writing.
4. This might appear rather restrictive in this context, but many real-world events can be described in terms of only two possible outcomes, for example legal judgements. The ideas outlined here in solving this particular problem have a much wider applicability.
5. This is one example of general portfolio construction which will be discussed more fully in Chapter 10.
6. Options, in reality, are written on large numbers of shares and the rounding up or down of the number of shares to be bought does not make a material difference.
7. Our approach to the binomial model and the Black–Scholes model suggests that there is a link between the jumps in the binomial model and the parameters of the Black–Scholes formula. It can be shown that if we denote the upward jump as u, such that if the share price before the jump is S it becomes uS after the jump, $u = e^{\sigma\sqrt{T/n}}$ where n denotes the number of jumps until maturity. Similarly a downward jump, taking the share price from S to dS, can be written as: $d = e^{-\sigma\sqrt{T/n}}$. The probability of an upward jump is $(\hat{R} - d)/(u - d)$ while that of a downward jump is $1 - (\hat{R} - d)/(u - d)$ where $\hat{R} = R^{T/n}$.
8. Strictly speaking the intrinsic value is the difference between the current share price and the discounted exercise price. However, this distinction is rarely made in practice.
9. The long put option position can be replicated by selling one-third of the share at t_0 and investing £38.4615 at the 4% risk-free interest rate on the same date. The net cost of this portfolio at t_0 will be £5.1282. The payoffs at t_1 will be £0 and £10.
10. It also works the other way around. If we know the price of puts, we can appeal to the same theorem to price call options.
11. The Black and Scholes formula for determining the price P of a European put option is:

$$P = [SN(d_1) - Xe^{-RT}N(d_2)] - S + Xe^{-RT}$$

Note that the formula is made up of three elements: the first part in the square brackets is the Black and Scholes formula for pricing a European call option, the current share price (S) and the present value of an amount equivalent to the exercise price of the options (Xe^{-RT}). These are, of course, the three elements that comprise the put-call parity in the text.
12. For completeness we have set out below a table, similar to Table 7.2, showing the direction of the movement in European put option prices following changes in the five determining variables:

Changes	Impact on put price
Increase in current share price	↓
Increase in exercise price	↑
Increase in time to expiry	↑
Increase in risk-free rate of interest	↓
Increase in volatility	↑

Chapter 8

1 We shall use $R_\$$ to denote the dollar-based interest rate for the appropriate maturity and R_{DM} to denote the Deutschmark-based rate.
2 In contrast to share options, interest rate options are settled at expiry in the form of a difference cheque. This payoff is, of course, equivalent to paying 10% and receiving the relevant spot rate if this rate is above 10%.
3 Many purchasers prefer to include the price of the cap in the interest payments that they have to pay on the loan. Thus, if the loan were priced according to LIBOR + spread, the capped loan would be priced according to LIBOR + spread + x%. Changing the quotation into this form involves calcplating x such that the net present value of the payments represented by x equals today's cash value of the options. To illustrate this, consider the case of the two period rollover loan which we have used in Section 8.4. The first interest payment is made at the end of year 1, while the second is made at the end of year 2. Suppose that today's cash price of a cap on the second interest payment on a £100 loan is £y. The alternative method of quoting the price would involve the calculation of x such that $y = [x/(1 + {}_0R_1)] + [x/(1 + {}_0R_2)^2]$.
4 This is not quite correct because settlements for the interest payments and payments under the cap are at the end of the interest rate periods. However, at the maturity date of each option the actual payments are no longer uncertain, that is volatility is effectively zero.
5 We need not concern ourselves here with the market assessment of volatility; we just insert a figure of 16% for illustrative purposes.
6 A full premium of £18.6926 for the compound option could also be paid upfront with a refund of £13.9978 at $t=1$ if the option is not exercised. If credit risk considerations are ignored, this does not alter the characteristics of the pricing of this option.

Chapter 9

1 We are dealing here with issues of cash flow. Some countries may require parties to show the contracts on their balance sheets, while accounting laws may require them to estimate their eventual value and to show any changes in their profit and loss accounts.
2 We shall assume that this rate is the market rate as quoted in newspapers, on Reuters screens and so on. Different rates will be quoted to different customers in order to take account of differing credit risks, but we shall not

Notes 231

bother with this issue here. In other words we shall consider deals made between institutions with the best possible credit ratings.

3 We are here taking into account interest payments, both when they accrue to the margin account (as at points B and A) and also when they are forgone on alternatives as the margin account requires topping up (as at points C and E).

4 That is, their net teiminal value will be equal to zero. Because the cash flows occur at different times, their absolute sum will be zero only in the most unusual circumstances.

5 In more technical terms, each is assembled at time $t=0$ from a string of consecutive one day forward contracts, known as forward forwards, spanning the period $t=0$ to $t=T$.

6 This type of discussion leads on to a debate – perhaps not very productive – on what are the fundamental materials from which the instruments can be constructed. Smithson (1987) tends towards the view that there are five basic building-blocks: a foward, a future, a swap, a call option and a put option. Other authors see the two options as the fundamental materials. By pairing a short European put and a long call with the same exercise price one can construct a forward; by taking strings of option pairs one can construct a future or a swap. Other authors follow the Black and Scholes (1973) methodology and argue that the fundamental materials are a forward contract and a riskless security. Combinations of the two produce synthetic options and combinations of the options produce the other three building-blocks.

7 However, remember that a high market price only reflects the high volatility of the underlying currency of the option, given the option is fairly priced.

8 In this section we have discussed the use of financial instruments to modify an initial exposure. This seems to fit the situation of the typical corporation which demands financial engineering to deal with exposures which result from its business activities. The instruments can, of course, be used to create rather than modify exposures. This might fit the situation of a typical speculator. Thus, for example, a speculator who had no exposure but who wanted to gain from dollar volatility could still construct the V-shaped payoff shown in Figure 9.24 but would use a different combination of building-blocks. Without an initial exposure, the V payoff would be produced by the purchase of one call option and one put option each with an exercise price equal to the forward rate. In this context, the combination is often known as a straddle. In general, any payoff produced from an initial exposure plus some building-blocks can also be produced from building-blocks alone. This is clear both in theory and also on the grounds that the initial exposure can itself be thought of as a building-block, namely a short forward.

9 However, it was not impossible for agents to make special one-off arrangements with banks to fix interest rates in advance and so to provide forwards.

Chapter 10

1 We are interested here in getting an estimate of the population statistic. When using sample data, the best estimate of the population statistic is calculated by

dividing through by $n - 1$ observations. In other words we should be dividing through by 11 rather than 12. In calculating these statistics it would be usual to take many more observations, perhaps 60 or more. In such circumstances, it does not make much difference whether we divide through by 59 or 60!
2 Remember $(a + b)^2 = a^2 + b^2 + 2ab$.

Chapter 11

1 Recently the market has seen Eurobonds where the issuer has bought currency options from the investors.
2 For example, the route of borrowing abroad might be helpful for companies which have low cash flows at the outset of a project.

References and Further Reading

General

The following texts cover many of the topics discussed in this book in a general way and will not be cited again in the individual chapter lists.

Antl, B. (ed.) *Management of Currency Risk*, Euromoney, 1989.
Antl, B. (ed.) *Management of Interest Rate Risk*, Euromoney, 1988.
Redhead, K. and Hughes, S. *Financial Risk Management*, Gower, 1988.
Robinson, J. N. 'The growth of financial engineering', *Business Economist*, vol. 19, no. 1, 1987, pp. 5–21.
Solnik, B. *International Investments*, Addison-Wesley, 1988.
Walmsley, J. *The New Financial Instruments*, Wiley, 1988.

Chapter 1

Bank for International Settlements *Recent Innovations in International Banking*, 1986.
Cooper, I. Introduction to the 1987 Gilbart Lectures on Banking, reprinted in *New Financial Instruments*, Chartered Institute of Bankers, 1987, p. vii.

Chapter 2

Copeland, T. E. and Weston, F. J. *Financial Theory and Corporate Policy*, 3rd edn, Addison-Wesley, 1988.
Flood, E. and Lessard, D. R. 'On the measurement of operating exposure to exchange rates: a conceptual approach', *Financial Management*, vol. 15, no. 1, 1986, pp. 25–36.
Lessard, D. R. 'Finance and global competition: exploiting financial scope and

coping with volatile exchange rates', in Porter, M. E. (ed.), *Competition in Global Industries*, Harvard Business School Press, 1986.
Martin, I. J. *Accounting in the Foreign Exchange Market*, Butterworths, 1987.
Oxelheim, L. and Wihlborg, C. *Macroeconomic Uncertainty*, Wiley, 1987.
Tiner, J. I. and Conneely, J. M. *Accounting for Treasury Products*, Woodhead Faulkner, 1987.

Chapter 3

Dodds, J. C. and Ford, J. L. *Expectations, Uncertainty and the Term Structure of Interest Rates*, Martin Robertson, 1974.
Douglas, L. G. *Yield Curve Analysis*, New York Institute of Finance, 1988.

Chapter 4

Dodds, J. C. and Ford, J. L. *Expectations, Uncertainty and the Term Structure of Interest Rates*, Martin Robertson, 1974.
Douglas, L. G. *Yield Curve Analysis*, New York Institute of Finance, 1988.
Heywood, J. *Foreign Exchange and the Corporate Treasurer*, Black, 1978.
McRae, T. W. and Walker, D. P. *Foreign Exchange Management*, Prentice-Hall, 1980.

Chapter 5

Fitzgerald, M. D. *Financial Futures*, Euromoney, 1983.
Kolb, R. W. *Understanding Futures Markets*, 2nd edn., Scott, Foresman, 1988.

Chapter 6

Bicksler, J. and Chen, A. H. 'An economic analysis of interest rate swaps', *Journal of Finance*, vol. 41, no. 3, 1986, pp. 645–55.
Henderson, S. K. and Price, J. A. M. *Currency and Interest Rate Swaps*, Butterworths, 1988.
Turnbull, S. M. 'Swaps: a zero sum game?', *Financial Management*, vol. 17, no. 1, 1987, pp. 15–22.

Chapter 7

Black, F. and Scholes, M. 'The pricing of options and corporate liabilities', *Journal of Political Economy*, vol. 81, May/June 1973, pp. 637–54.

References and Further Reading

Bookstaber, R. M. *Option Pricing and Strategies in Investing*, Addison-Wesley, 1985.

Cox, J. C., Ross, S. A. and Rubinstein, M. 'Option pricing: a simplified approach', *Journal of Financial Economics*, vol. 7, September 1979, pp. 229–63.

Cox, J. C. and Rubinstein, M. *Options Markets*, Prentice-Hall, 1985.

Merton, R. 'Theory of rational option pricing', *Bell Journal of Economics and Management Science*, vol. 4, no. 1, 1973, pp. 141–83.

Rubinstein, M. and Leland, H. 'Replicating options with positions in stock and cash', *Financial Analysts Journal*, vol. 37, no. 4, 1981, pp. 63–71.

Smith, C. W. Jr 'Option pricing: a review', *Journal of Financial Economics*, vol. 4, January/March 1976, pp. 3–53.

Chapter 9

Black, F. and Scholes, M. 'The pricing of options and corporate liabilities', *Journal of Political Economy*, vol. 81, May/June 1973, pp. 637–54.

Smithson, C. W. 'The LEGO approach to financial engineering', *Midland Corporate Finance Journal*, vol. 4, no. 4, 1987, pp. 16–28.

Chapter 10

Portfolio Theory and Asset Pricing Models

Brealey, R. and Myers, S. *Principles of Corporate Finance*, 3rd edn, McGraw-Hill, 1988.

Ross, S. A. and Westerfield, R. W. *Corporate Finance*, Times Mirror/Mosby College, 1988.

Sharpe, W. F. 'A simplified model for portfolio analysis', *Management Science*, vol. 9, no. 2, 1963, pp. 277–93.

Corporate Hedging Policy

Eckl, S. and Robinson, J. N. *Some Issues in Corporate Hedging Policy*, Accounting and Business Research, 1990.

Dufey, G. and Srinivasulu, S. L. 'The case for corporate management of foreign exchange risk', *Financial Management*, vol. 12, no. 4, 1983, pp. 54–62.

Shapiro, A. C. and Titman, S. 'An integrated approach to corporate risk management', *Midland Corporate Finance Journal*, vol. 3, no. 2, 1985, pp. 41–56.

Smith, C. W. and Stulz, R. 'The determinants of firms' hedging policies', *Journal of Financial and Quantitative Analysis*, vol. 20, no. 4, 1985, pp. 391–405.

Using Share Prices to Indicate Exposures

McFadden L., Robinson, J. N. and Thomas, D. *Corporate Hedging Decisions and the Identification of Financial Risk*, Working Paper in Financial Economics no. 3, Chase Manhattan Bank, 1988.

Index

accounting exposure, 11
 measurement, 14–20
 summary, 21–2
Accounting Standards Committee, 14
accounting values, 19
aircraft (World Air costs), 31–2
aircraft values, 34–5
American call option, 96, 123–4
American put option, 96
amortizing swaps, 94
arbitrage, 14, 182
 exploiting opportunities for, 212–14, 218
 pricing theory (APT), 201
 regulatory, 212–14, 218
 risk-free, 43, 44, 48–9, 52, 54–5
 trading, 76, 77–9
Asian options, 150, 151–2, 154
asking price, 43
asset pricing models, 200–1
assets
 monetary and non-monetary, 15–16
 value of, 12–13, 20
Association of British Travel Agents, 27, 36
at-the-money option, 118
average prices, options on, 150, 151–2, 154

back-to-back loan, 85
balance sheet
 accounting exposure, 11, 16–22

passim
 World Travel Group, 29, 30
Bank for International Settlements, 1
banks, 167–8, 223, 224
beating the market, 182–3
bid-ask spread, 43
bid-offer spread, 43–7, 55, 56, 61, 75
bid price, 43
Black, Fischer, 100
Black and Scholes model, 127
 formula, 111–14, 137
 introduction to, 98–103
 pricing on three-year cap, 144, 145–6
 sensitivity in 116–22
 share option pricing computer program, 143
bond futures, 78–9
bonds, long dated, 49–52
borrowing costs, 214–17
borrowing rates, posted (reducing), 218–21
Bretton Woods system, 2
British tour operator (case study), 25
 background, 26–8
 World Travel Group, 28–32
 World Travel Group (suggested exposure profile), 32–41
building-block approach, 10, 155–67
 as insurance policies, 178–81
business practices (tour industry), 26–7

call options, 95
  American, 96
  European, 96–7, 100
  expiration values, 96–7, 98
  on interest rates, 143–7
  pricing, 98–114
  put-call parity, 126–7
  values, 154
capital asset pricing model, 200–1
caps (pricing), 141, 143–7
case studies
  corporate exposures, 208–11
  financial engineering with currency options, 183–4
  identifying exposure, 25–41
  pricing of three-year cap, 144–7
cash bond, 78
cash flows (World Travel Group), 35–9
cash settlement date, 143–4
central banks, 223
central rates, 54, 56, 58
charter airlines (market share), 27–8
'cheap money', 219
Civil Aviation Authority, 27
closing rate method, 17–19
collar, 170
commodity futures, 71
commodity-indexed swaps, 91–2, 224
commodity price exposure (World Travel Group), 32–5
commodity price fluctuations, 2, 5, 20
company valuation, 12–13
competition, 44–5, 55
  perfect, 42–3
compound options, 147–50, 154
continuous price movements, 127
contract settlement
  forward contracts, 68–70
  futures contracts, 81–3
  share options, 131
  swap contracts, 91
convergence, 78
Cooper, I., 1
core business risks, 2, 7
corporate exposure, quantifying, 207–11
corporate hedging decision
  portfolio theory, 189–202

quantifying corporate exposure, 207–11
risk-return relationship, 185–6
statistics, 186–9
users (policies and activities), 202–7
correlation coefficient (corporate hedging), 188–9
cost of carry, 64, 78–9
covariance (corporate hedging), 187–8
simplified: Sharpe's Market Model, 194–200
credit arbitrage, 213
currencies
  forward market for, 54–8
  spot market for, 45
currency conversion facility, 215–16
currency forward contracts, 57–8, 65–6, 156–8
currency futures, 72–6
currency movements, 30, 31
currency options, 134–7
  financial engineering with, 183–4
currency swap agreement, 86
currency swaps, 84–6, 91, 160, 162
customer confidence, 203
cylinder, 170

dealing, 181–2
debt servicing, 214–17
deferred swaps, 93–4
delayed swaps, 93–4
delivery process, 78
demand for holidays (World Travel Group), 37, 38
deposits (spot market for interest rates), 46–53
derivative products, uses of
  building-block approach, 155–67
  case study, 183–4
  financial engineering, 167–78
  instruments as insurance, 178–81
  uses classified, 181–3
derivative products, uses of (increased range)
  borrowing costs/ability to pay, 214–17
  conclusion, 221–2
  exploiting opportunities, 212–14
  posted borrowing rates, 218–21

Index

time and tax transformation, 217–18
Deutschmark currency futures, 72
Deutschmark/pound spot rate, 2, 3
discount rate, 12, 35–6, 203
dividends (option values), 122–4
dollar–mark currency futures, 72
dual currency loan, 215–16
Dufey, G., 202

economic exposure, 11
  company valuation and, 12–13
  expectations and, 13–14
  measurement, 12
  summary, 21–2
environmental factors, 8–9
environmental risk, 2
equity (in company valuation), 12–13
Eurocommercial paper market, 218
Eurodollar interest rates, 2, 4
European call options, 96–7, 100
  Merton's model, 123, 137
  values (sensitivity of), 114–22
European currency call option, 137, 138
European monetary system, 223
European put options, 96, 97–8
exchange rate, 2
  agreement, 69, 75
  forecasting, 8
  forward, 7–8, 54–7
  stabilization policy, 223
  variability, 14–19
  see also foreign exchange
exercise price
  of interest rate option, 144
  option values and, 122–4
  put-call parity, 126, 127–8
expectations, economic exposure and, 13–14
expiration values
  forward contracts, 65–8
  futures contracts, 79–81
  payoff to an option at, 129–31
  share options, 96–8
  swap contract, 90–1
exposure
  accounting *see* accounting exposure
  corporate (quantifying), 207–11
  economic *see* economic exposure
  hidden (and total), 22–5

identifying (case study), 25–41
interest rate, 12–14, 35–9
profile, 7–9, 22–5, 155–6
profile (case study), 32–41
to transaction risk, 15
to translation risk, 15–19

financial engineering
  building-block approach, 167–78
  future development, 223–4
  with currency options (case study), 183–4
financial engineering (growth), 1
  instruments (supply of), 9–10
  volatility and demand for, 2–9
financial futures, 71
financial instruments
  derivative products *see* derivative products, uses of; derivative products, uses of (increased range)
  as insurance, 178–81
  pricing *see* pricing financial instruments (principles)
  supply of, 9–10
  see also forward contracts; futures contracts; share options; swap contracts
fixed assets (book value), 20
fixed-floating swap, 213, 214
floor-ceiling swap, 170
floors (pricing), 143–7
foreign exchange
  agreement, 69
  exposure, 7, 22–3, 39–41
  see also exchange rate
forward band, 170, 171
  construction of, 184
forward contracts
  as building-blocks, 156–8, 159, 162–4
  contract settlement, 68–70
  currency, 57–8
  forward market for currencies, 54–8
  forward market for interest rates, 58–63
  synthetic forward contracts, 64–5
  value at expiration, 65–8
forward exchange rates, 7–8
  calculation, 54–7

forward interest rates
  agreements, 61–3, 66–70, 158, 159, 205
  calculation, 58–61
forward market
  for currencies, 54–8
  for interest rates, 58–63
forward rate agreement, 61–3, 66–79, 205
FT-SE 100 futures contracts, 73, 79, 82
future rate agreement, 158
futures contracts, 71
  as building-blocks, 158–64 *passim*
  contract settlement, 81–3
  currency futures, 72–6
  interest rate futures, 76–9
  stock market index futures, 79
  value of (at expiration), 79–81

geographical trends, 224
German Government bond futures, 76, 83
German importer's exposure (example), 156–8
globalization, 1, 223
gold ingots (markets), 42–5
group of seven (G7) countries, 223

hedge ratio, 104, 106, 108–9
hedging, 22, 182, 183
  building-block approach, 155–6, 163–8
  call option, 163, 165–6
  unsystematic risk, 201–2
  see also corporate hedging decision
hidden exposures, 22–5
Hokkaido Grain Exchange, 71
Holiday Booking Index, 26
holiday receipts (World Travel Group), 37–9
home market, 7

imports, 7, 15
in-the-money option, 118, 171, 172, 217
industrial structure, 24
interest rate
  call options, 141, 143–7
  changes, 19–20
  exposure, 12–14, 35–9

forwards, 58–63, 66–70, 158, 159, 205
  futures, 76–9
  spot market for, 46–53
  subsidies, 214, 218, 219, 221
  swaps, 87–91
  three-month Eurodollar, 2, 4
interest rate options
  practical considerations, 140–3
  preliminaries, 137–40
  pricing caps and floors, 143–7
International Commodities Clearing House, 74–5
intrinsic value, 118

Japan, 224
Japanese Government bond futures, 76, 82
Japanese yen currency futures, 72

'kerosene-indexed swap', 92
Keynesianism, 2

leasing (World Travel Group), 36
LIBOR, 31, 36, 213–14, 218–21
loans
  back-to-back, 85
  dual currency, 215–16
  spot market for interest rates, 46–53
log-normal distribution, 113
London International Financial Futures Exchange, 71, 72–4, 76, 77, 83
long dated bonds, 49–52
long gilt futures, 76, 83
lookback options, 150–1, 152–3, 154

managers (corporate hedging decision), 202–7
margin funds, 80–1, 82
market capitalization, 12
market conventions (differing)
  loans and deposits, 48–9
  par yield loans, 52–3
market maker, 58, 59
market model, Sharpe's, 194–200, 207
market share
  charter airlines, 27–8
  package tours, 26, 27

Index

market value
 of firm, 12
 interest rate swaps, 88
 securities, 20, 22
market-wide index, 195
markets (and traders), 42–5
marking-to-market system, 74, 75, 160, 162–3
mean value (corporate hedging), 186–7
medium gilt futures, 76, 83
Merton, Robert, 123
Merton's model, 123, 137
monetarism, 2
monetary assets, 15–16
monetary liabilities, 15
monopoly, 44

net cash flows, 12–13
net investment method, 17–19
net terminal value, 129–30
New Zealand Futures Exchange, 71
non-monetary items, 15–16
notional principal, 66

off-balance-sheet derivative products, 9
off-market swap, 217
offer price, 43
oil indexation, 92
oil prices, 2, 5, 20–1, 24–5, 214–15, 216, 218–19
 case study, 32–5
operating costs (World Travel Group), 32–4
option delta, 119–21
option expiry date, 143–4
option gamma, 121
option kappa, 122
option lambda, 122
option premium, 100, 128, 129, 147
option replication, 115, 123, 134
 compound options, 150
 currency options, 136–7
 interest rate options, 139–40, 142–3
 introduction to, 140–6
option rho, 122
option theta, 121–2
option values, 122–4
option vega, 122

options
 as building-blocks, 163, 165–7
 see also share options
options (pricing), 132–3
 compound options, 147–50
 currency options, 134–7
 interest rate options, 137–47
 path-dependent options, 150–4
 out-of-the-money option, 118, 136, 171, 172–3, 217
overseas markets, 7
ownership (share options), 95

Pacific Basin, 224
package tour market share, 26, 27
par yield curves, 49–52, 53
participating swap, 172
participation, 172, 184
participation rate, 184
path-dependent options, 150–4
payoff profiles, 66–8, 80–2
perfect competition, 42–3
performance bond system (ABTA), 27, 36
plain vanilla swap, 219–20, 221
portfolio
 construction, 100–6, 126
 risk and return, 189–91
 selection decisions, 191–4
 theory, 189–202
 see also risk-free portfolio
posted borrowing rate (reducing), 218–21
pound sterling
 Deutschmark/pound spot exchange rate, 2, 3
 foreign exchange exposure, 39–41
price(s)
 asking, 43
 average, 150, 151–2, 154
 bid, 43
 commodity, 2, 5, 20, 32–5
 exercise *see* exercise price
 of raw materials, 7
 see also share prices
pricing
 asset (models), 200–1
 call options, 98–114
 caps and floors, 141, 143–7
 put-call parity, 126–7, 166
 put options, 124–8

pricing (*cont.*):
  three-year cap, 144–7
pricing financial instruments (principles)
  markets and traders, 42–5
  spot market for currencies, 45
  spot market for interest rates, 46–53
pricing of options, 132–3
  compound options, 147–50
  currency options, 134–7
  interest rate options, 137–47
  path-dependent options, 150–4
profit, 43–4
  arbitrage, 76
  corporate hedging decision, 203–6
  risk-free, 54–5, 64–5
profit and loss account
  accounting exposure, 11, 13–16, 18–21
  World Travel Group, 29
profit-share option, 172
profitability, 2, 7
purchasing power, 39, 41
put-call parity, 126–7, 166
put options
  American, 96
  European, 96, 97–8
  expiration values, 97–8, 99
  floors (pricing), 141, 143–7
  pricing, 124–8

range forward, 170
rate notation, 58, 59
ratio forward, 172, 175
raw materials, 7
regression line (corporate hedging), 195–200
regulatory arbitrage, 212–14, 218
replication strategy, 104–6
reset swap, 219, 221
revaluations, 20
risk
  core business, 2, 7
  environmental, 2
  management of, 8–9
  profile, 7–9
  and return, portfolio, 189–91
  systematic, 198, 200, 202, 204
  transaction, 14, 15
  translation, 15–19

unsystematic, 198, 200, 201–2, 204
risk-free arbitrage, 43, 44, 48–9, 52, 54–5
risk-free portfolio, 132–3
  compound options, 149
  currency options, 135–6
  interest rate options, 138–9, 142

sales revenue, 19, 24
Scholes, Myron, 100; *see also* Black and Scholes model
Sears PLC (case study), 209–11
securities, 19–20, 22
  World Travel Group, 36–7
securitization, 1
sensitivity (European call option values), 114–22
share options, 95
  contract settlement, 131
  dividends, 122–4
  expiration values, 96–8
  payoff to an option at expiration, 129–31
  pricing call options, 98–114
  pricing put options, 124–8
  sensitivity of European call option values, 114–22
  share prices, 13–14
  call options, 112–23 *passim*
  at expiration, 129–31
  put options, 124–8
Sharpe, William, 195
Sharpe's market model, 194–200, 207
short gilt futures, 76, 83
Smithson, C. W., 155, 175
Spanish peseta, 39–41
speculation, 182
spot exchange rate, 2, 3
spot market for currencies, 45
spot market for interest rates, 46–53
spot yield curve, 48–50, 52, 53
spread, 43, 53; *see also* bid-offer spread
Srinivasulu, S. L., 202
standard deviation (corporate hedging), 187
Statement of Standard Accounting Practice, 14, 15
statistics (corporate hedging), 186–9

Index

sterling currency futures, 72, 73–6, 80–2
stock market index, 2, 6, 79
subsidiaries, 15–19 *passim*
substitute product, 64–5
substitution effect, 24
swap contracts
  as building-blocks, 160, 162–4
  commodity-indexed swaps, 91–2
  contract settlement, 91
  currency swaps, 84–6
  interest rate swaps, 87–90
  value of, 90–1
  variations, 92–4
Swiss franc currency futures, 72
synthetic forward contracts, 64–5
systematic risk, 198, 200, 202, 204

tax transformation, 217–18
temporal method, 15–17
three month ECU interest rate futures, 76, 82
three month Euro-Deutschmark interest rate futures, 76, 82
three month Eurodollar interest rate futures, 76, 82
three month sterling interest rate futures, 73, 76–9, 82–3
time profile, tax transformation and, 217–18
total exposure, 24–5
tour industry (case study), 25
  British operations industry, 26
  British operators, 27, 28
  business practices, 26–7
  charter airlines market share, 27–8
  package tour market share, 26
  World Travel Group, 28–32
  World Travel Group (suggested exposure profile), 32–41
traders (and markets), 42–5
trading, 181–2
transaction exposure, 21
transaction risk, 14, 15
translation exposure, 21

translation loss, 18–19
translation risk, 15–19
tunnel, 170
Turkish lira, 41

uncertainty, 99, 112, 203
unsystematic risk, 198, 200
  hedging and, 201–2, 204
up-front premium, 147
US dollar
  exchange rate (impact), 7, 8
  exchange rate exposure, 22–3
  /sterling (foreign exchange exposure), 39, 40
US Treasury bond futures, 73, 76, 77, 78, 83

value-for-money solutions, 169
variance (corporate hedging), 187
variation margin, 74–6
volatility
  and demand for financial engineering, 2–9
  of financial prices, 223, 224
  interest rate option, 144
  path-dependent options, 150–1
  share options, 112–17, 122

World Air, 30–2
World Travel Group PLC, 28
  corporate hedging decision, 208–9
  exposure profiles (suggested), 32–41
  Sunnex Vacations PLC. 29–30
  World Air, 30–2
write-down, 20
write-up, 20

yield curve
  differing market convention, 48–9
  interpreting, 46–8
  par, 49–52, 53
  zero, 48, 49–50, 52–3

zero cost forward band, 184
zero cost option 170, 180
zero coupon instruments, 49, 53
zero yield curve, 48, 49–50, 52–3